The Choreographic

THE UNIVERSITY OF
WINCHESTER

Martial Rose Library
Tel: 01962 827306

To be returned on or before the day marked above, subject to recall.

The Choreographic

Jenn Joy

The MIT Press
Cambridge, Massachusetts
London, England

MIT Press books may be purchased at special quantity discounts for business or sales promotional use. For information, please email special_sales@mitpress.mit.

This book was set in Archer by The MIT Press. Printed and bound in Spain.

Library of Congress Cataloging-in-Publication Data

Joy, Jenn.
The choreographic / Jenn Joy.
     pages   cm
Includes bibliographical references and index.
ISBN 978-0-262-52635-7 (pbk. : alk. paper)
1. Dance—Philosophy. 2. Arts—Historiography. I. Title.

GV1588.3.J69 2014
792.8—dc23   2013047477

10   9   8   7   6   5   4   3   2   1

To J

Contents

Acknowledgments

To write is to fall into the outer spaces of thought and of language. What at one moment is a crystalline vision at another becomes only an enigmatic abyss; yet always it is a shifting terrain of possibility. During the final writing of this book, my beloved teacher, José Esteban Muñoz, passed away. José always valued what is gorgeously illegible and the urgency of choreographing spaces for these many intimacies, sensations, and hopes, and his generous spirit and fierce wit illuminate this writing and whatever is to come.

This project was years and lives in the making and owes many debts of gratitude to the community of artists, friends, and colleagues who challenged and sustained me. My thanks to Noémie Solomon who conspires with me on all things choreographic and without whose careful readings this book would remain lost and unfinished. Thank you to the brilliant artists whose many speculative cosmologies incited my initial hallucinations surrounding the choreographic and who so generously answered my questions over the years: luciana achugar, Hilary Clark, DD Dorvillier, James Foster, Miguel Gutierrez, Maria Hassabi, Heather Kravas, Ralph Lemon, Meg Stuart, Jeremy Wade.

Thank you to my teachers and collaborators for inventing radical possibilities for thinking and making along the limits of performance, dance, sculpture, ethics, life: André Lepecki, Ann Pellegrini, José Esteban Muñoz, Barbara Browning, Randy Martin, Rebecca Schneider, S. A. Bachman, Elizabeth Rossa. Thank you to Judy Hussie-Taylor for creating a visionary platform to enact these fantastical proposals in conversation and in public. Thank you to Ellen Driscoll, Dean Snyder, and my students at RISD for their engagement with these ideas. Many thanks to my editor at the MIT Press, Roger Conover, for his critical insights and support, to Julia

Collins and Kathleen Caruso for their meticulous editing, and to Erin Hasley for her elegant design.

Thank you to the constellation of friends and interlocutors who listened along the way: Gabriel Rivera, Caitlin Marz, Julian Hoeber, Allison Shields, Justine Delori Neely, Kim Rosenfield, Deb Levine, Trajal Harrell, Tere O'Connor, Luisa Kazanas, George Ferrandi, Tamara Johnson, Sara Shaoul, Sheila Pepe, Carrie Moyer, Stephanie Tamez, Youngja Yoo, Jamie Compton, Kerstin Park-Labella, Kesang Yhudon, Bill Durgin, Hilary Joy Harmssen, Matthew Joy, Jessica Myers Joy, Judy Joy, Ken Joy.

And thank you to Sian Joy Durgin, my dawn dance partner and collaborator in the imagining of new worlds. In answer to your question, are faeries real? Yes, faeries are real. They whisper in your ear of desires and dreams that are as real as the gestures of the quotidian. You cannot always see them as they fly so fast.

Introduction Opening to the Choreographic

You dance inside my chest where no one sees you, but sometimes I do, and this sight makes our dance.—Maria Hassabi

Why choreography now? What does choreography—as concept, as practice—offer in this particular moment of cultural crisis marked by deluges distinctly political and climatic?[1] Perhaps choreography invites a rethinking of orientation in relationship to space, to language, to composition, to articulation, and to ethics. To engage choreographically is to position oneself in relation to another, to participate in a scene of address that anticipates and requires a particular mode of attention, even at times against our will. Writing of the precarious state we find ourselves in now, Judith Butler acknowledges that this "demand that comes from elsewhere" structures the very possibility of discourse and dissent (Butler 2004, 130). Facing another we encounter precariousness as the condition of address; a scene rife with violence both of the event and of language (139). Yet if we engage this tenuous choreography we invent a more sensual counter-address to the legislative acts of consumption, erasure, and violence. I imagine the work of the choreographic as one possibility of sensual address—a dialogic opening in which art not only is looked at but also looks back, igniting a tremulous hesitation in the ways that we experience and respond. As Miguel Gutierrez explains, the "choreographic is a value that rises and falls . . . crests and receives"; a mode of dancing composed not only of movement but also light, sensation, sound, stillness (Gutierrez 2011). Trespassing into the discourses and disciplines of visual-sculptural-audial-philosophic practice, *the* choreographic works against linguistic signification and virtuosic representation; it is about contact that touches even across distances. The choreographic is a metonymic condition that moves between corporeal and cerebral conjecture to tell the stories of these many encounters between dance, sculpture, light, space, and perception through a series of stutters, steps, trembles, and spasms.

---

1. To evoke only a few of these events: Arab Spring, the wave of protests beginning in December 2010, Occupy Wall Street initiated in Zuccotti Park in New York City in September 2011, Hurricane Sandy in October 2012.

An opening scene: Maria Hassabi and Robert Steijn (figure I.1) stare into each other's eyes. They embrace and walk onto the sanctuary floor of St. Mark's Church in-the-Bowery.[2] Lit by a pile of black stage lights, they face each other. This will be the refrain of *Robert and Maria* (2010):[3] to gaze deeply into each other's eyes. Their "Eyes breathe. Like open wounds," as Rosmarie Waldrop writes (Waldrop 1998, 42). At once simple and gorgeous, the structured duration of their gaze renders a devastating address. It is not a gaze that reifies the cult of the visible, but rather transports me to a more sensuous moment of its undoing. As Hassabi stands in front of Steijn, looking up and into his eyes, tears flow down her cheeks not once but at various times throughout the performance. I am never certain if she is crying from emotion or physical fatigue or memory or any combination of these. Witnessed in *Robert and Maria*, the choreographic revels in microscopic detail as prismatic liquid light gathers in her eyes. A performance as address, the work demands a close quiet attention as it unfolds in silence and almost stillness.

As If a Bird in Flight

Often, when we pose our gaze to an art image, we have a forthright sensation of paradox. What reaches us immediately and straightaway is marked with trouble, like a self-evidence that is somehow obscure.—Georges Didi-Huberman, *Confronting Images: Questioning the Ends of a Certain History of Art*

Following philosopher Georges Didi-Huberman, my writing toward the choreographic is marked by "uncertainty" moving against the "closure of the visible

---

2. St. Mark's Church in-the-Bowery is home to Danspace Project, The Poetry Project, and The Incubator Arts Project. Danspace Project, directed by Judy Hussie-Taylor, presents new experimental works in dance and supports a diverse group of artists and choreographers (www.danspaceproject.org). Many of the works discussed were witnessed in some form at Danspace Project in St. Mark's Church and so this sanctuary as site returns throughout the writing.

3. *Robert and Maria* premiered as the final performance of *i get lost*, a 2010 PLATFORM curated by Ralph Lemon for Danspace Project. I witnessed this initial performance and then saw the piece again on January 10, 2012, also at Danspace Project in St. Mark's Church in-the-Bowery. *Robert and Maria* was created and performed by Hassabi and Robert Steijn, with lighting design and installation by Ji-youn Chang and Hassabi.

I.1 Maria Hassabi and Robert Steijn, *Robert and Maria*, 2010. Photograph by Antoine Tempe.

onto the legible and of all this onto intelligible knowledge" (Didi-Huberman [1990] 2005, 3) to open up more promiscuous and irrational, sensual and critical possibilities for the making and writing of art. In *Confronting Images: Questioning the Ends of a Certain History of Art* (1990), Didi-Huberman details his exorcism of domineering models of art history (specifically naming Giorgio Vasari and Erwin Panofsky) whose clear, clean, rational articulations over-determine the objects of their attention and he counters with a conception of representation as itself a productively failing and failed practice. I would suggest that this kind of rational, clean reading is not only specific to art history, but perhaps to aspects of dance history as well and that here performance studies and its promiscuous attention to the less visible, less legible moments of art, of history, and of knowledge production offers a productive disciplinary and discursive intervention.

Against what he describes as the "tyranny of the *visible* . . . [and] the *legible*," Didi-Huberman looks to the "the *visual* and the *figurable*," trading Panofsky for Sigmund Freud to unsettle questions of representation (Didi-Huberman [1990] 2005, 8; italics in original). Identifying in Panofsky's iconography a neo-Kantian addiction to reason and logic, an enclosing of art such that it closes off all confusion, enigma, and aporia, Didi-Huberman describes knowledge, particularly the forms produced by engaging with art, as a more gaseous and viscous surround like a sea spilling through a net or clouds mutating in the sky (170, 2). Casting our gaze toward an image would feel as if we were standing on the beach pulling a net in from the waves, watching as the water recedes leaving only bits of algae and frayed rope in our hands. Rather than consider these fragments as icons or symbols directing us to an intrinsic meaning, he describes the "work"[4] of these residual and fragmented images as "symptoms" of the inability of representation to represent (164, 161). Transposing Freud's conception of dream interpretation to aesthetics as a "*critical* paradigm," he reveals the paradox of "resemblance" as a contradictory "process" rather than a static "state" (7; italics in original, 150).[5] Didi-Huberman

---

4. Didi-Huberman uses the term "work" in contrast to Panofsky's "function," continuing to put into play an economics of image that participates in the productively negative or unworking of work described by Georges Bataille. The epigraphs for the book open with Panofsky on the "curse and blessing of *Kunstwissenschaft*" above Bataille's provocation that "*Not-knowledge strips bare*" ([1990] 2005, v).

5. Didi-Huberman is clear that his turn to Freud "concerns precisely the putting in play of a *critical* paradigm—and absolutely not the putting in play of a *clinical* paradigm" ([1990] 2005, 7).

speaks of the work of representation as a dialectical engagement of distortion, conflation, and repetition, breaking with art history as a series of categorical imperatives based on style, period, or history, to instead conjure "open structures full of holes, of knots, of extensions impossible to situate, of distortions and rips in the net" (170). Experiencing art is then less about interpreting a script and instead a mutually penetrating address.

For Didi-Huberman it is gesture that reveals the gaping impotence of representation. The gesture arresting representation is the "rend," the ripping of the net or what he describes as an opening or break within the image itself: "At the very least to make an incision, to rend. What exactly is in question? To struggle within the trap that all knowledge imposes, and seek to render the very gesture of this struggle—a gesture at bottom painful, endless—a kind of untimely, or better yet incisive value" (1990] 2005, 139).

To write of images under the influences of "the rend" is to call attention to the difficult distorting choreography at work in the image and simultaneously to the moving relations between image and viewer. Didi-Huberman explicates his concept of the rend against a backdrop of the developing history and science of iconography and its reading of crucifixion images—of wounded sacred flesh. His attention to punctured flesh, to the body as it torques away from presentation toward the more obscure aspects of representation left out of traditional histories continues his earlier attention to gesture—explicitly the gesture of seizure—captured in the immense archive of Jean-Martin Charcot's photographs of women housed in the Salpêtrière asylum in Paris. These are distinct histories and different objects, yet crossing both projects is an attempt to reveal the hypocrisies underwriting the scientific and historical aspirations in Charcot's science of hysteria and iconography's science of images. This undressing of Charcot and of Panofsky exhibits the inventive fictions of both discourses and the blind spots in the production of these modes of knowledge. Haunting the peripheries of both scenes is Freud. Standing in the shadows as Charcot delivers his Tuesday lecture-demonstrations at the Salpêtrière, Freud is "witness to obscenities, contortions, hysterical wails, and worse yet" (Didi-Huberman [1982] 2003, 79) and then evoked as

---

He is also quite clear that contrary to Freud's warnings that his ideas are not to be used as aesthetic theory, there is value in reframing Freud's conception of "figurability" as a critical hermeneutic for rethinking representation (155).

the interlocutor whose writings still speak against the repressed symptoms of art history. Freud's writings offer a critical hermeneutic that breaks with a science of images and reason, methodologically offering Didi-Huberman a way to see failure and incapacity as sites of knowledge and invention, a "counter history" of art ([1990] 2005, 187).

Didi-Huberman's writing revels in the accidents of flesh captured on film and on canvas to propose a concept of image read through gesture as an intertwining of historical, theoretical, and corporeal forces that in some moments feels distinctly phenomenological. He explicitly attests to the influence of philosopher Maurice Merleau-Ponty as seminal for his opening of the image and quotes from Merleau-Ponty's "Eye and Mind," to explain that the "duplicity of awareness"[6] is not only about leaving behind distinctions between media, but is also concerned with a reading of image as a chiasmatic field (Merleau-Ponty quoted in Didi-Huberman [1990] 2005, 142). For Merleau-Ponty and for Didi-Huberman, this turn to the moving work of the image on the viewer, such that the seer not only sees but also is seen, is not only a critique of vision but also a critique of the assumed objectivity of science (Merleau-Ponty [1961] 1964, 159). Merleau-Ponty's theory of the visible as a corporeal and carnal practice, what he explains as a "mobile body [that] makes a difference in the visible world, being a part of it" points to a choreographic understanding of the work of vision (162). Within this phenomenological encounter of looking and being looked at the static one-to-one correlation of representation to object shivers ever so slightly—not only because of the force of the object's own gaze, but also because it calls attention to what is supplementary within representation itself, a supplement marked by a subtle movement, stutter, or hesitating address.

Turning his attention to dance, as Israel Galván flamencos in front of him, Didi-Huberman sees a compelling dialectical force, a fierce anticipatory stillness that he compares to a bird hovering above its prey. He whispers his epiphany: "Here is exactly what dancing is, I then told myself: to make of one's body a subtracted form, even if immobile, of multiple forces. To show that a gesture is not the simple result of a muscular movement and a directional intention, but something much

---

6. In "Eye and Mind," this moment is also translated as the "duplicity of feeling" (Merleau-Ponty [1961] 1964, 164).

more subtle and dialectic[al]: the encounter of at least two confronted movements—those in this case of the body and the aerial milieu—producing, at the very point of their balance, a zone of arrest, of immobility, of syncope. A kind of silence of the gesture" (Didi-Huberman [2006] 2013). The bird as dancer or dancer as bird, is this what Hélène Cixous had in mind when she wrote of an "airborne swimmer" (Cixous [1976] 1980, 260)? I wonder. Both writers choreograph human touching animal touching substance, rendering the choreographic as an atmospherics of encounter along its violent and erotic edges as the bird dives to kill her prey, so the swimmer laughs her desire. Friedrich Nietzsche also spoke of birds as graceful metamorphosis, luminous innocent creatures breaking down barriers of thought and gravity—or so Alain Badiou will cite in his meditation on "Dance as a Metaphor for Thought" (Badiou [1998] 2005, 57). Extending Nietzsche's conception of dance as a series of forces—innocence, flight, light, verticality, and silence (57–59)—to Baruch Spinoza's question of the capability of the body, Badiou points to a radical possibility and a reactionary limitation depending on how one is to approach dance: as movement of thought or as the movement of body in and of space. He defines dance as neither gymnastics nor a submissive trained virtuosity, but rather, simultaneously "capacity" and "restraint"; "it is the bodily manifestation of *disobediance* to an impulse" (59, 60; italics in original). Badiou's fulgurant perception of dance is that of an extreme sensitivity, a thinking body reflexively exposing this process as it moves, breathes, flies, dives. Dance becomes event: "precisely what remains undecided between the taking place and the non-place—in the guise of an emergence that is indiscernible from its own disappearance. . . . Dance would then point toward thought as event, but *before this thought has received a name*—at the extreme edge of its veritable disappearance; in its vanishing without shelter of the name" (61).[7] This is the ontological lament of dance; it will

---

7. Miguel Gutierrez offers a contradictory power of dance as an act of naming or renaming the self toward eternity and against forgetting, when he writes: "you create things—things that have little discernable value other than to you and to a select group of people who have convinced themselves that these worthless things also have value. you create these things mostly so that these people will know your name, and so that they repeat it to others when you are not around. you hope that this game of name uttering—much like a phone tree—will continue uninterrupted for as long as you live and then way beyond that" (Gutierrez 2009a, 51).

disappear, its exquisite present vanishing before our eyes.[8] And yet, the dancer dancing, like the bird diving for her prey, remains breathing before us on and off stage. So how else might we think of choreography in flight or as brilliant intoxication that does not forget its material stakes?

Even a bird in flight casts shadows. DD Dorvillier taught me of these many perceptual qualities of choreography in *No Change, or, "freedom is a psycho-kinetic skill"* (2005) within which dance is a single contingent value with sonority, luminescence, color, atmosphere, temperature, shadow[9] (figures I.2–I.4). There is a moment near the end when she stands with her back to the audience, dressed in black skirt and sweatshirt with the hood pulled over her head, and Elizabeth Ward follows her with a light casting a looming shadow as Dorvillier bends, twists, arcs. A double duet of sorts—Ward with Dorvillier, Dorvillier with her shadow—rendering a virtuosic density as if all the gestures of the work condense into an absence of light or light displaced by her body drawn onto the space. It is a photographic capture, if we consider photography as a drawing with light that suspends Dorvillier's earlier investigations of the space (a photo studio on the edge of Greenpoint in Brooklyn), its curved back wall, black curtains, windows, corners, her play with acoustic apparatus of microphones, stands, cords, even a blue plastic bucket in her dance. Her choreography questions the use-value and function of objects, asks them to perform differently, to mean something else, perhaps. Ward returns in a white dress holding a white paper coffee cup in a momentary arabesque. She bends as if to place the cup on the ground again and again as Seth Cluett plays a sad refrain on the piano.

---

8. As Peggy Phelan writes of this disappearance: "The moving body is always fading from our eyes. Historical bodies and bodies moving on stage fascinate us because they fade. Our own duration is measured by our ability to witness this fading; writing is one way of measuring that duration. . . . History writing and choreography reflect and reproduce bodies whose names we long to learn to read and write. Our wager is if we can recall and revive these fading forms, our own may be recalled by others who will need us to protect themselves from fading. This repetitious dance assures our continual presence: We are the characters who are always disappearing" (Phelan 1995, 200, 209).

9. *No Change, or, "freedom is a psycho-kinetic skill"* (2005) opened at Context Studios as a Danspace Project Out of Space, New York. Performed by Dorvillier and Elizabeth Ward, sound by Seth Cluett, lighting by Thomas Dunn.

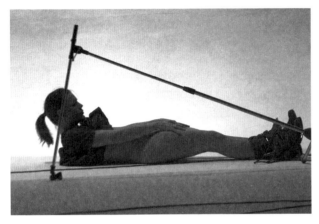

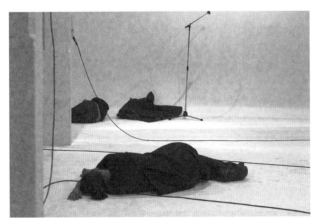

I.2–I.3 DD Dorvillier, *No Change, or, "freedom is a psycho-kinetic skill,"* 2005. Photographs by Thomas Dunn.

I.4 DD Dorvillier, *No Change, or, "freedom is a psycho-kinetic skill,"* 2004. Photograph by Eileen Travell.

Witnessing *No Change, or, "freedom is a psycho-kinetic skill"* again, I am not only reminded of its materialist plays with the technologies of the studio, stage, and institution, but also more deeply affected by its elegiac erotics. As Dorvillier struggles to remove her jeans and forces her body into the shape and space under a fallen microphone stand, all of this amplified by the microphone attached to her belt loop, she evokes a longing for communication in another mode, one that requires a physically energetic body in connection to more than itself. Dorvillier's work renders the intrinsically relational qualities of the choreographic. I cannot evoke its precarious qualities except as a series of constellations or encounters that sometimes collide, or whisper or fall or fade or fly or walk away from each other.

A Tenuous Genealogy

After Doris Humphrey: The Art of Making Dances

Consider the following image. A vast ocean, the surface black and

> *After Jacques Derrida: What Is Poetry?*

plain, any vibration on the surface appears to be a disturbance, fright.

> In order to respond to such a question—in two words, right?—you

It is night and yet on the beach stands a man, or Man, perhaps personi-

> are asked to renounce knowledge. And to know it well, without

fied as a young person hardly more than six or eight years old, in full

> ever forgetting it: demobilize culture, but never forget in your learned igno-

daylight. A girl. The beach slops upwards. In the background group-

> rance what you sacrifice on the road, crossing the road.

ings of summer cottages spread out in the landscape, a landscape we

> Who dares to ask me that? Even though it remains inapparent, since disappear-

know rests upon post-Fordist production, void of manufacturing, filled

      ing is its law, the answer sees itself (as) danced (dancing). I am a dancing, pro-

to the brim by organization and ubiquitous management. The black

      nounces choreography, learned through the body, guard and keep me, look

surface absolutely still now. Suddenly, the surface breaks, with an

      out for me, look at me, danced dancing, right before your eyes: soundtrack

enormous intensity and a black shiny body catapults itself out of the

      wake, trail of light, photography of the feast of morning.

ice-cold water. The body, in its entirety leaves the ocean behind and . . .

—Mårten Spångberg, "Why 'The Art of Making Dances' Now? Between "-What is . . ."
and Choreography"

Mårten Spångberg's text "Why 'The Art of Making Dances' Now? Between '-What is . . .' and Choreography" casts a picture of these difficult processes of encounter—of reading, of writing, of dancing, of imagining—in the moment of their intertwined (and almost illegible) relationship. Spångberg's writing describes choreography as a bodily practice, whose law is disappearance, and so must always remain in movement (as danced [dancing]) in an attempt to suspend this disappearance. Yet then another body intervenes, a shiny black creature (perhaps whale, perhaps butterfly) spit out of the ocean's surface that the girl on the beach attempts to capture, yet cannot quite contain. And these two encounters—the girl and the creature on the post-Fordist[10] beach, the attempt to define poetry as a crossing of the road (where later one might meet a hedgehog)—these wildly nonsensical or hallucinatory stories frame one attempt to describe the choreographic through

---

10. Post-Fordism refers to the contemporary model of production structured through specialized markets of scale, marking a shift from the mass production model of Fordism.

language without losing its errant physicality or its improvisational labor or its philosophical force.[11]

_____

11. Spångberg's "After Jacques Derrida: What Is Poetry" takes Derrida's text line for line (the English translation that is) and transposes the terms of dictate, dictation, poetry, poem, and poetic with variations of dance and choreography, a move that plays off Derrida's own attention to the intricacies of language and sound and the slipperiness of meaning. As the English translator Peggy Kamuf points out, the stresses of the "str" sound as if "the beast [itself is] caught in the strictures of translation" (Kamuf in Derrida [1988] 1991, 223). In the final lines of Derrida's text, he extends this question of poetry to the questions of history, epistemology, and philosophy (left untranslated as *"isotria, episteme, philosophia"* [237]). And he continues that the very asking of this question is a lament at the poem's immanent disappearance, its disappearance in the face of being named poetry as such. Instead Derrida wants to capture the "poematic," a quality of poetry as accident, one imaged as a hedgehog curling up into a ball in the middle of the highway, more eloquently rendered in French and Italian as a "hérisson" or "istrice" on the "autoroute" (233, 223, 231). With bristles out, the hedgehog places itself in a defensive position, turning its heart away from danger and yet in this same moment inviting death by stopping on the highway in traffic. This is the accident and danger of poetry, or a particular quality of poetry that is "poematic" (233). And this accident-inducing danger is a quality that Spångberg desires to capture as a quality of the choreographic—a quality that is also intricately interlaced with history and gesture and the play of both in the landscape. (This question of landscape will appear again in chapter 1.)

Spångberg's rewriting of Derrida's text appears graphically intertwined with and interrupted by "After Doris Humphrey: The Art of Making Dances," an inventive meditation on her book *The Art of Making Dances* (1959). Not published until after her death in 1958, Humphrey's text reflects on the shifting focus of choreography as concept and practice after World War I and offers prescriptive advice on how to decide if one might be a choreographer and if so how to make a dance that is not boring, or too long, or monotonous, or overly intellectualized, or two-dimensional (9). In her writing, dance becomes personified as Sleeping Beauty, yet one who is no longer content to passively sleep and to dream but abruptly awakens to the call of history. "Suddenly the dance, the Sleeping Beauty, so long reclining in her dainty bed, had risen up with a devouring desire. No Prince Charming was the answer. She awoke staring into the muzzles of the guns of World War I, and she was enamored of such unlikely things as machinery (mechanistic ballets), social problems, ancient ritual and nature (flowers, bees, water, wolves)" (Humphrey 1959, 16).

Humphrey's personification of dance turns allegorical when infused with contemporary concerns in Spångberg's writing. The after-effect of Spångberg's translation of Humphrey's book is its own event; one that draws on her descriptive personification of dance and its connection to historical conditions, yet moves it into the present such that we are now reading of a post-Fordist landscape marked by summer cottages on the edge of the beach. The ocean, we are told, is "the virtual, understood as a container for all the possible and impossible actualizations of the world that did not and have not yet been actualized" and the whale creature is "individuation, i.e. a theory of intensive processes of becoming . . . agitations of space, pockets of time, pure synthesis of speed, direction and rhythm" (Spångberg 2009, 31). Derrida meet Humphrey meet Deleuze.

In contrast to Spångberg's citational peregrinations, Boris Charmatz offers another score for a physical body that is also intrinsically theoretical:

The idea is to let oneself melt gradually and to allow unexpected detours, to insist on the most difficult transitions: eventual disturbances of equilibrium must not be ignored, nor the complications, the uncertainty of one who when his eyes are closed does not know any more when his knee will touch the ground. . . . Contrary to the pedagogy of sitting straight, one could find in this voluntary (if unexpected) sinking down a veritable openness to the anarchist movements of life. . . . Are you ready? (Charmatz quoted in Ploebst 2001)

Yes, or maybe not quite. The dramaturgy of melting, of asking my own exhausted limbs to experiment with the "openness to the anarchist movements of life," imagines a different encounter—one that breaks with seated postures and cerebral associations and embraces disjunctive transitions simultaneously conceptual and corporeal. To consider choreography through melting—arms shaking, legs trembling, slowly falling—interrogates the ways in which movements happen in space. My own participation also warns against the use of choreography or the choreographic as yet another theoretical turn; or intrusion into another abstract meditation or philosophical seduction with choreography where choreography becomes (if not necessarily intentionally) philosophy's malleable muse.

Choreography acts in these moments of philosophical drift as the unstable signifier that sometimes dances, that sometimes stands in for dance, that cannot be or is not named, or remains forever suspended in anonymity. Think of Jacques Derrida's too oft-cited conversation with Christie McDonald that begins with

---

The intertwining of these seemingly discrete projects and thinkers offers Spångberg a way to return to the pedagogical question par excellence asked by Immanuel Kant in 1784, "What is the Enlightenment?" (Kant [1984] 1996) without falling into the grip of an essentialist notion of knowledge or of aesthetics, one determined by dictation and mimesis, but rather opens up a weird play of allegorical experiences. What the "poematic" offers to poetry, so the "choreomatic" offers to choreography, a form learned not by heart, but of and from the heart, an "address itself to someone, singularly to you but as if to the being lost in anonymity, between city and nature, an imparted secret, at once public and private, *absolutely* one and the other, absolved from within and from without, neither one nor the other, the animal thrown onto the road, absolute, solitary, rolled up in a ball, *next to (it)self*. And for that very reason, it may get itself run over" (Derrida [1988] 1991, 223).

Please look before crossing the road.

feminist Emma Goldman's declaration, "If I can't dance I don't want to be part of your revolution." Derrida takes Goldman's prescription for a revolutionary embrace of dance as a way of reading woman and her history, as a way of pointing toward her condition of placelessness, her ability to dance out of her house arrest, and pushes this idea further toward a possibility for polyvalent sexual difference, as (and here he shifts the terms from dance to choreography) the "invent[ion of] incalculable choreographies" (Derrida and McDonald [1982] 1995, 154).[12]

Even when theory attempts to address itself to the material, or to the actual conditions of labor and laboring bodies, still here, the dancer remains an anonymous figure. In *A Grammar of the Multitude* Paulo Virno describes a new form of labor in terms of virtuosity and relies on juxtapositions of the piano player interrupting Karl Marx's narrative on productive labor in the *Grundrisse* (Marx [1939] 1986, 231), with the practices of contemporary pianist Glenn Gould, and with "the dancer" to elaborate on the performative structure of virtuosic labor as "an activity without end product [that requires] . . . a witness" (Virno [2001] 2004, 52). For Virno, this quality of labor has an intimate relationship to the conditions of politics; labor in this historical moment imitates politics. Virno's equation between labor and politics is indebted to Hannah Arendt's definition of politics written in the 1950s, which she describes as a deeply experiential and social process, as "the generically human experience of beginning something again, an intimate relationship with contingency and the unforeseen, being in the presence of others" (Arendt quoted in Virno [2001] 2004, 51).

---

12. Ann Cooper Albright has pointed to the theoretical possibilities that Derrida offers as a "form of communication predicated on the instability of the body and the resultant displacement of meaning" as productive for thinking on difference and discontinuity, yet she argues for a more corporeal and feminist attention to the specificities of dance through her own discussion of the performances of choreographer Marie Chouinard (Albright 1995, 157). André Lepecki also critiques Derrida's cooption of dance and choreography yet through the larger oeuvre of Derrida's own conception of writing as trace against the history of choreography as term and practice. Aligning Derrida's mobile writing with the dancing of steps becomes productive for a particular way of using deconstruction to address choreography in particular and the question of ontology in general. Yet, as Lepecki argues, when Derrida specifically names dance (in his interview with McDonald), he falls into a confusing bind such that dance remains an improvisational force and one that is always problematically gendered as feminine, further perpetuating a "hysterical-historical attachment" within feminine-writing-dancing-history that tethers dance's ontology to distance and disappearance, even as it gestures toward something else (Lepecki 2004, 137).

I draw attention to these seductive evasions as they reveal the importance of dance and of choreography as not only artistic strategies and disciplines, but also intrinsically theoretical and critical practices. Of course, seduction is never only one-sided; it faces the other direction as well. Thus dancers and choreographers are also performing philosophy evidenced in a strain of conceptual choreography happening in New York specifically, and in the festival circuit across Paris, Vienna, Utrecht, Zagreb, Brussels (as examples) where artists are not only addressing theoretical issues, but also dancing them.[13] Here choreography becomes an explicit form of knowledge production and distribution, an economy of transversal ideas. As choreographer Jérôme Bel explains: "choreography is just a frame, a structure, a language where much more than dance is inscribed" (Bel in Bauer 2008, 42).

Bel's answer to a question posed about his relationship to choreography articulates a provocative turn in the etymological and historical definition of choreography. Speaking in 2008 about his piece *Véronique Doisneau* (2004), which features the ballerina Véronique Doisneau executing extracts of dances she has performed as a member of the corps de ballet in the Paris Opera House, yet now alone in the corner of the stage, *her* corner as it were, Bel distances this piece from an idea of dancing to focus specifically on how it writes a specific body in a specific space and how this encounter narrates not only the relationship between dancer and company, but also between individual and society. Choreography, etymologically the intertwining of writing and movement, now becomes an intricate entanglement of relations, "a frame, a structure, a language" inscribing a social and serial accumulation. André Lepecki notes that the historical and etymological explanations of choreography still animate the critical work of contemporary choreography, functioning as distinct yet related apparatuses that suture writing and dancing under

---

13. A few specific examples of this dancing of philosophy or theory can be seen in Randy Martin's *Critical Moves: Dance Studies in Theory and Politics* (1998), André Lepecki's *Exhausting Dance: Performance and the Politics of Movement* (2006), and Noémie Solomon's discussion of the collaboration between philosopher Jean-Luc Nancy and choreographer Mathilde Monnier (Solomon in Lepecki and Joy 2009). The writings of choreographers including Xavier Le Roy, Jérôme Bel, and Boris Charmatz, among others, also evidence this concern. Daniel Linehan's brilliant and hilarious *Zombie Aporia* (2011) interrogates theory through voice, movement, image, and rhythm, and Noé Soulier's *Idéographie* (2011), a lecture as dance, attempts to dissemble the canons of philosophy and dance simultaneously.

the disciplined scrutiny of law and the church.[14] In a later text, Lepecki continues: "Contemporary dance discovers choreography as the polarizing performative and physical force that organizes the whole distribution of the sensible and of the political at the level of the play between incorporation and excorporation, between command and demand, between moving and writing" (Allsop and Lepecki 2008, 4).

This connection does not elide shifting conceptions and definitions of choreography, but rather reveals an underlying debt of dancing to inscription, as structures entangled with complicated networks of power. If we hesitate within the etymological for a moment, we see that this writing down of movements is never simply pure description or representation, but it is always a directive conditioned by prevailing notational devices, technologies, and pedagogical imperatives. And yet, these imperatives and demands and apparatuses never quite describe the thing they strive to define. As Laurence Louppe notes, choreography "contains a savorous hesitation in spelling, a delight for the modern semiotician: we read 'l'art de d'écrire,' almost as if, in English, one were to read 'the art of de-scribing'" (Louppe [1991] 1994, 14). To de-scribe would suggest a movement away from inscription, an escape from the very moment and movement of writing. Such that Louppe, following Raoul-Auger Feuillet's *Choreography, or the art of describing dance with demonstrative characters, figures, and signs* [*Choréographie: Ou l'art de décrire la danse*, 1700], explains this specific neologism as "to trace or to note down dance" (14). Yet here again, genealogy becomes convoluted as the attribution of choreography to Feuillet should probably be given to Pierre Beauchamp, whose notations Feuillet possibly took as his own (Louppe [1991] 1994, 134). As choreography has evolved as practice, it also has shifted in meaning, so that now the word refers more specifically to composition than to writing. And yet even the making and composing could not escape linguistic capture, as Louppe points out: "to compose, to create in dance, is designated in French by the verb *écrire*, to write" (14). However, the writing implicit within choreography is always already complicated by its many correspondences, as Louppe writes:

---

14. In *Exhausting Dance: Performance and the Politics of Movement* (2006), Lepecki establishes a genealogy of choreography that begins when dancing and writing meet at the shared table of a lawyer and a Jesuit priest and ballet master in 1589. A "peculiar invention of early modernity, as a technology that creates a body disciplined to move according to the commands of writing. The first version of the word 'choreography' was coined . . . *Orchesographie* by Thoinot Arbeau (literally, the writing, *graphie*, of the dance, *orchesis*)" (Lepecki 2006, 6–7). See also Arbeau 1589.

to a transformation of latent motor organizations, of the time and space they contain, and of the play of exchange between these interior polyphonies and the objective spatio-temporal givens . . . it is the ensemble of breathings, pulsations, emotive discharges or mass displacements which are focused on our bodies. It is the geography of the influxes diffused around us by the imaginary vision of space, it is the quality of the relations that we can have with the objective givens of the real—the very givens that movement "sculpts," embraces or disperses according to its own axes of intensity. (15–16)

Lingering within Louppe's description of choreography, I hear the expulsion of breath interrupting oppositional categories, to propose a more dialogic series of interruptions as space intersects time triggering affective exchanges across geographic and sculptural imaginaries. These many "savorous hesitations"—etymological, theoretical, ideological, biographic—reveal choreography as an intrinsically critical apparatus that requires an intimate attention to and negotiation of history and language and aesthetics. To speak of choreography, or to speak choreographically, is also to speak of history and of writing and of dancing as entangled forms.

Susan Leigh Foster imagines one such feminist history inscribed in the turning body as metaphor and as muse:

How to write a history of this bodily writing, this body we can only know through its writing. How to discover what it has done and then describe its actions in words. Impossible. Too wild, too chaotic, too insignificant. Vanished, disappeared, evaporated into thinnest air, the body's habitats and idiosyncrasies, even the practices that codify and regiment it, leave only the most disparate residual traces. And any residue left behind rests in fragmented forms within adjacent discursive domains. (S. L. Foster 1995, 4, 8–9; italics in original)

In her articulation of a "bodily theoretics"—a mode of writing history as a bodily writing that evokes both these performative and theoretical forces simultaneously—Foster invents a dialogue between her academic historian voice and her poetic personal voice that interrupts the text both rhetorically and graphically, set off by italics and spacings (8, 20). Her writing reflexively performs dance history to include the historian's body and her fantasies within the text as we would also include the choreographer or the dancer's body.[15]

The image of the vanished and broken dancer as site of choreography's re-imagining of history also animates dance scholar Gabrielle Brandstetter's account of "Choreography as a Cenotaph: The Memory of Movement" (Brandstetter 2000), which begins with her meditation on Rainer Maria Rilke's sonnets lamenting the death of a young dancer. Yet for Brandstetter this mourning takes on a distinctly different form. It is less about negotiating or reiterating loss in a reparative sense and more nearly about composing a "requiem"; choreography is a mode of the body writing both spatial and temporal constantly shifting between life and death (104).

The hypermobility of the body reveals an impression which is nearly impossible to comprehend: beauty of vanishing form—a "poetry of disappearance"—in the rejections and punctual deformities of movements that risk the unexpectable. . . . The task of memory—that double ReMembering—is divided among those moving and those watching the movement. And this process thus always becomes a journey of remembering through the phantasms of one's own body history. And is this landscape not also marked by deformity? By misunderstanding and misreading, which—in the limbo of subjective memory—rebuilds the rules of language and allows a world of spirits to arise out of it? (130)

Brandstetter calls attention to the retrospective qualities of choreography as "ReMembering," drawing on William Forsythe's claim that "your kinosphere functions as a memory" (Forsythe 1995, 39) to explicate the spatial and temporal and corporeal qualities of memory as well as the particular way he deals with the dissolution and suspension of gesture through improvisation. Here Brandstetter extends the topographical analysis of memory proposed by Freud and the phenomenological saturation of memory articulated by Henri Bergson through the voice and form of the choreographer. Out of breath and out of time, the body of the

---

15. Another important feminist intervention—written by a dancer and scholar who looks specifically at difference as a resistant political mode embodied in dance—is Ann Cooper Albright's *Choreographing Difference: The Body and Identity in Contemporary Dance* (1997). Albright, in a move similar to Foster's, describes her turn from the abstract narratives of dance history articulated by dance critics like John Martin (*The Modern Dance*, 1933) and philosopher Susanne Langer (*Feeling and Form: A Theory of Art*, 1953) toward the particularities of her own dancing practice and those of her contemporaries as part of the emergent interdisciplinary version of dance history on the move.

dancer and the spectator historically align with movement as an index of the pervasive shifts in technology, industry, culture, and as philosopher Peter Sloterdijk would add, with capitalism (Sloterdijk [1989] 2009), such that body intertwines with movement as its very ontology. Brandstetter argues that this intimate braiding of choreography, particularly in the works of choreographers Forsythe, Meg Stuart, and Xavier Le Roy, unsettle this seamless intertwining through a paradoxical relationship to representation and to language as they fall out of movement, in gestures like Forsythe's "virtuoso limp" and Stuart's "corporeal stutter" (Brandstetter 2000, 124). These improvisational disturbances of movement or choreographic hiccups engage what scholar Andrew Hewitt has called "choreography as catachresis" (Hewitt 2005, 14):[16] the operation of aesthetic and ideological undoing.

Describing the exhaustion of a certain kind of dance, Lepecki writes of "still acts" as "a performance of suspension, a corporeally based interruption of modes of imposing flow. The still *acts* because it interrogates economies of time, because it reveals the possibility of one's agency within controlling regimes of capital, subjectivity, labor and mobility" (2006, 15; italics in original). Lepecki values the still act because it breaks with dance as always beholden to movement; dance takes on a critical and political force in its stillness as it suspends temporal flow. Adrian Heathfield responds to this constant negotiation of stillness when he intimates: "Choreography is the impossible attempt to re-move the paradox of the stillness inside movement. Choreography is a transaction of flesh, an opening of one body to others, a vibration of limits. Choreography is given to the erotic: it tests out, seduces, and proposes without ever saying anything. Choreography is a corporeal passage in which the body is both a question and an inaccessible answer" (Heathfield 2007).

---

16. Hewitt follows a trajectory of thinking about the aesthetic through the body that resonates with Terry Eagleton's book *The Ideology of the Aesthetic* (1990), yet Eagleton remains uncannily absent from Hewitt's book. Together their works present a compelling argument about the relationship of aesthetics to ideology rather than offering a history of dance or of aesthetics that sides with the body. As Eagleton writes: "Aesthetics is born as the discourse of the body. . . . of the body's long inarticulate rebellion against the tyranny of the theoretical" (Eagleton 1990, 13). And both examine the aesthetic at its moment of collapse, which as Eagleton describes, is the very nature of the aesthetic itself: "Aesthetics is thus always a contradictory, self-undoing sort of project, which in promoting the theoretical value of its object risks emptying it of exactly that specificity or ineffability which was thought to rank among its most precious features" (2–3).

Rather than attempt another dance history or read dance only in terms of the visual, I am interested in extracting a concept of the choreographic out of this larger discursive field that has come to be called choreography and to linger in its corporeal paradoxes and vibrations. At moments, the choreographic risks illegibility, in the way that Roland Barthes speaks of the "filmic" as a specific mode of film that alludes to a disguise or instability of meaning.[17] To push this conditional play further across discipline we might invert Carrie Lambert-Beatty's question "What does it mean to say a dance is photographic?" (Lambert-Beatty 2008, 155) to ask instead: What do we mean by saying a photograph is choreographic? Her provocation draws on a reading of Yvonne Rainer's work through a photographic lens and an attention to issues of vision and spectatorship embodying a shifting definition of art (meaning all visual arts) in the 1960s "from a mindset that seeks art's essence in inherent aspects of the work, to one that finds art's definition contingent upon structuring conditions of its appearance" (Lambert-Beatty 2008, 38). How does dance encounter other media (photography, sculpture, as examples) materially and conceptually to undo notions of media specificity? If we extend Lambert-Beatty's reading to contemporary choreographic strategies we not only see the visual in dance but also stage both practices as mutually constitutive.[18]

Here the choreographic pressures the very writing of these histories, following Michel Foucault's exquisite dramaturgies of flesh and intellect that chafe

---

17. The filmic is "disturbing as a guest who persists in staying at the party without uttering a word, even when we have no need of him" (Barthes [1970] 1985, 48).

18. Taking both mediums seriously as connected to and contingent on each other is not simply to use dance as a foil for the visual, but also to think along complementary and provocative lines. The seduction of the visual arts by dance has now been fully established as museum institutions create exhibitions that foreground the historical links between these practices. Artists move easily between both practices, identifying as visual artists when their work appears to be "dance" and here Los Angeles-based artist Kelly Nipper comes to mind. Other recent examples of relevant museum exhibitions include *Move: Choreographing You* curated by Stephanie Rosenthal at the Hayward Gallery in London, October 2010–January 2011; *On Line: Drawing Through the Twentieth Century* curated by Cornelia Butler at the Museum of Modern Art, New York, November 2010–February 2011; *Dance/Draw* curated by Helen Molesworth at the Institute of Contemporary Art, Boston, October 7, 2011–January 16, 2012; *Danser sa vie* curated by Christine Macel and Emma Lavigne at the Centre Pompidou, Paris, November 2011–April 2012; *Some Sweet Day* curated by Ralph Lemon and Jenny Schlenzka at Museum of Modern Art, New York, October 15–November 4, 2012.

against techniques of body and of power. The labor of dance, a specific technology of the body, participates in the unsettling Foucault requires in his concept of genealogy, as an alternative to the writing of history, challenging any linear narrative and the very conception of a solo. Genealogy instead produces a crowded mediation on belonging and affiliation. What Foucault describes as "a field of entangled and confused parchments, on documents that have been scratched over and recopied many times" (Foucault [1971] 1977, 139) becomes particularly resonant for my own intervention into critical dance studies[19] as it negotiates a complicated relationship between bodies and the histories and discourses that create, legislate, and describe them without falling into essentializing terms. Tracing genealogy as a movement of "descent" that "disturbs what was previously considered immobile; it fragments what was thought unified; it shows the heterogeneity of what was imagined consistent with itself . . . descent attaches itself to the body. It inscribes itself in the nervous system, in temperament, in the digestive apparatus; it appears in faulty respiration, in improper diets, in the debilitated and prostrate body" (147). Foucault diagnoses the body under duress, falling and failing, against the constraints of power written into the documents of history. His analysis looks to the functions of the corporeal body, taking its temperature, sensing its tensions and energies to locate or "expose" the effects and affects of history's imprisonment and containment of this body. Genealogy's "task is to expose a body totally imprinted by history and the process of history's destruction of the body" (148); it is a description that speaks directly to the concept of the choreographic as an uncomfortable convergence of body and history, bodies and writing.

---

19. In "Choreographing History," Foster also calls attention to Foucault's writing of bodies as intertwined within history, yet she sees his work as too caught within the machinations of power to wield much agentic force of its own. She turns instead to the choreographer, as both literal and metaphorical counterpart of the historian, to create a history of bodies as generative of ideas, of writing, of "physical and semantic" agency (S. L. Foster 1995, 15). Other dance historians who draw on Foucault's thinking include Danielle Goldman in her "Conclusion: Exquisite Dancing—Altering the Terrain of Tight Places" in *I Want to be Ready: Improvised Dance as Practice of Freedom* (Goldman 2010). Mark Franko also invokes Foucault's discussion of absence, or the absence of madness from discourse as a marker of its presence, deployed in his own discussion of the myth or mistake of describing dance as a language, as a "mute rhetoric" that is not discussed in terms of its patterns of signification or communicative effects in his "Introduction" to *The Dancing Body in Renaissance Choreography* (Franko 1986, 9–10).

Miguel Gutierrez's *Retrospective Exhibitionist* (2005) explicitly elides a static conception of history and of the retrospective as an exhibit of the artist's oeuvre, foregrounding a genealogy of retrospection—a turn toward the past within the present—staging a saturated temporality composed of history, memory, legacy, and present tense. As Gutierrez describes it: "There's history in the present. There's inner life, there's off stage, there's shitting and eating and sleeping and fucking and wanting something and not getting it. . . . [There is] no such thing as transitions: this exists and then this exists" (Greenberg and Gutierrez 2006). The choreographic speaks of this temporal saturation as well. All of the works I include not only dance a history of their invention but also respond to the very contemporary surrounds of dance and of art. Inside the immediacy of the event, the peripheral and contingent are never relegated to an outside or offstage, but flash up unexpectedly within the duration of the piece. History resides in the video screened of Gutierrez as a child engaging in a slow muted dance, inscribed on the adult dancer's body as memorized movements, his own, and a series drawn from over 100 choreographers including John Jasperse, Simone Forti, Steve Paxton, Benoît Lachambre in Meg Stuart's *Forgeries, Love and Other Matters*, "British choreographer who did that thing with PJ Harvey," Neil Greenberg. . . . Each indexical movement slides into the next—high kick to still profile, tricep shaking, on the ground he stiffly balances on his side, mouth gaping open, flash of his back reflected in the mirror as he leaps to land on the floor—the phrasing reminiscent of Rainer's *Trio A* in its refusal to accentuate any movement regardless of its difficulty or pedestrian quality. Gutierrez's virtuosic embodiment of the languages of Joe Goode, Pina Bausch, Lucinda Childs, Sarah Michelson, guys in Union Square, J.Lo, and Aunt Verne embodies a virtual genealogy of historical, contemporary, celebrity, intimate, dance, pop-culture figures from New York and beyond, filtered through past conversations, all rendered simultaneously across the immediate composition of the stage and the dancer.

Here the choreographic takes on critical force. Dance extends beyond the limits of performance into the social to "expose both a political specificity and an entire political horizon" (Martin 2008, 14).[20] In speaking of the participatory and agentic force of dance, Martin does not fall into the trap of presence, which would argue that only in the moment of the performance could this kind of social

---

20. Mark Franko also writes of dance as labor, of dance as a social and cultural work in *The Work of Dance: Labor, Movement and Identity in the 1930s* (2002).

engagement happen, but importantly speaks simultaneously of the object (performance) and also what exceeds that specific performance (44). Tracing a line between Nietzsche's critique of the present and Marx's explication of labor as also conditioned by history, Martin describes choreography (as representation and temporal labor) as enabling a dialectical linkage between "agency and history" that "provide[s] methodological insights for recognizing politics where it would otherwise be invisible" (45–46).

My conception of the choreographic follows Martin's call situating the gestures of choreography within a discursive framework that writes against the traps of static history and disappearance.[21] This function of enunciation, of the what is said, is not then only an aspect of the linguistic, but also as Spångberg argues a "choreographic utterance as well" that points toward "a shift from a statement-making practice where 'signifying' is everything towards . . . a 'simple enunciative' practice in today's choreographic landscape" (2002, 35–36). These choreographic enunciations are often performed as a question. As Una Bauer writes in her discussion of Jérôme Bel:

A question that inspires a dialogue: a question that asks not what choreography is and what it is not but what are the processes of its construction and understanding as choreography, how is choreography constructed? And a proposal is framed: choreography is not constructed through the successful stages of particular representations, or through the impossibility of their staging (and thus, through the success at staging abstract movement) but through the movement of embodied thought which refuses to fix itself in particular recognizable types of oppositional discourses, or oppositional response structures. (Bauer 2008, 41)

Following Bauer's call for a mobility of thought, I trespass across a constellation of works, artists, writers, philosophers, and dancers to argue that the choreographic is

---

21. Here Carrie Lambert-Beatty's excellent critique of Marina Abramović's retrospective at the Museum of Modern Art, New York, offers another important framing of performance art (not dance explicitly but useful in comparison) as functioning "differentially, relationally, centrifugally" such that instead of "celebrating liveness (or anything else) as performance art's signal contribution, this model of performance is interested in multiple and changing temporalities" (Lambert-Beatty 2010, 211). Rather than extending performances' "propensity to spread," Abramović negates these "changing temporalities" through the re-performances and literal durational presence of the artist serving only to glorify the artist in rigid stasis (212).

not only a critical discursive force, but always already explicitly social, historical, and political.

The opening chapter mediates on a writing of history through the landscapes along which we move, breathe, and think, curating a precarious logic as Walter Benjamin, Pina Bausch, Werner Herzog, Francis Alÿs, Cormac McCarthy, James Foster, Fionn Meade, and Giorgio Agamben dance together. Chapter 2 traces the force of the choreographic as an explicitly feminist undoing of linguistic and corporeal imperatives from laughter and toward desire as witnessed in the choreographies of DD Dorvillier, Meg Stuart, La Ribot, luciana achugar, and Heather Kravas. The desiring work of the choreographic finds its ecstatic dissemination in chapter 3, which asks how these practices and improvisations of extreme experience not only propose more alteric modes of dancing and living, but also model other forms of communicability and pedagogy through the projects of choreographers Jeremy Wade and Miguel Gutierrez. Dancing into the outer spaces of desire and violence, chapter 4 looks to the cosmologies of science fiction writers Samuel R. Delany and Kim Stanley Robinson as so many perceptual avatars to dance with Ralph Lemon, Meg Stuart, Marianne Vitali, Janet Cardiff and George Bures Miller, and Massimiliano Gioni, among others.

Come. Dance with me. Let's get lost.

1 **Precarious Rapture** Lessons from the Landscape

To subordinate ourselves to the POSSIBLE is to let ourselves banish stars, winds, and volcanoes from the sovereign world.—Georges Bataille, *The Unfinished System of Nonknowledge*

Tell me which infinity attracts you, and I will know the meaning of your world. Is it the infinity of the sea, or the sky, or the depths of the earth, or the one found in the pyre?—Gaston Bachelard, *Air and Dreams: An Essay on the Imagination of Movement*

Come. Walk with me. Let's get lost.[1]

Walking along the deserted streets of Brooklyn near the East River, my son asks: "What would happen if the wind blew away all the buildings and cars and people and all that was left was sidewalks and streets and you and me?" A child's anxious fantasy of intimacy and vulnerability—will we still be together when the wind tries to take it all away? But also, perhaps, a premonition of shifting topologies and an acknowledgment that we always move in relation to the history of these transitions, whether they are emotional, architectural, ecological, or climatic.

"Is it scary?" he asks.

---

1. Walking as philosophical tactic has a long genealogy: we might step from Charles Baudelaire to Gustave Flaubert to Walter Benjamin's arcadian flâneur to Michel de Certeau's wanderer along the streets of New York City who illuminates the "act itself of passing by" through a "pedestrian enunciation" (Certeau [1980] 1984, 97, 99). For Certeau, walking as reading collapses the rhetorical and spatial, the paroxysms of urban street life with the cosmos to propose an "erotics of knowledge" (92)—an erotics, not a hermeneutics, as Susan Sontag called for years before (Sontag [1964] 1966, 14). Walking will be our refrain—as movement and metaphor—as we proceed through this constellation of works and texts. We will enact a kind of "wanderlust" to borrow Rebecca Solnit's title for another meditation on the aesthetics and histrionics of walking (Solnit 2000). And along the way these footnotes act as a parallel trajectory of footsteps or perhaps activate what Jacques Derrida calls a "parergon" in his circling around painting (Derrida [1978] 1987). My parergon traces and repeats a series of spirals around sculpture.

It is more or less safe:[2] a precarious condition staged across urban streets, grassy dunes, burnt and burning oil fields, smoking barren roads, shimmering black pyres. An oscillation between safety and premonition, expectation and hope, a movement between what is known and what is not, what is certain and what is never quite so. A story narrated in dirt, dust, smoke, fire, stars.

The stories that follow trace the improvisational and ambulatory forces of the choreographic, attending not only to its spatial effects, but its exquisitely temporal ones as well. Written under the influence of multiple discrete landscapes—spatial terrains and topographic representations—these peregrinations happen in the present with an eye always turned toward the past. Drawing attention to the ways we place ourselves in relation to history[3] in the present and how we make sense of

---

2. These words are credited to Rebecca Brooks and are inscribed on a small photograph emailed to me by choreographer Heather Kravas. The photograph—a small portrait of Kravas's face obscured by a ski mask and shot in a bathroom—was part of a series of gift exchanges, the research for our collaborative performance lecture (ski mask, glitter glasses, knee socks, love letter . . .), 2011.

3. To narrate these encounters under the influence of landscape is a specifically performance studies project that attempts a different direction than Allen Weiss's elegant *Unnatural Horizons: Paradox and Contradiction in Landscape and Architecture* (1998) and draws on the various ways history has been written methodologically and discursively in performance studies scholarship. Performance studies encounters history differently than art historical or linear or teleological models and has a more suspect relation to paternity and legacy. As the bastard stepchild of anthropology and theater now more intimately aligned with queer studies, feminism, psychoanalysis, and critical theory (these discourses being the ones I am most invested in), performance studies places itself on the periphery and speaks from an oblique angle of analysis. Over the course of its development, different scholars have considered the workings of history in relation to anthropology and ritual as distinct from theater (see Richard Schechner, *Between Theater and Anthropology*, 1985; Johannes Fabian, *Time and the Other: How Anthropology Makes Its Objects*, 2002); through an attention to the erased subjectivities in the archive and repertoire (see Diana Taylor, *The Archive and the Repertoire: Performing Cultural Memory in the Americas*, 2003); as a corporeal attention to movement and psyche (see Barbara Browning, *Samba Resistance in Motion: Arts, Politics of the Everyday*, 1995; Peggy Phelan, *Mourning Sex: Performing Public Memories*, 1997); and witnessed as a stuttering within the temporal architecture (see Homi Bhabha, *The Location of Culture*, 1994; Gayatri Chakravorty Spivak, *A Critique of Postcolonial Reason: Toward a History of the Vanishing Present*, 1999). These conceptions of history diverge in their narrative structure and political intent, yet aspire to a radical impulse, an attempt to locate the fault lines of traditional narratives as Walter Benjamin in his flash of awakening and Karl Marx with his search for revolutionary timing sought to do in an earlier moment. To propose a choreographic articulation of history, I draw on the thinking of Karl Marx, Walter Benjamin, Homi Bhabha, Peggy Phelan, Gayatri Spivak, and Michel Foucault to witness the unveiling of

these connections through language and through art is never obvious or direct but is quite precarious and tenuously situated. To feel the precarious,[4] to be held under its sway, is to breathe in history as present tense and sit within it in fields of grass or scarred arid deserts or under buzzing white gallery lights. For me this is the promise of art—to imagine strategies for articulating something like precariousness through "a blazing shape, a sudden shock" or perhaps a moment of rapture that is missing from our current thinking (Didi-Huberman 1996, 52).[5]

I imagine the choreographic as a set of dispersive and generative strategies, calling our attention to these shocks and seizures and spasms within the contemporary. Perhaps like the qualities of art that Georges Didi-Huberman sees in the "blazing shapes," the choreographic also acts as a mode of provocation and address, one that requires a more transitive quality of writing to articulate its theoretical-aesthetic-ethical horizons. And so these encounters with and within landscape attempt a writing as walking that navigates the precipitous edges of art to expose something of the precarious situation of the present. Asked to identify an underlying tendency in art from 2000 to 2010, art historian Hal Foster invokes the "precarious" in describing a "political and aesthetic apparatus [that] implies this state of insecurity is not natural but constructed—a political condition produced by the power on whose favor we depend and which we can only petition. To act out the precarious, then, is not only to evoke its perilous and privative effects but also to intimate how and why they are produced" (H. Foster 2009, 209).[6] Extending Foster's

---

history not only as a temporal event, but as an explicitly spatial turning toward the sites and spaces within which these histories take place. Let's walk.

4. Writing on the work of artist Lygia Clark, Eleonora Fabião cannot speak of the precarious, but of the reiterative status of "precarious, precarious, precarious" (Fabião 2005). Multiple echoes, listen. For Fabião, this transitive quality of the precarious conjures a spatial and temporal intertwining of aesthetic and political forces to "slow down specularity [...] to speed up relationality" and acts as a "biopoetics" that "defers from and adds to ephemerality and the transitory" (Fabião 2009).

5. And here Georges Didi-Huberman is explicating the work of the dialectical image in Walter Benjamin's writing that we will arrive at later in this chapter.

6. Hal Foster's essay was written as a response to the question of what defines the art of the last decade. Not linked by any conceptual project or formal alliance, he cites the work of Paul Chan, Isa Genzken, Thomas Hirschhorn, Robert Gober, Mark Wallinger, and Jon Kessler, as examples of this mode of precarious art.

analysis to other modes of contemporary artistic practice and back through the histories of sculptural discourse, I propose that it is not only a condition of the precarious that the artists[7] I will discuss are now speaking to, but also that this quality is aligned with something of the sublime or rapturous. There is always an oscillation or movement within the work and within our encounter that must negotiate the tension between the construction of a furtive instability and a ravishing of "time and knowledge" (Bhabha 1996, 8). Between something public and social and something incredibly personal and interior there lies a synaptic tic of experience. It is evidenced in particular artworks as a rupture within knowledge that Homi Bhabha refers to as an ambivalent distance between "aura and agora" (8). Writing of a perhaps similar dis-synchrony between the terms "negotiating" and "rapture," Bhabha begins: "Nothing, *at first sight*, is less negotiable than rapture. . . . Nothing, *at first sight*, is less rapturous than negotiation" (8; italics in original). And yet, as his exegesis proceeds, he finds these terms mutually constitutive in their evocation of a mode of interpretative address that trespasses across the noise of the quotidian and the silent sublime (10). If we "force rapture's lips, press the silent, sublime word to speak and disclose its agency, which is, after all, the task of negotiation [we can then] unveil an uncharacteristic moment of radical uncertainty of selfhood and subjectivity in the 'unquiet' trade of negotiation" (10). To locate this alterity, the space in between rapture and negotiation, aura and agora, Bhabha turns back to the landscape, specifically the view of the harbor from a hill depicted by Peter Bruegel the Elder, which captures the moment when the tiny figure of Icarus falls out of the sky. *Landscape with the Fall of Icarus* (1558) becomes for Bhabha the metonymic image for interpretative work as it reveals the miraculous within the landscape that no one is able to see, so focused are they on their own labors.

Perhaps rather than turning away from the miraculous to look down at one's own shoes, so to speak, we might turn toward the topographic details of the landscape itself to see what might be enunciated in this shift of vision and attention.

---

7. This constellation includes Francis Alÿs, Pina Bausch, David Brooks, Tacita Dean, Don DeLillo, James Foster, Werner Herzog, Ursula Le Guin, Cormac McCarthy, Robert Smithson, Meg Stuart, and Marianne Vitali.

Here the critical function of landscape in my own writing now grounds, quite literally, the theoretical drift by calling attention simultaneously to location and peregrination, to a place and a mode of transport through it.

Come. Walk with me. Let's get lost.[8]

While place identifies a certain specificity or location, it is also informed by the context of the space that it resides within and is contingent to it. My alignment of place and movement follows Henri Lefebvre as he follows Karl Marx to reveal how space is not simply a natural or nondiscursive entity but is in fact produced. If, as Lefebvre writes, "Marx's great achievement" was the "successful unmasking of *things* in order to reveal (social) relationships," then perhaps Lefebvre's great achievement was the unmasking of *spaces*, explicitly what he calls social space, as a network or cluster of relations, an urban "*mille-feuille*" of sticky interlaced planes (Lefebvre [1974] 1991, 81, italics in original; 86, italics in original). Social space organizes a relational matrix through the forms of "encounter, assembly, simultaneity" that generates an "incessant to-and-fro between temporality (succession, concatenation) and spatiality (simultaneity and synchronicity)" (101, 70–71). This description of space as a choreographic machine, a function of both time and movement, is intimately tied with a valuation of the labor of making art. Lefebvre's writing becomes productive in thinking choreographically as it performs a dialectical tension between art and theory using space as the crucible. As he writes, Lefebvre circles around the distinction between a work and a thing, as two contingent social practices. This distinction becomes important as it allows Lefebvre to articulate a mode of labor, of working, that "unleashes desires" to

---

8. Walking, of course, is a movement through space that also produces space in its passage. And so here this work might approach what Trevor Paglin calls "experimental geography," a practice that ties the modernist etymologies and mythologies of the experimental to a self-reflexive production of space not only as a "critique" but also as a "'position' within the politics of lived experience" (Paglin 2008, 33).

open up new relationships, new spaces, new social engagements, new kinds of knowledge (97).[9]

As Lefebvre reminds us, to pass through a landscape is not only a spatial affair, but also explicitly temporal—passing takes and makes time. Paul Virilio extends this concept in *A Landscape of Events* (1996) when he writes: "A landscape has no fixed meaning, no privileged vantage point. It is oriented only by the itinerary of the passerby . . . the myriad incidents, minute facts either overlooked or deliberately ignored. Here, *landscape is a passage . . . the only relief is that of the event*" (Virilio [1996] 2000, xi; italics in original). These events, or anecdotes, or encounters within the landscape articulate its horizon, defining a spatial and temporal presence. For the conspiracy theorist in Virilio the landscape can only be articulated through its interruption, by the events, objects, architectures, sculptures strewn across it. Perhaps this immersive experience within the surrounding landscape initiates a different kind of correspondence between body and earth, artwork and thought, suggesting spiraling trajectories charged with the aura of science fiction. As Ursula LeGuin intones in *The Left Hand of Darkness*: "We creep infinitesimally northward through the dirty chaos of a world in the process of making itself" (Le Guin 1969, 245).

A world that is making and unmaking itself as we walk across it: What would this look like? How might it feel? The making of a world touches on a kind of utopia,

---

9. Lefebvre's conception of social-spatial labor draws on detailed descriptions of everyday actions within urban experience and artistic provocations, specifically the work of the Situationists, to theorize new possibilities for spatial production and to imagine new ways of taking up and thinking space simultaneously. Not reducible to mere illustration, practices like *psychogeography* (an approach to drawing and collage, and a conceptual program) aligned modes of artistic and pedestrian inscription (as representations and actions in real space) to decipher the histories and oneiric surround of the spaces lived in and passed through. The Situationist *dérive*, a practice of walking through the city while communicating via walkie-talkie to create a sense of simultaneity between different spaces, attempted to perform a "synchronic history . . . [to] unify what has a certain unity, but a lost unity, a disappearing unity" (Lefebvre in Ross [1983] 2002, 280). Conflating movement with thick description, choreography with narrative detail, practices like psychogeography and the *dérive* evolved into explicitly disruptive tactics as the Situationists' interest in connective urban practices dissolved into actions that agitated against what they described as the city's—Paris or Amsterdam—ideological force. This shift in emphasis marks an important turning point in their process as the Situationists' defection from the making of art, or labor of art, to instead generate anti-art events. But at this point, Lefebvre and the Situationists had already parted ways as Lefebvre's theory of moments was too broad for Guy Debord's manifesto on situations.

the something missing from the present situation, which Ernst Bloch names (following George Brecht) in "Something's Missing: A Discussion between Ernst Bloch and Theodor W. Adorno on the Contradictions of Utopian Longing" (Bloch [1964] 1996). Utopia is a model, wish, anticipation for something that is not here but might be. It is spatial and historical; a science fiction with critical force that offers Bloch and Adorno a basis upon which to articulate a critical aesthetics. Imagining the multiple terrains over which we travel as so many literal, philosophic, and aesthetic grounds, my choreographic attention to landscape seeks not to tether the works to the sand or cement—the grounds—but instead to activate a mobile utopic thinking that participates in the uncertain writing of walking, making, witnessing, thinking, cruising[10] around and around again.

These encounters demand an experiential writing;[11] a writing under the influence of vertiginous canyons, towering skyscrapers, pleasurable vistas, staggering rock faces, and blinding icy tracks faced along the way. If we are not too careful we might approach what Immanuel Kant names the sublime, an event that produces in us a "movement [that] may (especially in its beginnings) be compared to a vibration, *i.e.* to a quickly alternating attraction towards, and repulsion from, the same Object" ([1790] 2000, 120; italics in original). Standing on the edge of the precipice like Caspar David Friedrich's *Der Wanderer über dem Nebelmeer* (Wanderer above the Sea of Fog) (1818), we feel something of the "dynamically sublime" (Kant [1790] 2000, 123). This dynamically sublime, as opposed to the "mathematically sublime," appears in "threatening rocks; clouds piled up in the sky, moving with lightening flashes and thunder peals; volcanoes in all their violence of destruction; the boundless ocean in a state of tumult" (125). These natural events,

---

10. Cruising, of course, is another highly motivated or intentional without specific intent mode of walking (or driving) through space. It also contains its own unique temporality, one with explicitly queer and utopic potential, as José Esteban Muñoz brilliantly details in *Cruising Utopia: The Then and There of Queer Futurity* (2009).

11. We might also imagine this writing as engaging in what Certeau names the "texturology in which extremes collide—extremes of ambition and degradation, brutal oppositions of races and styles, contrasts between yesterday's buildings, already transformed into trash cans, and today's urban irruptions that block out its space" (Certeau [1980] 1984, 91).

witnessed as Kant explains at a close range—not too close so we miss the sense of scale and architecture, but close enough to see the details of the shifting clouds,[12] bubbling lava, and white-capped waves—cannot be merely sensed but in fact force us into an encounter that does "violence to the Imagination" (103). In these moments, we participate in a kind of topographic spasm an inchoate experience, especially given the shift in scale and relation. Working against qualities of beauty and form, these spasms strive to articulate something more formless or boundless, precipitating a trembling encounter. As Kant proceeds through his halting explanation of the sublime, his writing repeats and returns, stumbling over these rocky barriers. His examples can mostly be found in nature but then he slips again and adds as well that the sublime, the dynamic sublime, might also be a way to speak of war (127). War too exhibits an extreme contrast in scale, forcing us to apprehend something much too large so that our perspective is laid bare in its own smallness. In this intrusion of human-made violence, Kant's critique reveals the intricate and often catastrophic relationship of landscape to history; neither history nor landscape exist simply as natural ideas or spaces but are both constructed under the influence of cultural, historical, geographic, and climatic forces to produce or mitigate specific qualities. And often the revelation of both happens only in extreme moments of crisis of witness or interpretation. What follows then is another approach to Kant's dynamic sublime or to Friedrich's contemplative wanderer conjuring a choreographic aesthetics that takes landscape as a frame, a parergon, through which we encounter history in the present.

Come. Walk with me. Let's get lost.

Facing the abandoned graffiti-covered bunkers along the Atlantic Wall between the years of 1958 and 1965, Virilio experiences a Kantian epiphany of his

---

12. In *A Theory of Clouds: Toward A History of Painting* (1972), Hubert Damisch traces the appearance of clouds in the history of painting, describing the cloud as a "surfaceless body" that "contradicts the very idea of outline and delineation and through its relative insubstantiality constitutes a negation of solidity, permanence, and identity that define shape" (Damisch [1972] 2002, 184, 15). Clouds present a representational paradox as they are atmospheric zones, indeterminate and constantly moving, a series of vanishing vanishing points.

own.[13] As he turns away from the oceanic expanse, he realizes that the events within landscape are not only spatial encounters but also specifically temporal markers. A threshold between sand and water and sky, the beach exists for Virilio as a series of intersecting mobile horizons that speak to the relationship of landscape to history and of the writing of these sublime encounters—with the monoliths or butterflies that one might find there.[14] Yet over time, even the monolith (like the butterfly) follows its own center of gravity, falling, tilting, turning under the constant warp of wind, tide, and receding sand. And this too is part of the "scandal of the *bunker*," he writes in retrospect (Virilio [1975] 1994, 13). Not only do the monoliths erode under the influence of time and water, but also their very proximity to images such as butterflies or picnics or tan lines is in itself darkly scandalous. Virilio's conflation of a "summer of seaside bathing and the summer of conflict" was announced at a moment that was too soon and too close (again history touching present too intimately) (14). The juxtaposition of sun-tanned bodies and acts of war gives a more contemporary spin on Kant's epiphany in the landscape of the sublime. Something about the vertiginous landscape calls to mind human-made violence and war. Following his epiphany, Virilio continues stalking these concrete domes like

---

13. In this moment in his career, Virilio is still practicing and aligned with architecture. Yet this project, which he refers to as "solely archaeological," already signals his later attention to the apparatus of the war machine as a determining condition of social and aesthetic life (Virilio [1975] 1994, 11). Not until 1968 does he renounce architecture for cultural critique and theoretical writing over building.

14. Under the influence of Virilio's militaristic imaginings of the beach, Mårten Spångberg's image (that appears as an extract in my introduction) of the girl on the beach watching a creature turned butterfly turned umbrella might seem naïve. Yet, both peregrinations across the sands image writing as wandering that carefully rhetorically navigates these shifting landscapes across distinct different years and different beaches. In order to imagine his butterfly, Spångberg too requires an architecture, what he calls a "teleological panopticon"—the machine from which the butterfly flees (Spångberg 2009, 37). And what is the function of a bunker, except as a teleological panopticon par excellence? Designed by Jeremy Bentham, the architecture of the panopticon equated control with spatial partitioning and surveillance, an apparatus that Foucault translates into a perfect ideological machine for simultaneously aligning spatial and interior dominance. And this spatial and internalized power relation is the concept of Choreography, of History, of Knowledge that Spångberg desires to write, to choreograph his way out of. Remember that the history of Western dance is one intimately coupled with imperatives of military and training for war, from Louis XIV onward (see Anderson-Davies 2012).

Albert Camus's stranger staggering across the sand gun in hand.[15] The bunkers propose a quest and itinerary that grounds much of Virilio's later thinking about the relation of war to experience as the determinant apparatus of the contemporary world. Formally, the structures take on the expansive qualities of the ocean and others mimic the surfaces of the dunes. In one instance, the concrete was poured directly onto to sandy surface and then excavated from underneath so that the entire process remained hidden, secreted away beneath the earth itself. Gray monuments to a paranoid and defensive projection, the bunkers, like the ideology that required them, appear almost hidden, camouflaged and aged. Their form, Virilio writes, "anticipates this [geological] erosion by suppressing all superfluous forms; the bunker is prematurely worn and smoothed to avoid all impact. It nestles in the uninterrupted expanse of the landscape and disappears from our perception, used as we are to bearings and markers" (44). The bunker not only anticipates the shapes and imperatives of modernist architecture and sculptural form but also the cultural clouds under which these forms will emerge. "One of the rare modern monolithic architectures," the bunkers evidence a new military space and a "new climatic reality" that responds to the transformation of "the earth into a pseudo-sun, through a momentary return to a gaseous state" (37, 39). For Virilio, the bunker acts "as a survival machine, as a shipwrecked submarine on a beach. It speaks to us of other elements, of terrific atmospheric pressure. Of an unusual world in which science and technology have developed the possibility of final disintegration" (39).

Virilio's manifesto in *Bunker Archaeology*, as much a travel journal as an archive of falling and fallen monuments, anticipates in uncanny ways the paradigm shifts of sculptural discourse as sculpture breaks with the logic of the monument and begins to reconcile itself with landscape and with history in more irruptive and radical ways. Narrating the shift from classical to modern sculpture, art historian Rosalind Krauss turns to Sergei Eisenstein's film *October* (1927–1928), specifically the sequence of the rioting proletariat tearing down the head of the monumental

---

15. Albert Camus writes of this existential walk: "It was this burning, which I couldn't stand anymore, that made me move forward. I knew it was stupid, that I wouldn't get the sun off me by stepping forward. But I took a step, one step, forward" (Camus [1942] 1988, 59). Transposing the existential crisis of the subject to that of the landscape itself, artist David Brooks describes the relationship between environment and sculpture and social as a kind of "environmental existentialism" (Brooks 2011). It is a process evidenced in his *Preserved Forest* (2010), an installation of rainforest trees coated in sprayed concrete included in MoMA PS1's Greater New York exhibition in 2010.

portrait of the Russian czar, Nicholas II, to figure this moment of classical sculpture's beheading. In Eisenstein's film, monumental sculpture becomes an actor, a series of material signifiers of the ideological (rather than only mimetic) imperatives of aesthetics. Yet, Krauss is suspect of a too-monolithic assessment of the ideological work of sculpture and draws our attention to the inclusion of Auguste Rodin's work in the film, sculpture that she argues figures a different relationship to rational presumptions of neoclassical sculpture and linear narrative.[16] While these early passages trace her initial critique of the ideological implications of sculpture and her movement away from the strict codes of Greenbergian modernism[17] through her own description of the "dam[ming] up of time" through repetition and shadow, her analysis still returns to a static or as she writes "contracted" version of the "meaning of history" not so far from its rational points of departure (Krauss 1977, 15, 37).

It is perhaps her reliance on a tight semiotic and structuralist methodology that limits the interpretive potential of her writing as we witness again when she defines sculpture in terms of an "Expanded Field" (1978). If we locate Krauss's critique of a too easy historicism within the folds and valleys of the landscape, her severe axes begin to fall apart, implode, as if following the entropic invitations of the very work she describes. Written after *Passages of Modern Sculpture*,[18] Krauss's "Sculpture in the Expanded Field" eloquently misses the point of this disjunctive relationship to landscape. The essay is decisive as a critique of an impulse to identify (and therefore legitimate) present work in terms of past practice. As these

---

16. With the advent of August Rodin's *Gates of Hell* (1880–1917), Rosalind Krauss argues that modern sculpture frees itself from its subservience to painting, from its pedestals and plinths, from a purely spatial formalism, from linear narrative to a condensed and dynamic representation of time as space "is congealed and arrested; temporal relations are driven toward a dense unclarity" (Krauss 1977, 23).

17. "Greenbergian" refers to the discourse of art critic and historian Clement Greenberg, whose writings about artists like Jackson Pollock, David Smith, and Anthony Caro defined the terms of modern painting (as a move toward flatness and opticality) and modern sculpture (as the break with figuration, volume, representation, the culture of the pedestal to embrace a new relationship to syntax, linearity, opticality, horizontality, transparency) (Greenberg [1961] 1989).

18. Anne Wagner notes in her critique of Krauss through an analysis of Gordon Matta-Clark's work that Krauss's essay was dated 1978, yet published in *October* 8 (1979): 30–44, and that an earlier, less polished version of some of the ideas appeared in Krauss's catalog essay *John Mason Installations from the Hudson River Series* (1978) (Wagner 2004, 44).

analogies began to fill the pages of art criticism, she finds that the "word sculpture became harder to pronounce" (Krauss [1978] 1986, 279). Sculpture, as medium and as term, Krauss warns, is indeed in danger of "collapse" (279).[19] Proclaiming that modernist sculpture has become "homeless" and "nomadic" as it becomes unhinged from its pedestals and plinths, she proposes an expansion but also a limit. In her version of a Klein diagram, sculpture triangulates between not-landscape and not-architecture suspended on the bottom point of the dotted lines connecting landscape, architecture (and their negative foils) to marked sites, axiomatic structures, and site construction (284). And yet, at every turn the work she describes shifts against the gravity of her rational argument. Listen to her opening sentences:

Toward the center of the field there is a slight mound, a swelling in the earth, which is the only warning given for the presence of the work. Closer to it, the large square face of the pit can be seen, as can the ends of the ladder that is needed to descend into the excavation. The work itself is thus entirely below grade: half atrium, half tunnel, the boundary between outside and in, a delicate structure of wooden posts and beams. The work, *Perimeters/Pavilions/Decoys*, 1978, by Mary Miss, is of course a sculpture. (Krauss [1978] 1986, 277)

Really? Or yes, it is a sculpture if one remains at a distance noticing its formal composition without taking account of the uncertain invitation to descend into the ground or leaving aside the uncanny mound surrounding it. There is something incredibly unsettling about this exposed hole in a Long Island field that calls itself a perimeter or decoy (two quite distinct terms that signify two quite different stances). Is it a barrier or boundary, that thing Martin Heidegger calls "that from which *something begins its presencing*—that same thing that Bhabha requires in his assessment of postcolonial practices (Heidegger quoted in Bhabha 1994, 1)? *Perimeters/Pavilions/Decoys* is a constantly doubling event. It feels like a cavern, underground cage, or grave. I imagine climbing into it I would experience an intense

---

19. Remember this is the constant fate of sculpture, to be ignored, to always have to justify itself against painting. Think of Honoré Daumier's print *Salon de 1857* (1857), that beautiful and hilarious rendering of a screaming sculpture in the center of the room that all of the visitors turn their backs on to focus instead on the hanging paintings. Or think of Barnett Newman's infamous quip that sculpture is the thing "you bump into when you back up from a painting." (I have always thought that this was the joke implied in the MoMA placement of his *Broken Obelisk* [1963], in the initial installation in the new atrium across from Claude Monet's *Water Lilies* [1914–1926].)

smell of earth and heat. I might feel claustrophobic or trapped or sheltered. It might be consciousness altering, but perhaps this is only a ploy, a ruse as the title suggests. Yet, these are not Krauss's concerns. Rather as art historian Anne Wagner points out, this is perhaps the "denial" implicit in Krauss's critique (Wagner 2004, 30).

Describing Krauss's writing, Wagner notes: "The wish is that art history might yet become a human science, on a par with others of that ilk. The idiom of sculpture might thus be plotted and structured, schematized and categorized, so that what is new and relevant in ongoing practice could be cleanly and confidently intelligible, its proper place laid open to view" (Wagner 2004, 30–31). Art history might aspire to be a science, but not one that is too human, or at least too bodily. Then Wagner points to a possible "parent text," Gene Youngblood's visionary treatise, *Expanded Cinema* (1970) that includes a weirdly evocative introduction by Buckminster Fuller about the impending strike of the Womblanders (babies in utero) organized through telepathic exchange (Wagner 2004, 30). Youngblood follows this uncanny introduction with his own assertion: "When we say expanded cinema we actually mean expanded consciousness. . . . Expanded cinema isn't a movie at all: like life it's a process of becoming, man's ongoing historical [hysterical] drive to manifest his consciousness outside of his mind, in front of his eyes" (Youngblood 1970, 41).

A new form of consciousness, one that takes in the exterior, the landscapes of experience, requires a new aesthetic and more explicitly choreographic practice—a discourse of the body's interiority, breath, residues, smells, taint of flesh and emotion, moving alongside affective traces of the landscape itself. Rather than use the landscape and architecture merely as rational foils, or "negative conditions," what Mary Miss invites and Wagner accepts and pursues in her analysis of Gordon Matta-Clark is the distinctly bodily irruption of sculpture against the imperatives of monumentality, of architecture, and of minimalism.

I want to hold onto these questions, and then also to complicate their affective force locating them in the landscape as corporeal, perceptual, and sculptural irruptions. This is not to reassert another expansion of the field that messes with Krauss's own terminology, but rather to take seriously the affective, cultural, and social work of landscape as participating in a shifting aesthetics—an aesthetics of impending and present catastrophe of seduction of devastation of desire of violence and of extreme beauty. For me this is crucial to opening toward an alteric discourse and practice around art (and specifically sculpture) that breaks with a simplistic description of the formal qualities or the too-easy uptake of historicism (that Krauss and Adorno similarly despised) or a prophetic endgame.[20] It is also to propose, again following Krauss, that our attention to distinct works of art tells us something quite specific about the structure of our historical moment, its "cultural determinants," and its "conditions of possibility" (Krauss [1978] 1986, 290).

---

20. In recent attempts to narrate the state of contemporary sculpture, Krauss and Adorno become an unlikely polemic; Krauss's discourse on expansion has now "collapsed" and Adorno instead offers an aesthetic matrix that positions sculpture as a resistant work that is not aligned with "false consciousness and political idiocy" (Adler 2011). One example of this occurred on the panel "Us and It: Sculpture and the Critique of Display Cultures" at the 2011 College Art Association Conference in New York. In his introductory remarks, Dan Adler attempts a definition of contemporary sculpture "composed in expansive and sprawling ways" that distances itself from installation. He explains that installation is now beholden to "demands of eye candy," "immersion," "monumentality for its own sake," "stimulating an amused passivity"; these qualities James Meyers also identifies in his *Artforum* essay "No More Scale: The Experience of Size in Contemporary Sculpture" (Meyers 2004), which begins with a critique of Olafur Eliasson's *The Weather Project* (2003) installed in Turbine Hall at the Tate Modern, London. Meyers contends that these exhibitions become merely backgrounds and destinations and evidence of the "instrumentalization of the phenomenological tendency itself, within a scenario of unrelenting global museological competition" (226). Sculpture no longer agitates against the system, but now actively participates in producing it. Meyers traces this argument through the evolution of Richard Serra's work and installations at Dia:Beacon, ending on a more hopeful note with the work of Charles Ray. In Ray's *Ink Box* (1986), Meyers sees the minimalist interest in scale as a bodily proportion along the lines of Robert Morris's performative objects returns "in the phenomenological sense as a formal quality capable of inducing awareness and provoking thought"—critically resistant, spatially and somatically resonant. (Stay tuned for more on Ray's *Ink Box*.)

Adler doesn't go into as much detail as Meyers's argument, yet it is important because the relationship to landscape—and here Kant returns to us—is always measured in terms of size and scale, so that Adorno and his more contemporary interlocutor, Susan Buck-Morss, offer Adler a critical vocabulary with which to identify this recent and resistant sculpture marked by "material specificity," "gaps between image and reference," "semantic switching" evidenced in pieces by artists Isa Genzken and Rachel Harrison, as examples. These works exhibit, Adler explains, a "fragmentary and abused logic that resists motives of original production, advertising and sales" (Adler 2011). Following his brief mention of Meyers, Adler then cites Isabella Graw's argument that if art is liberated from function, it can then become even more closely embedded in commerce. Yet many of his claims seem suspect, as the only artists he cites are already established art celebrities, meaning that their work is not only deeply embedded in the economics of the art market, but also drives and defines it in certain respects.

Come. Walk with me. Let's get lost.[21]

So . . . where do we go? . . . [Sound of car tires on the road as she reads the directions again.] Read what we should do again . . . Intersection . . . See lake . . . Now we know where the sheriff lives . . . Another road to Rozel Point . . . What an excellent trip this has been . . . designed to be this way . . . Go 5.6 miles again and see if we get to an intersection . . . Cattle guard #1. Absolutely, call it #1. Pass four cattle guards until you reach Rozel Point and the Spiral Jetty. This leads to a locked gate. Great. The other road . . . 1.3 miles . . . very accurate . . . [She takes a picture as the car idles.] Who took the time to do this? . . . Here it is now . . . trespassing. [She takes another picture.] . . . Another choice, another agency . . . No trespassing. You must take a picture of that. That's a jetty? What? This piece of land right here. [Sneezes.] I think I see a jetty. Not the Spiral Jetty . . . Look, the trailer. The trailer is the key to finding the road to the Spiral Jetty. This is not much of a road . . . Go slow . . . There are relics of the oil drilling thing. Wow. That's the amphibious war machine. Is it still running? [Reads directions] . . . As you drive turn immediately left and onto a two track. I have to change film. Now onto the color slide film . . . I have the trailer in the rearview mirror . . . Do you think he wrote this? . . . Reread the last part . . . Look at the water glistening. Who told you it had sunk and risen again? A guy in New York who worked at the gallery. Looking kind of like high tide to me. How are we going to get out of here? Have to drive backwards . . . Maybe its just about getting people to come here. Its such a beautiful place . . . It can't be underwater . . . See look at it from here . . . I think that might have been it . . . [Car hits a rock. Laughter.] Naughty, naughty, naughty. Can you see? Is it serious? Think we need to go backwards not forwards . . . Shouldn't move the car . . . back the car up and then walk. [Car bottoms out again. Stop the engine and get out.] . . . This doesn't look particularly like something the military would build . . . Looks more and more like it is rising and sinking . . . I'm not sure this is the Spiral Jetty . . . Haven't gotten to the Jetty yet. Beginning to look more and more like it has been underwater . . . And that the whole

---

21. Hamish Fulton writes: "I am a walking artist, not a sculptor. Walking is not an art material. On city streets and mountain slopes. Walking is an art form in its own right." I transcribed (almost illegibly) this quote from the wall text of the *Land Art* exhibition at Hamburger Bahnhof: Museum für Gegenart in Berlin, July 2011. Exhibition dates: March 26, 2011–January 15, 2012.

rising and sinking theory might be true . . . Salt ponds turn into true puddles . . .
[Walking, sound of steps.] . . . I'm not sure this is the Spiral Jetty.[22]

Tacita Dean's *Trying to Find the Spiral Jetty* begins and ends with a
hesitation: "So . . . where do we go? . . . I'm not sure this is the Spiral Jetty." Listening,
I become confidant and silent witness to her conversation with her companion Greg
as they follow the written instructions in search of Robert Smithson's *Spiral Jetty*
(1969–1970). Against the mythic framing of Smithson's own filmed document of the
Spiral Jetty, his seminal work constructed just off Rozel Point in the Utah Salt Flats,
Dean's audio piece records a more stumbling disorientation, intimately humorous
while also openly self-reflexive. Conflating a casual chatty presence to the expansive
grandeur of the landscape to the enigmatic ruin of the artwork located within it,
Dean evokes a temporal hesitation (an echo), a "belatedness" (Stewart 2005, 76) that
speaks not only to her encounter with the compellingly absent presence of the
submerged *Spiral Jetty*, but also of our relationship to the historical forces at work
in art, more generally establishing a precarious positionality of our own relationship
to history. *Trying to Find the Spiral Jetty* embodies what Susan Stewart describes as
Dean's role as "coincidence keeper" (75). In her work, "coincidence preserves
experiences and knowledges from the ephemerality of time passing, making them,
by their intersection, cohere as events and phenomena of significance" (76).

Dean's attempted viewing of the ruin or rune of *Spiral Jetty* ends in a missed
encounter that plays off the entropic aspirations of the work itself while countering
Smithson's more mythological and cosmological associations articulated in the film.
A flaming sun, a ticking metronome, a speeding truck on a dirt road, torn white
pages floating against a blackened quarry wall, Jurassic maps, archaic skeletons
cast in blood red hues, a horned lizard sunbathing on a rock (an animal that defends
itself by shooting blood from its eyes)—these images shift from solar to archaic to
terrestrial, constructing a montage of associations, a spiral, in effect, of affiliation
that turns and turns and turns again as the trucks (also referred to as dinosaurs)
dump piles of rock onto an circling plane.

As I looked at the site, it reverberated out to the horizons only to suggest an
immobile cyclone while flickering light made the entire landscape appear to quake.
A dormant earthquake spread into the fluttering stillness, into a spinning sensation

---

22. My fragmented transcription of Tacita Dean's *Trying to Find the Spiral Jetty* (1997).

without movement. This site was a rotary that enclosed itself in an immense roundness. From that gyrating space emerged the possibility of the Spiral Jetty. No ideas, no concepts, no systems, no structures, no abstractions could hold themselves together in the actuality of that evidence. My dialectics of site and nonsite[23] whirled into an indeterminate state, where solid and liquid lost themselves in each other. It was if the mainland oscillated with waves and pulsations, and the lake remained rock still. The shore of the lake became the edge of the sun, a boiling curve, an explosion rising into fiery prominence. Matter collapsing into the lake mirrored the shape of a spiral. No sense wondering about classifications and categorizations there were none. (Smithson [1972] 1996, 146)

Smithson's epiphany in the salt flats recalls those of Kant and of Virilio, yet rather than simply standing on the sublime precipice, he produces something within the vast landscape, transplanting a hieroglyphic cipher that marks the convergence of a Southwest Native American belief in the spiral as a "representation of whirlwind and word . . . and the legend of a whirlpool at the bottom of the lake" (Gilbert-Rolfe 1985, 132). The spiral acts as a "peripheral form" that not only draws into itself these references, but also becomes "the symbol of every vital force, of every deployment of generative energy, of every primordial vibration" (133; Gaudibert quoted in Gilbert-Rolfe 1985, 132). It is metonymic not only in its mode of signification, but also in its composition; as Jeremy Gilbert-Rolfe

---

23. Smithson's "Dialectic of Site and Nonsite" included in the footnotes of *Spiral Jetty*:

Site	Nonsite
1. Open limits	Closed limits
2. A series of points	An array of matter
3. Outer Coordinates	Inner coordinates
4. Subtraction	Addition
5. Indeterminate certainty	Determinate uncertainty
6. Scattered information	Contained information
7. Reflection	Mirror
8. Edge	Center
9. Some place (physical)	No place (abstract)
10. Many	One

Source: Smithson [1972] 1996, 152–153.

notes, it is not a "true" mathematical spiral because it is too evenly spaced (120). Focusing on the technique of *Spiral Jetty* in conversation with Thomas Pynchon's *Gravity's Rainbow* (1973), Gilbert-Rolfe argues that these two works[24] are explicitly historical and psychological and reads them as a "defamiliarization of the state of the artistic device[25] at a particular moment (a declaration of what is credible and what is not), and simultaneously, and of course unavoidably, an embodiment and record of a series of involuntary acts. It is an historical object that the work of art is most accountable and most mysterious" (Gilbert-Rolfe 1985, 15). While Gilbert-Rolfe's essay is often cryptic, it succeeds in performing the accumulative and repetitive techniques that he identifies in Smithson: his writing constantly oscillates between linguistic and material so that "physical facts like any others [are] sedimented, etymologically and archaeologically, within the geologies of words and things"—in the landscape (87). This alignment of words and things, what Smithson himself will specify as "words and rocks," enunciates the ways in which material itself is interpretive and self-reflexive; a reminder that we cannot ignore the tendencies or behaviors of the medium as these "contain a language that follows a syntax of splits and ruptures" (Smithson quoted in Weiss 1998, 7). Perhaps this is obvious, or blatantly modernist in terms of its return to technique or device as interpretive hermeneutic, and yet, these behaviors—desiccation, entropy, pulse, vibration, submersion—are what distinguish the work from a simply modernist conception of self-generating autonomy (the very thing that contemporary curator Massimiliano Gioni argues a strain of work is doing).

The epic (rational) proliferation Gilbert-Rolfe and Krauss formally propose becomes more complicated (and fragile perhaps) at the end of the film and as witnessed in Dean's visitation. In these moments Smithson, dressed in a white shirt, walks, runs, stumbles along the spiral until he reaches the central point and all of this is set to a helicopter soundtrack reminiscent of Francis Ford Coppola's *Apocalypse Now* (1979). Smithson's movements appear unstable, governed by the uneven topographies of the work. Reflecting on this passage he writes: "Swirling

---

24. Against the framing of Smithson's work in terms of an emergent postmodern position in Krauss's "Sculpture in the Expanded Field," Gilbert-Rolfe argues that *Spiral Jetty* and *Gravity's Rainbow* are explicitly "modernist" in their deployment of self-generating technique, and further that reading *Spiral Jetty* in terms of *Gravity's Rainbow* makes this apparent (Gilbert-Rolfe 1985, 87).

within the incandescence of solar energy were sprays of blood. My movie would end in sunstroke. Perception was heaving, the stomach turning, I was on a geologic fault that groaned within me. Between heat lightning and heat exhaustion the spiral curled into vaporization. I had the red heaves, while the sun vomited its corpuscular radiations" (Smithson [1972] 1996, 148).

Narrating the process of entropic collapse not only as a sculptural or geologic condition, but as vertiginously corporeal as well, Smithson's writing verges on phenomenological science fiction. Landscape alters consciousness as Youngblood might agree; sculpture has now exited the safe axes of the double negatives[26] of landscape and architecture and trespassed somewhere quite else.

Come. Walk with me. Let's get lost.

What did'st thou say? What, how, where, when? Is this love nothing now or all? Water? Fire? Good? Evil? Life? Death? (Sebald [1988] 2002, 110–111)

Two riders were approaching

and the wind began to howl

("All Along the Watchtower" [your choice: Bob Dylan or Jimi Hendrix])

A vortex of dust and dirt spirals up from the desert as a small figure runs toward its center. And now the spiral becomes ungrounded, dirt into air, a relentless

---

25. Curator Fionn Meade also draws attention to the role of "artistic device" in his exhibition *Knight's Move* at Sculpture Center, returning to Victor Shklovsky's essay "Art as Device" in *Theory of Prose* ([1929] 1990). For Meade, Shklovksy, Smithson, and Gilbert-Rolfe the internal logic of the work of art can be read through language—language that is materially and historically located. As Shklovsky reminds us in his preface: "Nevertheless, the word is not a shadow. The word is a thing" (vii).

26. I cannot help but wonder how Michael Heizer's *Double Negative* (1969) worked to undo the very conception of the double negative of its title and of Krauss's proposal; or in a distinct, and more spectacularly violent way, Jean Tinguely's *Study for an End of the World, no. 2* (1962). Considered an early Land Art piece, Tinguely set up a series of contraptions composed of doll parts, wires, and tiny rockets—Rube Goldberg-esque machines in the Las Vegas desert—and blew them up.

spinning energetic wind. Dressed in white, the man, the artist, labors against the force of the tornado until he reaches its interior. Sounds of footsteps and heavy breathing interrupt swirling static of wind. Now the screen is filled with brown wind, bits of dirt and debris, and the sound screams and whistles. Somehow sitting on the carpeted gallery floor of the Museum of Modern Art, New York, we are inside the eye of the storm. Or at least this is one approach to Francis Alÿs's *Tornado* (2000–2010). A less immersive view appears muted through a small aperture cut into the gallery wall.

From 2000 to 2010, Mexico City-based artist Francis Alÿs walked into tornados, smallish swirls of dust and dirt outside of the city. In the film he often holds the camera, so I only see him in flashes of feet, whispers of breath, silenced by the roar of the wind and dark inside the vortex. *Tornado* seduces sonically, visually, haptically as it slows down and accelerates my sense of timing through the shifting scale of the tornados. I am drawn in, captured, and held at attention as Alÿs repeats his encounter again and again. The approach, the immersion, the exit—these become refrains of the film. Repetition is integral to the force of the film as it registers some sense of the duration of this experiment and also the compulsive attraction of danger or being out of control, of submitting to an external force. His encounter is not simply a nihilistic giving up, but more nearly a willingness to suspend expectation and rationalism, to place himself inside a natural billowing, dirty vortex. There he is saturated by circumstances, yet only momentarily, for then the tornado passes by and we see the whirling cone recede in the distance. And then we wait until another appears on the horizon and we chase after it again.

There is something in this process that feels akin to how we experience and make sense of the world, our place, and our history. Perhaps witnessing Alÿs engulfed in the rising dust and swirling atmospherics offers a vertiginously corporeal image of our relationship to historical events. Writing about *Tornado*, curator Mark Godfrey describes the repeated gesture[27] as a "representation of a

---

27. Alÿs's gestures act as poetic ciphers that gain power as they are disseminated as anecdotes and myths into social space. His work is allegorical, yet also explicitly physical, allowing himself to be overtaken by circumstances and landscapes, putting himself into precarious situations—taking a different drug every day for a week, walking the streets of Mexico City with a visible gun, pushing a block of ice until it melts, tracing a line in paint through Jerusalem, running into tornados. Each gesture offers a different level of risk and correspondingly a different commentary on the spaces within which he walks, falls down, flees.

response to disaster . . . compulsively reentering the whirlwinds" (Godfrey 2010, 28), one that he aligns with an experience of history. This endless repeated litany of events and tragedies, listed together one after the other, is not only how we experience history, but also the present, as reading the newspaper becomes a reading of history, of the minutes, hours, days just passed, a catalog of disasters momentarily interrupted by other quotidian or perhaps even quixotic events.

This swirling, spiraling movement toward history, toward destruction, imaged in *Tornado* (and evoked in Smithson's blood-heaving gyrations) resonates with the concept of the omega point as conceived by Pierre Teilhard de Chardin, a French philosopher and Jesuit priest, who trained as a paleontologist and geologist. For Teilhard de Chardin, the universe itself is structured as a spiral composed of love and matter constantly evolving to the maximum point of complexity, the end of the world as we know it, the rapture—this moment is the omega point.[28] Teilhard de Chardin believes that the magnetic force of love is not only poetic and psychical but also cosmic and gravitational.

Driven by the forces of love, the fragments of the world seek each other so that the world may come to being. This is no metaphor; and it is much more than poetry. Whether as a force or a curvature, the universal gravity of bodies, so striking to us, is merely the reverse or shadow of that which really moves nature. To perceive cosmic energy "at the fount" we must, if there is a within of things, go down into the internal or radial zone of spiritual attractions. Love in all its subtleties is nothing more, and nothing less, than the more or less direct trace marked on the heart of the

---

28. Refracted through Don DeLillo's novel *Point Omega* (2010), the spiraling magnetism of Teilhard de Chardin's omega point inverts simultaneously inward as one man tries to escape from the seductions and delusions of history and outward as a meditation on making art. (Thank you to James Foster for this insight.) Thoughts spiral across the desert. Landscape becomes vastness itself: a parched monochromatic space to look out into, to meditate on, an almost emptiness where thoughts evaporate desiccated by the heat, caffeine, dust, and alcohol. For DeLillo, landscape becomes a container for the confessions of the filmmaker and the philosopher as they attempt to make sense of their own histories, delusions, aspirations, and all of these peregrinations— physical, emotional, intellectual follow the spiral around and around again. They talk of a film that will be one take with no edits, one man, Richard Elster, against the wall, just talking. There will never be a film, yet this cinematic quality of portrait of a man (men) against a wall or an emptied out landscape confessing returns again and again in subtly different ways—sometimes with a scotch in hand, sometimes water, sometimes a cigarette, sometimes coffee, sometimes with Elster's daughter hovering in the periphery until she too disappears into the landscape—a young, beautiful apparition seduced and consumed.

element by the psychical convergence of the universe upon itself. (Teilhard de Chardin [1955] 1975, 264–265)

As I witness *Tornado*, there is something of this energetic force happening. Not only figuring a body pushed into other bodies, although it is intriguing to watch other audience members leaning into and away from the screen, but this singular body of Alÿs willingly participating in a kind of communion, rapture by dust, alone in the desert.

Come. Walk with me. Let's get lost.

For a long time I boasted that I possessed all possible landscapes . . . I made rules for the form and movement of every consonant, and with instinctive rhythms, I flattered myself to have invented a poetic verb accessible, sooner or later, to all these senses. I reserved the translation. It began as a study. I wrote of silences, nights, I noted the inexpressible. I fixed the vertiginous whirls. (Rimbaud in Casid 2011, 97)[29]

And where have these illicit trajectories taken us? Through a "turbulent alchemy" as words and things, ideas and rocks, wind and dust, verbs and nouns exchange and change places (Casid 2011, 98). It is in this whirling space that artist and art historian Jill Casid finds the feminist and queer potential of landscape as a verb. Against the static bucolic romance of landscape as art historical archive, Casid invites "ruin, that is, if ruin means theorizations based in embodied, sensate encounters with landscape that involve mucking around in the pleasures, difficulties, same, and desires of the differences within and without" (99). In her theses on landscape Casid plays a semantic bait-and-switch to illuminate a performative and material understanding of landscape as never only representation

---

29. I want to foreground the work of citation and influence and affiliation in this first chapter. And to mark that this epigraph by Rimbaud comes from the epigraph of Jill Casid's "Epilogue: Landscape in, around, and under the Performative" (Casid 2011) included in *Women & Performance: A Journal of Feminist Theory*. This issue on "Feminist Landscape" was edited by Julia Steinmetz and Katie Brewer Ball. Thank you to Ann Pellegrini for suggesting this text at a crucial moment in the writing.

but always already messy and dirty.[30] Casid's alchemical turbulence offers another way to think across this constellation of spatial terrains and topographic representations, modeling a sensate trespassing with critical force and one that returns us to the choreography within the choreographic (98).

Pina Bausch's film *Die Klage der Kaiserin* (1987–1989)[31] opens with a woman struggling with a leaf blower. Wrestling the weight of the machine against the unevenness of the ground, she haphazardly blows clouds of leaves in different directions. In her Sisyphean labor, her dress comes undone, as all Bausch's costumes do,[32] falling off her shoulders as she staggers through the park attempting to clear a ground from which the narrative might begin. The sound of a funeral march continues as the scene cuts to two dancers walking in the woods with large dogs, then to a dancer in an erotic black bunny costume, taking her shoes on and off as she staggers down a dirt hill. She walks as if falling.[33] Knees buckle at each step as she almost collapses against the uneven surface. Later, two old men in overcoats and hats will methodically climb this hill together. Later, the bunny dancer will appear running up a narrow road cutting between the fields of overturned dirt. In a different scene in the forest, a man raises a small boy up into the air with a rope tied

---

30. Wandering in the Ramble in New York City's Central Park, Bob Nickas and John Miller attempt a not-unrelated documentation (in writing, in photographs) of a gay "eroticized landscape, a libidinous site," yet their collaboration records a cool and deserted terrain, one that withholds more than it reveals, which seems perhaps its intent (Nickas [2003] 2008, 45).

31. Pina Bausch's film *Die Klage der Kaiserin* (Lament of the Empress) was produced from October 1987 to April 1989. Why return to an obscure film by Bausch now? As one of the dancers in Wim Wenders's film *Pina* (2011) repeats: *dance dance dance, otherwise we are lost.* Or perhaps it is a nod to my own coming to dance while watching her company perform *Nelken* (1982) at UC Berkeley in 1999 and later other epics at BAM and in formative discussions in André Lepecki's seminar on Bausch, which confirmed my seduction with dance and intrigue in the atmospheric and geographic textures of landscape and theory. And perhaps we are not now witnessing a lament of the empress, but a lament for the empress herself. . . . Am I missing Pina?

32. Here Fionn Meade's description of a different work gives us a telling image: they "hide and reveal their raw materiality at the same time like a loosely tied hospital gown" (Meade 2010, 80).

33. A refrain from Laurie Anderson: "You're walking . . . and you don't always realize it but you're always falling. With each step . . . you fall. You fall forward a short way and then catch yourself. Over and over . . . you are falling . . . and then catch yourself. You keep falling and catching yourself falling. And this is how you are walking and falling at the same time" (Anderson 1987, 69).

to the tree.[34] In another, old men carry crying children through a forest of numbered trees. A man struggles to carry a wardrobe tied to his back with thin rope across a deep green field. Another man shaves in the gutter of a busy street. A woman dances in a state of almost undress under the falling snow and the camera captures the moment just preceding as she hands her coat to an off-camera assistant.

There are a few scenes shot inside—within a lush greenhouse a man covered in mud slowly circles his hips or smokes, an indifferent yet cruel ballet teacher forces repetitions of movement and word in the studio, a dancer wanders through an empty white room under a huge painting of a violent storm—yet these scenes appear more as subtext or rehearsal for the outdoor scenes shot in and around Wuppertal where Bausch's company is based. The interior scenes feel less primary and much less fugitive. There is less a sense of illegitimate trespassing, or erotic betrayal, or traces of violent altercations in the ways that the dancers encounter the landscape. This coupled with the theatricality of the film foregrounds a reimagining of history through a constantly shifting and repeating topography and passage. It is as if the instability of these dirt hills, dimly lit forests, snow-covered fields, empty industrial roads act as participatory translators suggesting a more affective and anecdotal spatial and historical narrative terrain.

It is critical to attend to the landscape within *Die Klage der Kaiserin* to reveal a disruptive correlation between past and present that is explicitly poetic and coincidental. Looking at this work now,[35] it seems prescient that from October 1987 until April 1989, Bausch periodically exited the studio for the woods and fields of Wuppertal to shoot these haunted scenes of arduous walks through the forest, tragic exiles across dangerous terrains, or risky balancing acts. This last image often is negotiated by a male and female dancer as one attempts to stand on the other's shoulders without holding on to each other or the woman momentarily balances only to fall off again and again, almost caught by waiting men as she falls to the floor. These are all poetic and associative leaps to think about the "fall" or

---

34. These scenes haunted me in the earlier writing of this chapter as a lecture for CREATURE FEATURE at the Hebbel Theater in Berlin in August 2011. As I ran everyday along the dirt trails through flickering shadows in the Tiergarten these ghosts felt especially close.

35. Also in light of Wim Wenders's film *Pina* that seems to take *Lament of an Empress* quite seriously as an uncanny model of fragmented narrative. "What are we longing for? Where does this yearning come from?" asks one dancer in the Wenders's film, and yet she could be speaking for both films—was in both, actually.

dissembling of the literal wall separating East and West Berlin in November 1989, and yet . . .

As cultural theorist Paul Carter writes:

To take account of the lie of the land is not simply to seek to ground historical knowing differently; it is to break down the opposition between history and poetry. What if, say, the manner of going over the ground were itself a poetic act, and not merely a prosaic means of getting from one place to another? . . . It is in this cloudy, kineasthetic realm that historical events turn out to obey a spatial poetics, and that poetry, the making of marks, turns out to be performative and historically implicated. (Carter 1996, 295)

Writing to unearth an awareness of the multiple betrayals and erasures of Australian colonial history and specifically the infiltration of Aboriginal art by a Western interpretative lens, Carter seeks to break with a concept of aesthetics that is beholden to mimesis and the fixity of art historical models of writing. Instead his writing as walking acts as an anti-"enclosure act," one that embodies a paradoxical drift and contingency of displacement and movement (Carter 1996, 292). To enact his methexic model, Carter trespasses across songs, dances, ballistics, falconry, love, and violent storms. Describing the arc of a spear in flight as a relational connection between two spaces made visible through its passage, he suggests that this too is the work of poetry, as a mode of thinking and of writing (328). A word or poem "can be likened to the echo which gives back to the caller his voice modified by the lie of the land, the dimensions, forms and textures of the environment" (328). Bausch's lament is one such echo or series of echoes resonating across the landscape and history.

I spoke: you are my life

She spoke: I'll end it soon

I spoke: come soon moon

She spoke: My moon adorns the sky

. . .

I marvel not why someone dies outside his lover's tent

I marvel though when someone loves and still goes on with life

Let us make creatures of all kinds, he urged, and she did not say nay

Little sister, I am thirsty

I could find a little brook

I would go and take a drink

I think I hear one murmuring: how fares my child, how fares my love

Twice shall I come and then never more

(Bausch 1987–1989, spoken in German by dancer Mechthild Grossman; translation mine)

These words, spoken once in a fragmented version in the middle of the film and again in the final scenes as the dancer, Mechthild Grossman, rides an empty suspended tram car through the desolate streets of Wuppertal, become quite literally an echo, repeated in her journey across the spaces of the city; a plaint that calls out to the celestial and natural, moon and river and sky, as interpreters of her difficult, violent desire. Listening to the Empress's lament attunes us to a more tremulous attention to a history of the ground; its fugitive even amnesiac qualities whisper across what is now overgrown, rebuilt. Remember that Wuppertal, like many cities in Germany, was devastated by the bombings near the end of World War II,[36] explosives dropped between the steep granite banks of the city ignited into uncontestable firestorms. Writing in *On the Natural History of Destruction*,[37] W. G. Sebald describes the ruins of cities like Wuppertal as "the terra incognita of the war"; landscapes of ruin that few contemporary writers or witnesses could account for (1999 [2003], 31). Quoting Alexander Kluge's response to encountering Wuppertal, "on that dreadful day when our beautiful city was razed to the ground," Sebald suggests that this is "no more than a gesture sketched to banish memory"

---

36. The Royal Air Force-led raid hit Wuppertal the night of May 29, 1943.

37. Sebald's text draws on lectures presented in Zürich in 1997 detailing the relation between "Air War and Literature" or rather the lack of literature describing these events. His collage of photographs, intricate journalistic details, and limited literature casts a disturbing portrait of the events and simultaneously an inability of the literature of the time to articulate them. One exception he notes is Henrich Böll's *Der Engel Schweig (The Silent Angel),* yet while this was written in 1949–1950 it remained unpublished until 1992.

and one written twenty-five years after the fact (25).[38] So while he compiles a series of impressions, Sebald's deeper concern is that we "forget what we do not want to know" and so now must approach with a more "synoptic and artificial view" (41, 26). Sebald points to a particular quality of forgetting, one that perhaps speaks to Georges Didi-Huberman's reminder that "to remember one must imagine" ([2003] 2008, 37, 30). Meditating on four photographs "snatched" from within the gas chambers at Auschwitz (3), a very different scene from the same war, he argues against any easy rejection or obfuscation of what is given to be seen even if it seems impossible to comprehend. These breathless or "metaphorically, out of breath" images evoke a visceral condensation of past implicating present, forcing us to focus on the blacked-out corners and distant out-of-focus figures as evidence of extreme conditions of physical, emotional, and psychological torment (37). And yet, in spite of all this, he wants us to sense that "this urgency too is a part of their history," something stronger than ghosts emanating from the images, from the landscapes (38).

And while, of course, Bausch's lament does not speak directly to these catastrophes, this is, I believe, the power of a choreographic intimacy with ground as alchemic translation of the violent impossibilities of experience, sensation, event, so that we must encounter the past in the present as so many trespassing, still fugitive acts accumulating historical force even as they speak to a distinct present context.

Come. Walk with me. Let's get lost.

Nights dark beyond darkness and the days more gray each one than what had gone before. Like the onset of some cold glaucoma dimming away the world. His hand rose and fell softly with each precious breath. He pushed away the plastic tarpaulin and raised himself in the stinking robes and blankets and looked toward the east for any light but there was none. In the dream from which he'd wakened he had wandered in a cave where the child led him by the hand. Their light playing over the

---

38. These comments by Kluge were included in his "The Air Raid on Halberstadt on 8 April 1945" and were written around 1970, describing what Sebald claims were his impressions of Wuppertal, Würzburg, and Halberstadt (24–25).

wet flowstone walls. Like pilgrims in a fable swallowed up and lost among the inward parts of some granitic beast. (McCarthy 2006, 3)

Written in a deeply visceral language, scarred and laid bare like the landscape itself, Cormac McCarthy's novel tells the story of a boy and a man crossing a barren burning wasteland on their way to the ocean. McCarthy never admits what cataclysmic event has decimated the countryside, but only hints at it in moments when he writes of howling winds, shifting tremors of the plates moving, hinting at the sounds, smells, vistas of geologic time seizing. Instead he focuses on the quotidian details of passage, of walking, of eating, of sleeping, of "carrying the fire" without falling victim to madness, violence, or fear (McCarthy 2006, 129). This is a choreographic writing of the landscape dilated and emptied out, a durational intensity within which memory and future collapse in the tedious horrors of the present. A nightmare, a fiction, not projective but descriptive as science fiction writer Ursula K. Le Guin reminds her reader: "Distrust everything I say. I am telling the truth" (Le Guin 1969, xvii). The Road focuses not on the violent event—of war, of total devastation (which remains unnamed only hinted at and evidenced in the burnt out terrain)—but instead on the boy and the man's passage, closing in on their bleak precarious journey along the empty roads, dying trees, ruptured bridges. The cryptic gravity of McCarthy's writing effaces its own violence or perhaps as Eyal Weizman explains: "Violence is a kind of performance that does not take place within the fixed grids of space, but actually remakes it" and so this emptied out telling reflects the suffocating preciousness of language as its own kind of sustenance, one that can barely be spared even in explication (Weizman et al. 2009, x). If violence, as Weizman explains, takes over a power of dissembling force, then what kind of language—of words, of gesture, of images—might be capable of response?[39]

Haunting all of these encounters from Kant to Virilio to Bausch to Smithson to McCarthy is the specter of a very specific kind of violence—that of war—whether rendered up close or at a distance that determines the precarious structure of our

---

39. As if attempting to answer a similar question, Didi-Huberman ends his chapter "In the Eye of History" with Samuel Beckett: "No trace anywhere of life, you say, pah, no difficulty there, imagination not dead yet, yes, dead, good, imagination dead imagine" (in Didi-Huberman [2003] 2008, 208, 47, taken from Beckett's "Imagine Dead Imagine"). To process, we must repeat, return, reiterate, and continue on.

contemporary moment. Across these disparate landscapes and events, there exists an uncanny resonance between the scale and dimensions of architecture, of sculpture, of bunkers, of desolate mountain trails, of concrete towers, yet also of ruins and wreckage. This is not to imply that the very distinct historical (and geographic) conditions precipitating acts of war are the same, not at all, but rather to suggest that the fact of such pervasive violence requires our attention particularly when we are thinking about implications for aesthetics and art. Writing of what he calls a forensic aesthetic in postwar art, curator Ralph Rugoff notes that the first use of aesthetics in English appeared in an essay by Thomas De Quincey written in 1827 and titled "On Murder Considered as One of the Fine Arts" (Rugoff 1997, 70).[40] Rugoff highlights this intimate correlation between violence and aesthetics, Kant's own fraught dialectic of the sublime, without romanticizing it. Rather, he uses this dark complicity to argue against existing strictures of artistic discourse, foregrounding the exquisite, if fragmentary, materiality of the work to call attention to what is not given to be seen, not only the events (represented or the labor required in their making), but also "the absent bodies that remain forever off stage" (85).[41] One potent juxtaposition from the catalog pairs Hans Haacke's *Germania* (1993), a torn-up concrete floor framed by the title hung in block letters on the wall created in the German Pavilion at the 1993 Venice Biennial, with a photograph of wreckage from US Air flight 427 scattered in an airport hanger.[42] As witnesses, we are called on to make sense of these contingent and provisional clues not only as a process of investigation, but also as a way of mourning (98). Under the influence of this conception of aesthetics, a choreographic attention to writing and to art making provokes another way of moving and being moved by art, sensing seduction, devastation, grief, as not always political but also perhaps ethical or social concerns, reverberations of our precarious state.

---

40. Rugoff notes that his reference comes from the Joel Black's work *Aesthetics of Murder: A Study in Romantic Literature and Contemporary Culture* (1991).

41. This essay appears in the catalog for the exhibition *Scene of the Crime* that traces a strain of West Coast artists including Paul McCarthy, Chris Burden, Edward Ruscha, Edward Kienholz, Lyle Ashton Harris, Vij Celmins, Nayland Blake. The exhibition ran from July 23 to October 5, 1995, at the UCLA Armand Hammer Museum in Los Angeles.

42. *Germania* refers not only to Hitler's name for Nazi Germany but also his visit to the same pavilion in 1934. Haacke includes a photograph of this event at the entrance of his installation.

These conditions exist not as natural states, but as results of actions and encounters; they are constructed conditions for which we must prepare and to which we must respond. And for curator Massimiliano Gioni, this is one of the powers of art (and particularly sculpture) as its own enigmatic event that is always explicitly historically grounded and anticipatory.[43] Taking its title from W. G. Sebald's novel *After Nature* ([1988] 2002), Gioni's exhibition *After Nature* (2008)[44] returns us to the precarious conditions of the present, unveiled in the landscapes of painting, of barren arctic seas, of the artist's own mind. It is as Gioni writes: "an exhibition of landscapes—it tells the story of offended sceneries and scorched earth. It is nature after a trauma, a violent loss of uncertain origins" (Gioni 2008). His provocation lies not in the aesthetic identification, but in his assertion of art's predictive power to not only imagine landscapes, invent worlds, but also prefigure cultural climates—again science fiction with critical force, an agenda that becomes more devastatingly clear in *After Nature*:

Animals dangling from the wall, dying trees supported by crutches, the light of the stars trapped on paper, the surface of the moon carefully scrutinized. And idols sculpted with animal skin and straw, mutant bodies encased in glass sarcophagi, plants bathing in artificial lights, nuclear explosions and obsessive litanies

---

43. Gioni makes a similar claim in *Unmonumental*, his previous exhibition that opened the new New Museum in 2007. Marked by a promiscuous accumulation, a repurposing of pop and social imagery, and a consumption of the pedestal, the aesthetics of the unmonumental reject all monumental ambitions and devices of modern sculpture to embrace a state of more dispersive precarious ruin. The essay opens with the allusive statement: "The century had barely begun when its foundations started to tremble. The millennium opened with the sound of rubble falling to the ground, smoke enveloping the city. This new century began in a ruin" juxtaposed with images of the Paris Vendôme column falling (1871), Mario Merz's *Giap's Igloo* (1967), the urban field of flowers of Princess Diana's memorial outside Kensington Palace (1997), and a nod to Krauss's nod to Eisenstein, David Hammon's *In the Hood* (1993) (Gioni 2007, 64). A tour de force of citation much like the work it surrounds, *Unmonumental: The Object in the 21st Century* opened at the New Museum in 2007. This exhibition also falls into a genealogy of the dispersive accumulative aesthetics of contemporary sculpture explored in *Thing: New Sculpture from Los Angeles* curated by James Elaine, Aimee Chang, and Christopher Miles (2005); *The Uncertainty of Objects and Ideas* curated by Anne Ellgood at the Hirschhorn Museum (2007); and the qualities Hal Foster identifies in his article on the precarious (as discussed earlier).

44. The title of the exhibition references W. G. Sebald's *After Nature* ([1988] 2002) and the exhibition catalog consists of a foldout cover that wraps around a paperback version of Sebald's book.

scribbled in the midst of a frenzy. Rituals, dances, propitiary rites. . . . It is a world caught in a moment of fibrillation. It is the land of wilderness and ruins that exists in an imaginary time zone between a remote past and a not-so-distant future. (Gioni 2008)

Describing a world in spasm—"in a moment of fibrillation"—that jumps from earthly to celestial to human to animal to future to the past in a series of sublime seizures, Gioni opens with an epigraph borrowed from Werner Herzog's film *Lessons of Darkness* (1992). "The collapse of the stellar systems will occur—like creation—in grandiose splendor" (Pascal in Gioni 2008). The entropic velocity and scale of this premonition casts a long shadow over all of the work in *After Nature*[45] yet is perhaps best articulated along the desolation of McCarthy's roads and the vertigo of Herzog's film (included in the exhibition) that share an uncanny resonance with the images of Virilio's bunkers and Bausch's surreal parables.

Herzog's documentary of the burning and bubbling oil fields in Kuwait ignited by the retreating Iraqi soldiers driven out by coalition forces in the aftermath of the Gulf War is gorgeous and seductive and horrific. Composed of images intensely shifting in scale (tire tracks that appear like a smoking mountain ranges), occasional voice-over by Herzog, and an operatic sound score, it serves as lament and requiem without assigning specific blame. This textured ambivalence made the film quite controversial during its premiere release, as some in the audience felt the use of these images for poetic and ambivalent means to be unethical (Herzog and Beier 2010). Yet *New York Times* film critic J. Hoberman claims it stands as Herzog suggests as "ecstatic truth" (Hoberman 2005). Ecstatic or sublime, Herzog renders a world seeming unlike our own, yet is explicitly that. *Lessons of Darkness* projects what theorist Brian Holmes names "proliferating monsterous effervescences"—the potential for art to produce or visualize something in the world that is untimely or out of joint (Holmes 2011). Shot from a helicopter, the aerial views produce a vertiginous perspective sweeping over the swollen

---

45. T. J. Demos's essay "Art After Nature: The Post-Natural Condition" identifies a mode of artwork that addresses the impact of economies on ecologies through a myriad of interactive technological paradigms and processes. He writes: "'Nature' cannot be objectified as separate and external, because living and nonliving objects are embedded within a 'mesh' of social, political, and phenomenal relations" (Demos 2012, 194). His is a provocative explication of the unnatural of nature and the contingent structuring processes of financial and legal sector on what we still call the natural world.

concrete bubbles that tower over the sprawl of the city and the emptied out landscapes punctuated by fires, smoke, temporary shelters, and men wandering in hazmat suits in the midst of the flames. The helicopter casts its own shadow on the arid gray ground as Herzog intones: "all we could find were traces"—tire tracks, hand signals from these "creatures" (cleanup crew), and "dinosaurs" (their gigantic earth-moving equipment). The workers appear against walls of orange flames and then in the few moments that they stand against the toxic gray clouds, one throws a torch back into the stream of oil. Herzog observes again in his deep romantic monotone: "now they are content, now there is something to distinguish again." Not only calculated ironic distance, his sparse remarks illuminate the uncanny seduction of the flames and the desire even on the part of the cleanup crew (often featuring close-ups of the U.S.-based crew from *BOOTS* and *COOTS* that merged with Halliburton in 2010[46]) to sustain the devouring flames.

In the section titled "Protuberances," the camera closes in on fallen blackened tree branches submerged in slowly twitching bubbles of oil. This microscopic view of boiling sludge evokes a darkened sea, toxic and otherworldly, an eruptive landscape under siege. It is a powerful image in its confusion of reference. Editing out the saturation of spectacle, these images lend a political and prophetic power to this film. As Herzog explains: "When I look out here I see that everything is cluttered. There are hardly any images to be found. Images are no longer possible. One has to dig deep down like an archaeologist to find images in this offended landscape" (Herzog in Gioni 2008).[47]

In Herzog's film (and McCarthy's writing), landscape functions multiply as ground and mise-en-scène, pointing to the provocation of this searing documentary that doesn't mention specific cultural events precipitating the devastation and as a result stands as historical, present, and projective image. Something immanent resides within the landscape itself, something that Herzog seeks through his excavation of the literally burning monuments. It is not that Herzog's film resists specificity but rather that it is so specific as to signal the constant deluge of cultural catastrophe. "All too soon, there will be something else to talk about: the next massacre, the future failed revolution, a fresh cycle of economic collapse, the

46. See http://www.bootsandcoots.com/members/history.html (accessed June 20, 2013).

47. The Herzog quote was taken from Wim Wenders's *Tokio Ga* (1985) and translated for the catalog by Gioni.

renewed disappointment of democracy, environmental cataclysms, another looming pandemic," writes curator Cuauhtémoc Medina on the relentless failures in contemporary life while questioning how art might respond (Medina 2009, 28–29). *Lessons of Darkness* articulates and anticipates this something else through the montage of images, enacting what Walter Benjamin calls a dialectical image:

It's not that what is past casts its light on what is present, or what is present its light on what is past; rather, images is that wherein what has been comes together in a flash with the now to form a constellation. In other words, image is dialectics at a standstill. For while the relation of the present to the past is a purely temporal, continuous one, the relation of what-has-been to the now is dialectical: is not progression but image, suddenly emergent.—Only dialectical images are genuine images (that is, not archaic); and the place where one encounters them is language. Awakening. (Benjamin [1940] 1968, 462)

The force of the dialectical image incites recognition of the failures of the past as explicitly connected to the present; it clarifies something of history necessary for a realignment of the present. The dialectical image draws together Benjamin's materialist leanings and mystical thoughts, an aesthetic theory of spiritual and political consequence. And it is very personal as well, as much of Benjamin's work was. For Benjamin, history was not some abstract machine, but words whispered into your ear and images staged before your eyes from which you could not look away: "The true picture of the past flits by. The past can be seized only as an image which flashes up at the instant when it can be recognized and is never seen again. . . . To articulate the past historically does not mean to recognize it 'the way it really was.' It means to seize hold of a memory as it flashes up in a moment of danger" (Benjamin [1940] 1968, 255). Benjamin's prophetic warning doesn't advise that we stay away from meteorological or geologic or historic crises, but rather that within these maelstroms we notice, we pay attention to our position and response. We must walk up close.

For Benjamin, history, and our relationship to it, has an intimate relationship to facial gesture. He describes it in one moment as witnessed through the eyes of Angel Novelus, an image based on Paul Klee's childish drawing of Angel Novelus that hung in Benjamin's flat and becomes an avatar for the dialectical image. In another moment, he conveys in a letter to his dear friend Max Horkheimer in 1935 an image of history as a gesture, a sensual swoosh of air lightly kissing your cheek or disappearing into your ear. The "vanishing point" of history, he explains, is "contained in the ticking of a clock whose striking of the hour has just reached *our* ears" (Benjamin [1935] 1994, 509; italics in original).

Drawing on this moment from Benjamin's letters as he explains the logic of his exhibition *TIME AGAIN* at Sculpture Center, curator Fionn Meade makes a subtle, likely unconscious gesture as he explains: "the vanishing point of history is right behind your head" (Meade 2011).[48] He pulls his hand from behind the nape of his neck to illustrate how it is that history vanishes and perhaps to offer a way to reclaim it. Meade then turns to Matthew Buckingham's *Image of Absalon to Be Projected Until It Vanishes* (2001), a slide projection of a photograph of the monument to Absalon taken from behind so we only see the horses tail and the back of the man wielding an ax (figure 1.1).[49] From this perspective, Absalon, the controversial Danish warrior-bishop whose reign was marked by constant military campaigns supported by this stolen wealth, appears dwarfed by the swirling clouds (Meade 2011, 6). This slide is to be projected until the image burns out and for Meade points to an almost literal vanishing, a dimming of sight, an experience of history as duration in the present; imagining history not as the thing behind you that you cannot see or remember but the events right before your eyes that blur and fade until they vanish.

In *The Archaeology of Knowledge*, Michel Foucault writes of a similarly corporeal relationship to the monuments of history. Yet instead of being tied to the terms and imperatives of history he speaks of discourse as an alternative to history that anticipates its own limits. Inside the discursive paradigm, Foucault witnesses his own subjective decentering—his own impending death:

Is not discourse, in its most profound determination, a "trace"? And is its murmur not the place of insubstantial immortalities? Must we admit that the time of

---

48. *TIME AGAIN* ran at Sculpture Center from May 9 to July 25, 2011, Long Island City, NY.

49. Witnessing Buckingham's dimming monument, I recall the literal turning of the monument—another man astride another horse—that sits in Ban Josip Jelačić Square in Zagreb, Croatia, and that I walked past daily while there in June 2009. Created by Antun Dominik Fernkorn in 1866, and one of the first public monuments in Zagreb, this sculpture of Ban Josip Jelačić was originally positioned with the sword raised toward Hungary as a reminder of the victory but was removed in 1947 by the Communist government at the time. It was then reinstalled and reoriented to face away from Hungary in 1990 after the dissolution of Yugoslavia and elections in Croatia. See http://en.wikipedia.org/wiki/Ban_Jelačić_Square (accessed June 20, 2013).

1.1 Matthew Buckingham, *Image of Absalon to Be Projected Until It Vanishes*, 2001.
Continuous slide projection and framed text, dimensions variable. Photograph © Matthew
Buckingham, courtesy of Murray Guy, New York.

discourse is not the time of consciousness extrapolated into the dimension of history, or the time of history present in the form of consciousness? Must I suppose that in my discourse I can have no survival? And that in speaking I am not banishing my death, but actually establishing it; or rather, that I am abolishing all interiority in that exterior that is so indifferent to my life, and so *neutral*, that it makes no distinction between my life and my death? (Foucault [1969] 1972, 210; italics in original)

Discourse's efficacy resides in this displacement of subjectivity and of time and here Buckingham's dimming slide projects another ghostly image of this displacement. The impossibility of survival opens up the question of history's temporality, breaking from continuous, chronological representations of objects and subjects under the rule of history's causal laws, and foregrounds discontinuity and dispersion as conditions for a rewriting of history that Foucault names archeology.

In Foucault's thinking, classical history's compulsive search for origins, patterns, and continuity served only to force an incomplete and dominant legibility legislated by power that could not account for interruptions of less visible, less legible subjects and subjectivities. Monuments from the past were selected and taught to speak, turned into documents that fit neatly into predetermined dusty archives (Foucault [1969] 1972, 7). Foucault calls for a reversal of this process, an attention to the intricate details of the monument itself. In a sense he urges us to turn history (and its monuments) around, upside-down, to look as Buckingham's image does at the monument from behind or from below, to read the gestures of the man on the horse against drifting clouds. The examination of these particularities reveals previously given but "unthinkable" discontinuities that Foucault takes as his object of analysis, asking how to "conceive of discontinuity (threshold, rupture, break, mutation, transformation)?" (5). The objects of this archeological approach will not be artifacts or ruins, but statements. Unlike the sentence or the question, the statement, for Foucault, is not a grammatical function but a modality or "fact of language" that is "something more than a series of traces, something more than a succession of marks on a substance" (107). It takes a definite position in relation to other statements and other verbal performances and has a "repeatable materiality" (109). The "something more" is the excessive quality of the statement, an inhabitation of language by an other, a distance, within which what is said and the mode of saying it are joined. In the process of signification the object, its meaning, and relationship to the subject are suspended in the statement itself.[50] In this move, Foucault conflates the acts of speech and writing to offer a new locality from which to analyze history. Responsive to but distinct from structuralism, psychoanalysis, or phenomenology, discourse is rendered as a fold touching interior to exterior; discourse always verges on disappearance. It is a surface of discrete local affects and experiences revealing the conditions of subjectivity and knowledge under the influence of power; its time is the future anterior. The time of the future anterior— what will have been—is not only an imagined time or place but also hints at the spaces within which we walk and wander. How do we see? What images and events and worlds catch your eye? How does history live in the landscape and what does it anticipate?

Come. Walk with me. Let's get lost.

Holes in a fence are for peeping.
    I would establish boundaries and then let others be cowed, or look skyward, or investigate the situation and find the physical and mental points of egress that lead to topography, to cairns and to the highway. To suddenly feel surrounded should give the viewer pause, but to assess in that moment the height of the enclosure should elevate the viewer above the construct—like projecting oneself over a maze to find the missed turn, but then stopping to consider that one was, in fact, aloft. (J. Foster 2011b)

    To trace the subtle workings of historical force through an attention to topography, to landscape, is a vertiginous proposal, requiring a suspension of the limiting logics of representation and orientation in order to enter instead a more immersive terrain. It is also to ask how "we place ourselves in relation to history?" (J. Foster 2012). Following Benjamin, we understand these histories are never only

---

50. Foucault clearly differentiates the multiple qualities of the statement from a psychoanalytic notion of latency and posits instead that it is "neither visible nor hidden" (Foucault [1969] 1972, 109). The nature of the statement must be paradoxical. If the condition of discourse is one of "traces," it requires an object that overflows and offers something more to attach itself too, something that is equally unstable. Marking out a position for language that is not anthropological or transcendental, Foucault names the ontological quality of language "a statement" (113).

distant cultural hallucinations but are quite intimately experiential as well—whispers, echoes, shadows, reflections that might only be apprehended up close.

Standing in front of artist James Foster's *All Along, My Watchtower* (2011) is a compromised perspective; it is a safe intermediary zone allowing only a partial view, for from here you cannot really see it in whole or detail (figures 1.2–1.3). Playing with boundary as concept and composition, the sculpture demands a hesitation. You must step back or draw even closer, inciting a shift of perspective that turns inward, bends underneath, looks up. From one perspective it appears as a fence post growing out of the slick purple cube, broken appendages that once might have been part of a double helix are now distended and severed, bleeding black resin from their post holes. A small rock outcropping interrupts the surface of inky black resin that seems to fill or perhaps seal the cube's interior. Yet, this is not ink (think Charles Ray, *Ink Box*, 1986) or a riff on the notorious neutrality of minimalism's myriad manifestations of cube-ness (think Donald Judd, Robert Morris, Carl Andre, Tony Smith, Eva Hesse, Anne Truitt),[51] but a strange pedestal that is simultaneously seductive and withdrawn, perfect fetish finish as terrain for a decoupage of signification. The rungs suggest a broken spiraling architecture interrupted by the detailed attention to the interior surfaces that hide a photograph of a meteor landing, a huge hollowing of the earth's surface, refracted by the lower surface of mirror interrupted with circles of black plexiglass. The exterior surfaces of the posts are coated in black plexiglass inlaid with a half-moon shard of mirror and a smaller photograph of a moon or a planet. Embedded within the surfaces, the images propose a sedimentation of disparate topographies and temporalities—geologic, planetary, art historical—that interrupt the surface and momentarily flatten the sculptural into the pictorial, casting blind spots or blackouts within the work itself, affecting a disorientation of horizon as the structure itself proliferates through reflection on the surface of the black resin. These intimate shifts of scale and site

---

51. Here one could meditate on the contemporary resonances of Donald Judd's definition of the "Specific Object" (1965), a definition that was far less specific than its name, or Robert Morris's "gestalt" explained in his "Notes on Sculpture, Parts I–III" that responded to Judd's initial provocation. For Morris, the gestalt was an almost monadic contraction of perception possible in the form of the cube that when installed in a gallery setting with other cubes or shapes achieved a kind of phenomenological presence—the very notion of presence that Michael Fried ran from in horror in his hysterical essay "Art and Objecthood" (1967 in Fried 1998) about the impending doom of sculpture becoming theater. See also Annette Michelson's essay "Robert Morris: An Aesthetics of Transgression" ([1969] 2000).

1.2–1.3 James Foster, *All Along, My Watchtower*, 2011. Wood, epoxy, mirror, plexiglass, found photos, stone, pigment. 34 × 34 × 86 inches. Photographs courtesy of the artist.

affect a disorienting vertigo that mirrors the spiraling movement of the architectural limbs: an uncanny monument that becomes ladder, passage, beacon, and watchtower.

All Along, My Watchtower proposes a series of trajectories connecting rocks to stars, mirrors to meteors, cellular to architectural to invent its own topography where the boundaries between terrestrial and celestial appear, at moments, not so distant, perhaps. This confusion of orientation recalls Smithson's conflation of time in space such that time might take on the qualities of sedimentation and space those of reflective horizon: "A horizon is something else other than a horizon; it is closedness in openness, it is an enchanted region where down is up. Space can be approached, but time is far away. Time is devoid of objects when one displaces all destinations" (Smithson [1972] 1996, 119). Part of the enchantment of Foster's work (like Smithson's) is its seductive deployment of a crystalline opacity, a seeming transparency that foregrounds its own material virtuosity while withholding its secrets and depths. It acts, as Foster explains, as a "koan" (J. Foster 2011a). This koan is an enigmatic gift. As Avital Ronell describes: a koan "requires the recipient both to answer to it and to let it go. A koan is an enigma with which one has to contend, almost existentially but without the ontological question mark. . . . Cohabitation with a koan must also provoke a crisis, an experience at the limit of conceivable tolerance on the part of the body and mind. . . . The koan is your intimate persecutor" (Ronell 2010, 35). Not only an intellectual conundrum, the koan intertwines physical with perceptual with theoretical to scale experience through our bodies—the disorienting site from which Smithson and Foster depart. For Ronell a koan vivisects a concept of philosophy as bodiless discourse, contaminating further what phenomenology sets in motion. Her agitation toward the corporeal offers something for a choreographic reading of sculpture that illuminates the intensely affective apparitional presences conjured in these works; seeing is only ever one part of the encounter. Foster reminds me of this provocation in his parenthetical and titular gesture, it is not *the* watchtower (of Bob Dylan or Jimi Hendrix) but *All Along, My Watchtower*, possessive and possessed.

And yet what is it that we are called upon to watch, to witness, to feel? Foster's *At Middle Distance* (2012), a broken leaning gallows inscribed with shards of glacial mountains evolving from swirling martian terrain offers a possible response. A forensic attention might incite so many stories of violent altercations in distant landscapes, apparitional figures fallen, buried, or consumed. *At Middle Distance* shifts the terms of *All Along, My Watchtower,* unleashing the latter's controlled clash of temporalities and materials into something more precarious, an idea of sculpture not beholden to the language of monuments or unmonuments, sites or nonsites (if we want to return to the terms of Krauss, Gioni, Smithson, et al.). A paradoxical tension resides within the sculpture itself; surface details literally materialize through magnetic forces of attraction (obsidian pigments gather on black marbles) while the composition (broken fence inverted into distended gallows) enacts an entropic dramaturgy that becomes more explicitly violent and violated when exhibited as a screen for Brendan Majewski's manic video montages—riot police, a baby politician, goth teens blacking out their eyes or coughing up razor blades, atomic bomb tests and collapsing cities, teenage beatings, a flock of birds, bedridden women holding hands, high-speed trains and office mutinies—edited into a furious flickering dystopia.[52] Yet even alone in the studio absent the devastating fury of Orphan's sound and Majewski's videos, *At Middle Distance* emanates a dark elegiac power in its looming scale and fractured logic, offering up a twisted dialectics closer to what artist Steven Parrino identifies as "a collapse of history . . . a post-punk existential" (Parrino 2003, 35).[53] While Parrino pays explicit homage to Smithson, positioning art "toward an expansion of the post-modern," he also returns

---

52. *At Middle Distance* was included in the exhibition "A Child's Guide to Good & Evil" at Ramiken Crucible, July 14–August 12, 2012, in New York City including videos by Brendan Majewski, soundtrack by Orphan, and screens by Nicholas Brooks, Graham Caldwell, Gardar Eide Einarsson, James Foster, Jacob Kassay, Amy O'Neill, Steven Parrino, David Ratcliff, and Jim Jim Train.

53. Steven Parrino's "Toward Expanding the Post-Modern (after Robert Smithson)" (2003):
-Toward an allegory of the chaotic.
-Toward an anti-systemic.
-Toward a Process Church of Final Judgment.
-Toward a collapse of history.
-Toward an abstraction of apocalyptic vision.
-Toward a responsible anarchy.
-Toward a structure in dissolve.
-Toward a Stealth Satanic.
-Toward a post-punk existential.
-Toward a supersession.
-Toward a psychedelic meltdown.
-Toward a hall of mirrors.
-Toward a totality of effect.
-Toward a resistant resonance.

us to the semantics of Rosalind Krauss and Gene Youngblood's haunted conscience as well. *At Middle Distance* evokes such distant expansive horizons, conjuring a black alchemy (of narrative and of matter) that is relentless, seductive, destructive. Such a choreographic perception of sculpture becomes then an aperture for history in its many points of contact along the landscape of experience.

Come. Walk with me. Let's get lost.

I have a thirst like the heat of the earth on fire. Mountains writhe. I see waves of flame. Washes, flashes, waves of flame. Thirst is in the rivers of the body. The rivers burn but do not move. Flesh—is it flesh?—lies beneath some heated stone. Lava rises in burned-out fields. Where, in what cavern, have such disruptions taken place? Volcanic lips give fire, wells bubble. Bone lies like rubble upon the wound. (Mailer 1983, 3)

There are hearts bigger than planets: black hearts that absorb light, hope, and dust particles, that eat comets and space probes. Motionless, sullen dirigibles, they hang in the empty space between galaxies. We can't see them, but we know they're there, fattening. (Jackson 2002, 3)

To ask how we place ourselves in relation to history is also to project ourselves into other scales, other perspectives, other landscapes to experience dirt, dust, smoke, fire, and stars as simultaneously intimately corporeal and cosmically vast. The flux between anatomical and topographical is of course allegoric and metaphoric, and yet it also calls attention to our own agency and orientation. In "What Is the Contemporary?" Italian political philosopher Giorgio Agamben asks a perhaps similar question of the relation, specifically of the poet or artist, to the contemporary—our present saturated with historical force and future promise. Explicating a poem by Osip Mandelstam, Agamben speaks of the contemporary as "the shattering, as well as the welding, of the age's vertebrae" (Agamben [2008] 2009, 43). Temporality takes on anatomical and sculptural form; under duress the contemporary appears fractured and distended like the rungs, perhaps, of Foster's broken spiral or severed gallows. And then Agamben gestures toward the artist to bear witness to these fissures in the hopes of offering some kind of recommendation or suture. This is not a heroic task or nostalgic turn to a more idealized past or

1.4 Marianne Vitale, still from *Burned Bridge*, 2011. Digital video. Photograph courtesy of the artist and Zach Feuer Gallery.

future, but requires that the artist look not at the light but into the shadows and darkness. Agamben's call reverberates across the work discussed thus far as it illuminates the darkness, violence, catastrophic qualities of the contemporary as that which the artist must look into and attempt to make sense of. "The contemporary is the one whose eyes are struck by the beam of darkness that comes from his own time" (45). This is a paradoxical position that requires a constant negotiation between distance and proximity (spatial and temporal) and casts the figure of the contemporary in a dis-synchronous relation to her own moment. Within this temporal "caesura," the artist creates a point of contact, a work of relation (52).

No longer must we look far out into the horizon for monuments or unmonuments or decoys or perimeters, instead we must turn to witness up close a leaking organic carapace, petrified forests, a muted gathering of bronzed boulders, burning bridges, fractured watchtowers (figure 1.4).[54] Sculpture as charred ruin or requiem. Art taken into the woods and torched. Aesthetics scarred by illegitimate trespassing, erotic betrayal, traces of violent altercation. This mode of contemporary work requires its own rapt discourse equally uncertain and oblique; rapture negotiated through a disorientation of vision, fragments of landscape and broken appendages, bleeding black resin, planets and blackouts.

We are still walking, even dancing, through the landscapes of the precarious. Are you lost, yet?

---

54. A constellation of works around Foster's could thus include Matthew Barney, *DJED* (2012); David Brooks, *Petrified Forest* (2010); Jim Hodges, *Untitled* (2011); Marianne Vitali, *Burned Bridge* (2012).

2 **Violent Desire** Writing Laughing

Dance involves breath, the respiration of the earth. This is because the central question of dance is the relation between verticality and attraction. Verticality and attraction enter the dancing body and allow it to manifest a paradoxical possibility: that the earth and the air may exchange their positions, the one passing into the other.—Alain Badiou, "Dance as a Metaphor for Thought"

For those who laugh, together become like the waves of the sea—there no longer exists between them a partition as long as the laughter lasts; they are no more separate than are two waves, but their unity is as undefined, as precarious as that of the agitation of the waters.—Georges Bataille, *Oeuvres complètes*

From landscape to liquid horizon, we now trespass from the scaffolding of sculpture into a more intimately corporeal terrain. Captured in the tremulousness of gesture—torqued, twisted, splayed out, laughing—we witness body becoming landscape becoming liquid becoming desire as so many openings toward another approach to the choreographic and to writing (the pressure of the choreo on the graphic, yet again). If chapter 1 asked how we encounter history in the present as we walk—feet tracing patters in dirt, eyes turned toward sky—this chapter attends more closely to the stumbles, stutters, and spasms of gesture, danced and laughed. In these encounters violence exists not only as shadowy surround, a series of symbolic and systemic contours that are deeply pervasive, ideological, and material, but is explicitly bodily as well. Under duress, whether gestural or emotional or historical, language falters, can only fail, leaving us in a volcanic abyss of sorts but also offering a possibility for escape. In these strangled moments, language, as much writing as speech, must search for a different transversal poetics that ruptures the imperative and known. Writing after the devastation and ashes of Hiroshima, Nagasaki, and the camps,[1] Georges Bataille evokes an "atmosphere of death, of the disappearance of knowledge" in the same breath and then attempts his own writing

---

1. In his introduction to Bataille's *The Unfinished System of Nonknowledge*, Stuart Kendall notes that Bataille published "Nietzsche's Laughter" in *Exercise de silence* in November 1942 at a moment when the war was finally turning against the Germans (Bataille 2001, xxii). Laughter

of nonknowledge or unknowing (*non-savoir*) as a never-ending process to uncover something of the impossible experience. Refusing the servile qualities of knowledge and of philosophy, Bataille seeks experience, intensity, as slippery sites to interrogate writing and thinking. A deeply paradoxical project, he acknowledges that nonknowledge must always exist in a "perpetual rebellion against itself" and must constantly seek out ways to elicit our own disorientation ([1951] 2001b, 129–130); laughter and tears offer two gestures that actively participate in such a vertiginous undoing of knowledge and of language.[2]

Laughter is convulsive: an "intimate overturning, of suffocating surprise" not only of our body and mind (and both simultaneously) but explicitly of knowledge as well (Bataille [1953] 2001, 133).[3] As Bataille writes: "*Laughing* and *thinking* at first

---

appeared in the midst of the horror and continued to echo across Bataille's thinking until his death in 1962.

2. Throughout this chapter, I refer to the translations of Bataille in *The Unfinished System of Nonknowledge*. Yet my initial reading began with Annette Michelson's translation of "Unknowing: Laughter and Tears" published in *October* 36 (Bataille [1953] 1986). I include an excerpt to reveal the slight discrepancies, most obviously the shift between nonknowledge and un-knowing: "Laughter is, let us say, the effect of un-knowing, though laughter has not, theoretically, as its object the state of un-knowing; one does not, by laughing, accept the idea that one knows nothing. Something unexpected occurs, which is in contradiction to the knowledge we do have. . . . He who laughs does not, theoretically, abandon his knowledge, but he refuses, for a time-a limited time-to accept it, he allows himself to be overcome by the impulse to laughter, so that what he knows is destroyed, but he retains, deep within, the conviction that it is not, after all, destroyed. When we laugh we retain deep within us that which is suppressed by laughter, but it has been only artificially suppressed, just as laughter, let us say, has the power to suspend strict logic" (Bataille [1953] 1986, 97).

3. Umberto Eco narrates the confounding confusion of laughter and knowledge in *The Name of the Rose* ([1980] 1983) through the character of the librarian who is so afraid of the potential contagion implicit in laughter that he hides away the only copy of Aristotle's exegesis on comedy and soaks each page in deadly poison. Of course, when the character of the monk-detective finds it, the librarian consumes every page and dies laughing in the midst of his burning library. Laughter figures as contagion to the sites and bodies of knowledge (literal and metaphoric), one so deadly that it must be contained and ingested lest it seep out off the boundaries of the page, the text, the library. And so for Eco's librarian, laughter and its discourse must be kept in the dark. This marks a distinct difference from Bataille, also trained as a medieval librarian, who in his secret societies and writings on the *Acéphale: Religion-Sociologie-Philosophie* and atheology celebrated the dark powers of laughter.

Also to note, the anecdote from Eco opens the "Introduction" by Jane Taylor to *The Anatomy of Laughter* (2005), an anthology of discursive texts on laughter including scientific assessments;

appeared to complete each other. Thought without laughter seemed mutilated, laughter without thought was reduced to this insignificance" ([1952] 2001, 153).[4] From within the experience of laughter, we witness something of nonknowledge as an opening to a messier ethics of dancing, of writing, of living. Such tremulous dances allow us an entrée into violence as gesture or act, a force (Walter Benjamin will use the word *Gewalt* to suggest both violence and force simultaneously[5]) warping speech and sense, sound and inchoate illegibility to produce another choreographic possibility. Within these precarious encounters, an incendiary corporeal logic undoes the rational along its insurgent and desiring edges, invasive and involved, I am captured in the glistening luscious viscera of spit sound speech. Such dances intoxicate: pleasure and horror and beauty are never singular but always multiple, echoing, stumbling, spasming, dancing.

Laughing

As she laughed I was aware of becoming involved in her laughter and being part of it, until her teeth were only accidental stars with a talent for squad-drill. I was drawn in by short gasps, inhaled at each momentary recovery, lost finally in the dark caverns of her throat, bruised by the ripple of unseen muscles.—T. S. Eliot, "Hysteria"[6]

---

metaphysical ruminations; speculations on humor that cross disciplinary lines of anthropology, ethnology, psychology, physics, and literary and cultural studies to foreground laughter as always already a strangely ambivalent mode of translation, one that breaks with an Cartesian division of body and mind. Is laughter possible to translate? What does it say? Where does it come from? But always laughter is deeply citational in its echoes, repetitions, refrains.

4. Even earlier, in 1946, when he was practicing yoga and organizing his principles for "Method of Meditation" Bataille wrote: "If I wish it, to *laugh* is to think, but this is a sovereign moment" (2001; italics in original).

5. See Benjamin [1921] 1996.

6. Anca Parvulescu concludes her introduction to *Laughter: Notes on a Passion* with a brief mention of this quote, as a reminder that laughter is never only joy but also terror. As laughter reiterates so it also incites citation and association. We become involved in these moments of the ecstatic trapped in the quotidian (Eliot is describing an interruption in an otherwise seemingly dull dinner date). Laughter's pleasure is always singed with violence.

Taking Bataille at his word, I begin again from experience. Here laughter and its many repetitions force a more promiscuous critical encounter with writing as laughing as dancing.[7] Entering the theater was my only initiation to this improvised action; dissembling spectator relations there would be no audience only participants in this one-hour performance of laughter. Laughing, coughing, smiling, doubled over, sweating, red faced, embarrassed, I awkwardly wander across the space. Part of the *Politics of Ecstasy/Altered States of Presence*[8] festival held at the Hebbel Theater (Hebbel am Ufer) in Berlin in January 2009, *A Single Action: Laughing* offers a provocative experiment of laughter as durational gesture through what choreographer Meg Stuart described as a "risky blissful experiment" of laughing together (Stuart 2009). Yet her joyful promise of laughing on an empty stage for one hour dissolves into a chaotic and excruciating event as we attempt to make each other laugh and then pull away. Tentative connections form as we test different forms of intimacy—tumbling, spinning, kissing, jumping, spilling water, crawling, undressing—touching and then recoiling out of exhaustion or confusion. Here the risk of ecstatic involvement requires an undoing of usual patterns of physicality and language. Entering this messy, sweaty experiment is sometimes an illuminating escape—momentary glimpses of community formed as friends collide with strangers—and more often unsettling as physical duress transforms into emotional betrayals.

---

7. Bataille was often accused of promiscuity, most blatantly by Jean-Paul Sartre, but for my purposes, I'm intrigued by Bataille's programmatic promiscuity that resists differentiation between life and thinking, particularly in regard to the process of non-knowledge. In his opening statements for his lecture "Consequences of Nonknowledge," he apologies for bringing anecdotes from the previous evening's conversation at the local bar to the lecture hall, thus admitting to "the embarrassment of beginning" (Bataille [1951] 2001a, 111). Let us continue.

8. *Politics of Ecstasy/Altered States of Presence* was curated by Jeremy Wade and Eike Wittrock in collaboration with Pirkko Husemann as the sixth edition of the CONTEXT-Festival at the Hebbel Theater in Berlin, January 23–31, 2009. Oscillating between religious fervor and sensual force, the artists, lecturers, and curators sought to develop a new language of experience, of identity, and perhaps of politics, while simultaneously calling attention to language's limitations. The ten-day festival of performance, music, film, lectures, and food aspired to an experiential intensification, which the curators described as a "magnification of perception [through] . . . trance, somatic exploration, intoxication, improvisation, club culture and ecstatic prayer" (Wade and Wittrock 2009). Artists and lecturers included DD Dorvillier, Miguel Gutierrez, Jeremy Wade, Ron Athey, Vaginal Davis, Reggie Wilson, Yasmeen Godder, Meg Stuart, Gabrielle Brandstetter, and myself, among others.

Bodies are thrown against each other, becoming projectiles conflating sensual and spiritual, aesthetic and erotic; my own conflicted participation evidenced in interior contractions as exterior encounters became less felicitous. One woman lies on the ground: her mouth open, eyes squeezed shut, sweat dripping off her face. Her mouth becomes vanishing point; a dark hole emitting joyful and toxic expulsions that animate her entire body and resonate against the nearby bodies. To be saturated by laughter and strange paroxysms of utterance feels more risky than blissful; the experience oscillates between a compulsion toward laughter and a resistance or wariness of being caught up in it. I feel something almost gravitational as laughter swoops through the crowd and instigates other acts. During some moments I require a narrative, an inner dialogue reminding myself of what makes me laugh, then laughing takes over my body, crying smiling gasping exhausting writhing, waves of pleasure and melancholy and excitement and curious confusion again and again. Then my dependence on narrative subsides, subdued in the tremulous shaking all around me. Laughing ceases to be a conceptual exercise and moves into a physical drive, a constant relay among concept, artifice, story, and gesture. This is perhaps laughter's theoretical and agonistic force—through excessive repetition, utterance and gesture contract in a precariously intense economy.

Laughter writes body as gesture and as language. In this intertwining, a surprising discourse on laughter (like laughter itself) contagiously spreads across theories of language, of violence, of the sublime, of gesture, to name just a few. Perhaps initially these connections seem almost accidental, but then not at all. When laughter speaks its words are doing something explicitly performative, yet it is not what J. L. Austin seemed to have in mind. Or perhaps it is one of the many things written into the peripheries of his book *How to Do Things with Words*. Translated from his notes and those of his students, a score for the lecturer's body in effect, the lectures record an elliptical series of possibilities of what a performative utterance might do or be. As he describes in the last minutes or final pages: "(1) producing a program, that is, saying what ought to be done rather than doing something; (2) lecturing" (Austin [1955] 1962, 164).[9] It is as if he is reminding us that

---

9. In an interview with Joan Richardson for *Bookforum*, Stanley Cavell speaks of Austin's program as also influenced by his work decoding military propaganda for British Intelligence in World War II, where Austin came to see philosophy as parallel to propaganda; accordingly his style of lectures and his program worked to disrupt these models (Cavell 2010). And this is perhaps part

we are reading as listening and so must go back through the text to listen attentively for utterances as well. This close listening will also reveal quiet laughter along the edges of his arguments, in the moments when his language becomes confused or he turns to puns and jokes to undercut what it is he is saying. In these moments, laughter reveals the fault lines of the linguistic performatives in Austin's writing, which later appear as an "excess of utterance" in Shoshana Felman's meditation on Austin through the literary figure of Don Juan in *The Scandal of the Speaking Body*[10] (Felman [1980] 2003, 80). Drawing on the writings of Baudelaire and Freud, Felman marks the interruption of laughter in Austin's text as shifting moments marking a "disparity of levels between theory and humor, between meaning and pleasure" (84). Laughter points not only to the asymmetrical shifting between these disparate qualities as thought meets body, as comedy meets tragedy, as Baudelaire meets Freud meets Austin, but also to our own complicity in the reading and response to these stumbles across uneven (theoretical, linguistic, psychoanalytic) grounds. Or as Freud would like to prescribe: "laughter arises if a quota of psychical energy . . . [requires] free discharge" (Freud [1905] 1960, 180). In Freud's analysis, it is required that only the witness of the joke laughs (laughter on the part of the teller of the joke would ruin the joke and thus the work of release). Yet in Felman's exegesis laughter not only offers a release from various kinds of tension but also more promiscuously participates in disrupting the differentiations between listener and speaker, between language and symptom, between psychoanalysis and linguistics, between pleasure taken in humor and the pleasure experienced in

---

of what Cavell describes as the impulse behind Austin's desire to uncover "philosophy's own scandal" as he writes in the foreword to Shoshana Felman's seductive mediation on Austin. A seduction he shares with Felman (Cavell in Felman [1980] 2003, xi). Yet again, the specter of war is undoing the ways we might speak, write, think.

10. The original title *Le Scandale du corps parlant* was altered in the 1983 English translation to *The Literary Speech Act*, which loses and "regains its body" as Judith Butler notes in her "Afterword" to the 2003 publication. An attention to the return not only of the body, but also of seductive citation and pleasure on the opening pages seems perhaps not simply a coincidental nod to Felman's own attention to the humorous pleasure that Austin takes in his own titles. And here coincidences are not just aleatory events, they are also ciphers of unconscious logic that perhaps (I propose) link to the allusive fires and mis-fires accompanying the multiple translations and publications of Felman's own work ([1980] 2003, 59). She points out three titles of different works by Austin—*How to Do Things with Words*; *A Plea for Excuses*; *Three Ways of Spilling Ink*—that act not only as punning innuendos, but also as ruptures in expectation and delivery, harbingers of the attendant pleasures in his economy of knowledge and its uncertain production.

desire. The pleasure in her text and in Austin's is not only that of humorous play with the possibilities of language, its felicitous and infelicitous relations to meaning and knowledge production, but also a more explicit negotiation of an erotics of knowledge through the repeated failures inherent in the notion of performative acts themselves. Laughter, she writes, is not only pleasurable but also "convulsive and brutal" (Felman [1980] 2003, 84). And thus, for Felman, Austin figures as Don Juan in his pedagogical perpetuation of scandal—a scandal of speech made bodily that speaks (and writes) against the logic of the constative and its philosophic assumptions (86); a difficult labor attempting to articulate a different economy of language, of pleasure, and of desire. Laughter participates in this sonorous scandal as testimony to the uncertainties attendant to pleasure and desire that often catch us unaware. Laughter contains excessive slippery motion and emotion illuminating the irruptive relationship of the performative to referentiality (84). Thus the choreographic scandal of the performative lies in its inherent multiple failures. Laughter gives rise to the limits of what gesture as language or language as gesture might mean and what it might do. Again Bataille reminds me that the problem posed by laughter to philosophy is one of repetitive failure;[11] laughter incites endless theories that can only miss the very act of laughing (Bataille [1953] 2001, 134). The perverse seduction of laughter and language is that to speak of it is to miss the very experience it undoes, similar perhaps to Bataille's thinking of death, an experience that we can know nothing of until we are in fact dead, an act rendering any knowledge impotent or so we project.[12]

In her eloquent meditation *Laughter: Notes on a Passion*,[13] Anca Parvulescu imagines her own "limited and fragile archive of laughter" that continues Bataille's

---

11. I imagine that Austin and Bataille might seem strange bedfellows, yet it bears pointing out that for both the proximity to and involvement in World War II marked an explicit shift in the ways each wrote and thought about philosophy. Violence forced an undoing of precedent and meaning.

12. Bataille will explain that in his comments about death, he collapses the death of thought and actual death, a problem that his interlocutor, Jean Wahl, calls attention to. And yet, he persists even while he admits that he is wrong to pursue this dialectic (Bataille [1951] 2001c, 124).

13. Parvulescu takes laughter as a hermeneutic to trace the conditions of race, feminism, philosophy, and cinema across the twentieth century and finds, particularly in the chapters on Bataille and Hélène Cixous, a compelling way to unthink community even as she imagines another community of laughers. Attending to Bataille's laughter returns us to Hegel while also opening to Jacques Derrida, Maurice Blanchot, and Jean-Luc Nancy as so many interlocutors of laughing philosophically.

interrogation of laughter as insurrection toward community, one in which laughter is simultaneously transgressive act and subject, "an opening in which self unfolds" as part of an antiphonal community of laughers and listeners (Parvulescu 2010, 5, 3). Importantly, this concept of community, like the discourse of laughter it bursts from, always renders a "perverse intimacy" as it repeats and echoes again and again (80). Perhaps in this way laughter as community escapes the traps of a sterile contract and instead comes closer to communication (89). And yet, laughter will always be a trembling, shaking, passionate, strange communication: a paradoxical mode that like language, as Slavoj Žižek writes, "the very medium of non-violence, of mutual recognition" also "involves unconditional violence" (2008, 65). So how might we negotiate a choreographic laughter on these terms, or what might an ethics of laughter look like, especially when we are not laughing alone?[14]

Stumbling

SHIT HERE . . . DESERT FLIGHT . . . DEADLINE . . . CLEAN LAUGHING . . . BRUTAL HELP . . . MUM'S DETENTION . . . BRUTAL MEMORY . . . MISSING BODY . . . TERROR CAMPAIGN . . . BRUTALLY STILL . . . MISSING CONTEXT . . . YOUR'RE DISTURBING . . . OVER 40'S MUM . . . ANONYMOUS DEATH . . . DRINKING HOLE . . . JUST ALIENS . . . STILL LAUGHING . . . —La Ribot, *Laughing Hole*

Laughter is a spasm—a movement of thought and of body, a trespassing between utterance and gesture, a pollutant of contained subjectivity—a dialectical force that reveals interior externalized in facial distortion and sonic relay as a critical choreographic strategy. When extended in duration, laughter becomes unstable in its form and signification. As witnessed in *Laughing Hole* (2006)[15] by Spanish choreographer La Ribot, laughter is simultaneously utterance and gesture, a material and linguistic outburst, out of context and unbounded by comic narrative

---

14. In "Laughter, Presence," Jean-Luc Nancy asks if "there is a laugh of aesthetics" (Nancy [1988] 1993, 371).

15. *Laughing Hole* premiered on June 12, 2006, at Art Unlimited at Art Basel 37, Switzerland, produced by Galeria Soledad Lorezeno, Madrid, Spain. Written and directed by La Ribot; performed by La Ribot, Marie-Caroline Hominal, and Delphine Rosay; sound design and performance by Clive Jenkins.

or humorous intent (figure 2.1). Over the course of four to eight hours, three women dressed in loose housecoats, flip-flops, sometimes kneepads, and bracelets of packing tape wander across an art gallery floor covered with 900 pieces of cardboard. Their task for the duration is to move the cardboard pieces from the floor to the wall while laughing. Crouching down, one dancer pauses, holding the card for the audience to read the two words written on one side: *DIE THERE* or *HELPING IMPOTENCE* or *STILL WAR* or *REMAIN ILLEGALLY* or *FEED TERROR*. The two words image a descriptive, but also an imperative. Language becomes a force, a deluge of images and associations. La Ribot rises and tapes another card onto the wall as the other dancer throws herself to the ground or stumbles on loose terrain. These movements become the refrain of the piece; each sequence prompts another approach to a different card held and displayed for reading.

Laughter echoes across the interstices of choreography and criticality, unsettling languages of physicality and of semantics. In a sense, La Ribot literally takes on and then amplifies this scenario in *Laughing Hole* as laughter signals the moment of language's failure. The floor is no longer a smooth surface for dancing on; it has been cut up or perhaps was never smooth at all,[16] but always already a myriad of scattered piles that must be returned to the wall. Lying on the floor, La Ribot displays another card: *KILLING OPERATION* another *GAZA STRIP* another *GUANTANAMO BEACH* another *DEAD LINE* another *FEED OCCUPATION* another *JUST SALES* another *DESERT FLIGHT* another *ME FALLING*. Language accumulates as the dancers move through the space, picking up one card, pausing, posing with it, cradling it, displaying it, revealing the illicit secret scrawled on the back, laughing throughout. Sometimes their laughter is slight or murmured, sometimes hysterical, cacophonous. Throughout the performance, their laughter is recorded and played back, conjuring an uncanny ghosting of sound and stumble. Laughter disturbs their labor, interrupting the placement of the cards on the wall, tripping them up as they fall; or perhaps it is their labor that disturbs laughter. The careful and almost tedious repetition of moving and fixing these signs reveals

---

16. Speaking in a post-performance talk at the Museum of Modern Art, New York, NY, choreographer Faustin Linyekula reminds us: "[To perform] in the Congo is about clearing a space of rubble and not only physical rubble. Then the colonial heritage of the proscenium theater is a blessing. The possibility of clearing space here [MoMA] is the opposite. The space is cleared already.... Oh no, even in the white box you have rubble. I come in with my own obsessions and build from there ... invent them.... The work is the same story over and over" (2012).

2.1 La Ribot, *Laughing Hole*, 2006. Photograph by Anne Maniglier.

laughter as less about comedy or humor, but more darkly about impotence, anxiety; laughter is a physical-linguistic utterance that performs the affective overwhelming condemnation of the words covering the walls and floor.

La Ribot's refrain—selecting, displaying, sliding, falling, pausing, attaching—conflates crucial gestures from her earlier works: performances that included taping of objects to the wall and performances that included cardboard as object and terrain. Describing the function of cardboard in her work, André Lepecki writes of its almost Proustian affects, an olfactory madeleine of sorts: "Smell blurred straight lines and folded flat planes; it vaporized the rigid striation of the grid. Smell performed the distension of the horizontal and the vertical planes into so many obliques, folds, and curves" (Lepecki 2006, 81). As he sits along the periphery of the gallery witnessing La Ribot's *Panoramix* (2004)[17] performed on a gallery floor covered with cardboard, Lepecki remembers "a small square piece of cardboard [carried] . . . always parallel to the vertical plane of her body" from *Pieza Distinguida #2 (Fatelo Con Me* [Do It with Me], *distinguished proprietor Daikin Air Conditioners, Madrid)* (1993) (82). He suggests that this small square of cardboard removed from the wall and walked through the gallery anticipates the cardboard floor in *Panoramix* or, if we extend it further, inverts the massive proliferation of cut-up pieces of cardboard piling up in *Laughing Hole* that are then taped (reapplied) to the gallery wall (82–84). The dramatic shift from the strict verticality of the first cardboard square to the flattened horizontality of endless sheets of cardboard in *Panoramix* performs, Lepecki argues, an unsettling of representational logic associated with visual art through a choreographic "toppling" that "privileg[es] aimlessness, meandering, drifting . . . [and] deterritorializes the striated, orthogonal *space* of the institutional gallery and turns it into a *dimension* both indeterminate and precarious" (Lepecki 2006, 77; italics in original). It is not only the presence of the cardboard that inspires these effects. However, cardboard is central to how La Ribot negotiates her interruption and displacement of choreographic and visual codes. When Lepecki returns again to the question of cardboard he laughs at the preposterous literality of taking the material so seriously.[18] And yet. Implicit in this choreographic toppling is also a critical stumble marked by an irruption of laughter: perhaps the philosopher's laugh anticipates the artist's laugh or perhaps it is the other way around.

The dense intertwining of laughter and language in *Laughing Hole* is difficult to traverse (physically, linguistically) and as the dancers stumble and fall, we as

---

17. *Panoramix* is a "durational performance" within which La Ribot performs all of her *Piezas Distinguidas 1993-2003* (Distinguished Pieces) (Lepecki 2006, 76). The version Lepecki describes was performed in March 2003 at the Tate Modern, London.

18. Like the stumble, laughter unsettles Lepecki's critical approach: "The question is this: where did all that cardboard covering the huge areas of gallery floor come from? First we laugh at the question, as laugh we must with several of La Ribot's incredibly humorous *piezas*. But if after the laughter we stay with the literal question for one more second, we find out it is not at all an unreasonable one" (Lepecki 2006, 82).

spectators struggle to make sense of this vertiginous vibrating world that is filled with laughter, and yet, never funny. Laughter, or is it language, trips us up constantly manifesting its "contradictory" force as Charles Baudelaire describes it; laughter disfigures categorical or aesthetic distinctions, instead inciting a "perpetual explosion" between the superior and the insane, the grand and the miserable, the satanic and human (Baudelaire [1855] 2008, 153). These moments of contradiction are figured by a stumble. The stumble over cobblestones (over cardboard) is both the mise-en-scène inciting laughter in the spectator[19] and—for my purposes, more intriguing—the discursive gesture that unsettles language and writing.

In his intricate genealogy of gesture in *Social Choreography,* Andrew Hewitt juxtaposes the stumble to that of dance and argues that "dance fails as gesture through an inability either to begin or to complete the gesture, and it figures a linguistic play that neglects the work of semiotic closure" (Hewitt 2005, 83). For Hewitt, choreographic gesture takes on its social and political force through its interrogation of action. He asks how gesture and its falling out of action in the moment of spasm renders subjects within the social: Is this spasm an intentional disruption of the social, a mode of resistance? Or is it an unexpected somatic rupture conditioned by the very hegemonic forces that seek to control it?[20] The stumble, a staggering step toward an almost falling, figures the dissolution of perfect poise and intention; it reveals the unevenness of ontological, theoretical, and literal grounds. This choreographic event communicates a critical breaking point, signaling toward an impossible legibility—the moment when gestures become spastic, when bodily expression becomes undone and unreadable. Hewitt witnesses this in Giorgio Agamben's alignment of gestural collapse with the naming of

---

19. The scene of the stumble appears in Baudelaire's text and also in the opening pages of Henri Bergson's *Laughter: An Essay on the Meaning of the Comic* as both a literal stumble and fall on the street and then as the "stumbling-block" that incites other kinds of laughter (Bergson [1900] 1999, 4–5).

20. Tracing the historical force of gesture and its undoing in the late nineteenth and early twentieth century in the writings of Honoré de Balzac, Giorgio Agamben, Henri Bergson, and François Delsarte, to name the most oft-cited, Hewitt suggests that these spastic gestures intertwine aesthetic and social ideals at the moment of collapse. Against bourgeois fantasies of democratic grace, he focuses on the stumble as the gestural and critical undoing of these Enlightenment aspirations (Hewitt 2005, 79).

Tourette's syndrome, suggesting that "embodied communication [performs] a crisis of writing and intentionality (a loss of control of gesture) and of legibility (the gestures no longer 'mean' anything)" (83).[21] The spastic stumble figures a crisis, not only as a bodily residue of repressed emotions or history or as a meaning-*less* movement, but also as a supplementary excess of corporeality, a somatic disturbance of the social and the linguistic.

Stumbling joins laughter as a critical hermeneutic marking decisive intervals in Hewitt's gestural topography that image a body within social space stuttering at the edge of balance. Drawing attention to the stumble that incites laughter in Henri Bergson's *Laughter: An Essay on the Meaning of the Comic* (Bergson [1900] 1999), Hewitt looks at the ways in which "immanent bodily community" forms when we laugh at the one who almost falls, repeating our laughter as another "form of sonic stumble" (Hewitt 2005, 99). The repetition and reiteration of writing of stumbling parallels the labor of laughter itself, which never appears as a singular act, but always as a multiplicity. As Bergson describes: "Laughter appears to stand in need of an echo. Listen to it carefully: it is not an articulate, clear, well-defined sound; it is something that would fain be prolonged by reverberating from one to another, something beginning with a crash, to continue in successive rumblings" (Bergson [1900] 1999, 3).

In this rare moment in his book, Bergson tunes into the vibrating sonic qualities of laughter as affective transmission to articulate its regulatory relationship to social space and communication. Bergson spends most of his treatise examining where laughter comes from, what incites our laughter, and why we laugh, but leaves aside an examination of laughter as gesture (sonic or anatomical) even though his definition of gesture sits within this laughter-filled text. Similar to Hewitt, Bergson is less interested in laughter as gesture itself, as anatomical distortion, but more compelled by its irruption within a social situation. And yet hidden near the end of *Laughter*, Bergson inserts very specific definitions of what gesture is: "By gestures we here mean the attitudes, the movements and even the language by which a mental state expresses itself outwardly without any aim or profit, from no other cause than a kind of inner itching. Gesture, thus defined, is

---

21. Here Hewitt is referring to Agamben's *Notes on Gesture* (1992) where he defines gesture in terms of dance.

profoundly different from action. Action is intentional or, at any rate, conscious; gesture slips out unawares, it is automatic" (Bergson [1900] 1999, 129–130).

Bergson defines gesture through what it is not—motivated action. While gesture may be initiated only by an almost passive "inner itching," it still maintains an "explosive" potential to "awaken our sensibility" (Bergson [1900] 1999, 130). In this moment, the gestures Bergson refers to are those of comedy—"the attitudes, the movements and even the language" of the comedian attempting to incite laughter in the audience. Yet, if we transpose his theory of gesture from the comedian's repertoire to laughter itself, then laughter becomes something quite complicated and even contradictory as an expression of both an internal impulse and that which "slips out" without our prior approval. Laughter irrupts, entangling physicality and language.

While Bergson, Freud, and Austin return to the joke, to humor, as the instigator for laughter, I am less interested in the joke that incites laughter, but rather in the laugh itself. The laugh as gesture performs a specific kind of work that calls attention to the messy physical aspects of corporeal movement even when it is written, painted, or uttered, and undercuts any attempt at a clean theoretical articulation.[22] The laughter in *Laughing Hole* does not come from outside the piece. It is not an antiphonal response of the audience to the staggering, slipping dancers or to the litany of language, but it is gesture itself. It is laughter that critiques the function of laughter. This laughter is not an open invitation to laugh with or a complicit avowal of another's slips and stumbles that incites laughter in the onlooker. It seems to work against laughter as cathartic release described by Freud and parodies Bergson's description of laughter as a moral and aesthetic "corrective" (Bergson [1900] 1999, 22). For Bergson, laughter is a "*social gesture*. By the fear which it inspires, it restrains eccentricity, keeps constantly awake . . . softens down whatever the surface of the social body may retain of mechanical inelasticity" (176; italics in original). Laughter, specifically that incited by the comic, points to the

---

22. Even in its representational form (I laugh on command) there is something about laughter that is infectious. Choreographer Antonia Baehr speaks of this contaminating and nomadic function of "laughing as laughing" that happens as "gestures wander possessing bodies on their paths," as witnessed in her performance *Rire* (Laugh) (2008) (Baehr 2008, 11, 6). Combining research on laughter in its various forms (yogic, comedic, personal, social, etc.) with scores given to her by friends for her birthday, Baehr developed *Rire* as a series of vignettes of her performing the scores. Within these scores, laughter acts as "a choreographic movement of emotion, as a material itself" (95). *Rire* is documented in *Rire/Laugh/Lachen* (Baehr 2008).

falling out of sociality or a becoming too mechanical, particularly the ways in which individuals stray from the human continuum that Bergson describes as a movement between "*tension* and *elasticity*" (22; italics in original), the ways in which we mold ourselves to fit within the evolving social structure. Laughter, for Bergson, is "social signification" (13) that stands outside the joke, against the stumble, highlighting the breaks or dissolutions of models of good, moral, upright living. *Laughing Hole* dissembles Bergson's conception of laughter as "social signification" as it glaringly illuminates through shattering tones and eerie echoing whispers that we too are complicit, indicted, involved somehow within this massive horizontal accumulation of language.

Seizure

Does laughter have an origin? A source or code? Or is laughter's seizing of power, the victorious cavalcade of its multiplicity, all that exists? An initial bursting out and its unmitigated echo. Laughter is a shadowy creature which after millions of years still feels at home beneath the outer shell of the human being. There it resides and moves about as chemistry, as network, as fungus, sprouts tubers and shoots, grows into dendrites and veins, waxes and wanes. Limited by this underground existence, it makes its appearance through eruption, swelling through pores or cracks; it breaks out of its mantle, gushes, gallops, stumbles, rushes, hovers. Laughter spreads like gas, like language, infects, advances like a herd, an electrical current or like an oil spill or slime, then oozes away in retreat once again, evaporates, flees, submerges, goes back underground.—Stefan Pente, "Laughter. Minus-Laughter"

Laughter is the philosopher's undoing; it leaves us writhing under the desk, rolling on the floor in ecstasy and anguish. Remember how unsettled Michel Foucault becomes in his Introduction to *Archaeology of Knowledge* when he hears Hegel's laughter echoing through his own self-interlocution: "no, no, I'm not where you are lying in wait for me, but over here, laughing at you?" (Foucault [1969] 1972, 17). This laughter appears just following Foucault's own admission of the "stumbling manner of this text: at every turn, it stands back, measures up what is before it, gropes toward its limits, stumbles against what it does not mean" (17), indexing yet another critical irruption of laughter in the mapping of a theory of language.[23] Foucault's words echo the choreographic quality of La Ribot's gestures, her constant struggle to move and make sense of the endless litany of inscriptions scattered across the floor, and simultaneously point to the self-reflexive questioning required of both his writing and her dancing/laughing in relation to the content of their performances. What they are both attempting to communicate (in distinct ways) demands a stumbling approach that participates in the decentering work of defining discourse (for Foucault) and defying discourse (for La Ribot). Remember for Foucault, discourse is an alternative to the writing of history and its condition is one of "traces" that like laughter requires an object that overflows and offers something more to attach itself too, something that is equally unstable such that in the process of signification of the object, its meaning and its relationship to the subject are suspended (107).[24]

This excessive instability becomes the ground and architecture for *Laughing Hole*. It is not that the words themselves represent statements, this would contradict both La Ribot's and Foucault's purpose, but rather what they do—hundreds of handwritten inscriptions about war, about torture, about economics, about family, about debt, about secrets, about politics, about love all performed while laughing— that hints at a different writing of history as a crucial undoing of its own descriptions, of its own monuments, moments, names, codes through association, and excess. *Laughing Hole* renders a messy convergence closer to the "neither hidden nor visible" (Foucault [1969] 1972, 109) facts of experience as MISSING SECRET overlaps HERE SOFT SELL ALIEN and CLEAN POLITICIAN obscures ECONOMIC making the second word unreadable or perhaps irrelevant. We are forced to read differently and listen to the distant silences.

Laughter repeats and reiterates; it is not singular but always a complicit multiplicity. It is a contagious refrain that "bursts," as Jean-Luc Nancy writes, the

---

23. Parvulescu points to another seminal moment of laughter that opens Foucault's *The Order of Things* when he cites Borges and the laughter that laughs (2010, 13). Interestingly in both cases, it is not Foucault who is laughing but either Hegel or the text itself.

24. Drawing attention to a slightly different alignment between Foucault's concept of discourse and contemporary European choreographic practice, Mårten Spångberg explains: "dance has been occupied with the transformations of techniques into utterances, utilising different loosely organised grammatologies to propose extra-discursive topographies where the danced utterance takes place, it thus positioned itself outside the realm of the archive" (Spångberg 2002, 35).

expected boundaries of responsibility and of meaning. While Nancy's burst points to the spontaneous explosive quality of laughter, this bursting also speaks to laughter's force of interruptive disorganization when it is performed as a score. Even as a performed gesture (and when is it ever not performed?), laughter distorts and explodes, it contracts and disfigures body, voice, and utterance. I cannot simply read or scan La Ribot's cryptic ciphers of recent catastrophic events, wars, secrets, or quotidian facts, without also feeling the anxious pressure of laughter circulating and amplified through the gallery. One dancer opens her mouth slightly, drawing near, and a quiet subdued laugh escapes, her whisper of intimation. Moments later her mouth gapes open, a dark hole emitting a crashing moan more animal than language. These sounds and textures, simultaneously voice, timbre, language, tenor, and body, all signal the multiplicity of which Nancy writes that undoes representational logic and the hegemony of visuality associated with representation; this is an explicitly choreographic project. Undoing the categorical distinctions between senses he writes not only of a mouth that bursts, but the eyes too (Nancy [1988] 1993, 373). There is a correlation between the eyes and the mouth in *Laughing Hole* as well in the intensity of La Ribot's screaming laughter. Her laughing mouth becomes a black abyss, so open, so stretched that her eyes squint. In these moments I desire to avert my gaze, yet laughter pierces my closed eyes conjuring an ecstatic awareness that is violent and abject. Laughter surrounds me, infiltrating my senses, dissembling expected boundaries between artwork, wall, spectator. It is a sensuous undoing that like the "certain laugh" that inspires Nancy's meditation—a painted red mouth of a woman in a Baudelaire poem—moves from word to color to paint to sound to philosophical and choreographic provocation (392).

Laughter becomes an affective indictment. I feel it, hear it, tremble with it, so that even as I might think: these words are not mine, this is not my "killing operation, my missing secret, me falling" laughter unsettles any easy evasion of responsibility and intention. La Ribot's explicit intertwining of laughter and language and violence conjures an incredible potency that resonates, perhaps too strongly, with Žižek's discussion of the "gesture of what is called fetishistic disavowal" at the paradoxical heart, or shall we say laugh, of ethics. "'I know, but I don't want to know that I know, so I don't know.' I know it, but I refuse to fully assume the consequences of this knowledge, so that I can continue acting as if I don't know" (Žižek 2008, 53). Like laughter, this gesture of disavowal, of forgetting, stutters, requires Žižek to repeat his radical provocation that ethics requires forgetting, particularly along its extreme edges. We are complicit not only symbolically but structurally as well. Language, he writes, "pushes our desire beyond proper limits. . . . Reality in itself, in its stupid existence, is never intolerable: it is language, its symbolization, which makes it such" (65, 67). Then Žižek offers me an image of a rioting crowd, burning buildings, and asks me to remember their "placards" (67) and I cannot help but return to the relentless montage of signs that La Ribot trips on and then raises above her head as she slides down the wall in the final hour of *Laughing Hole*.

Intoxication

Laughter bursts without presenting or representing its reasons or intentions. It bursts only in its own repetition. . . . The "burst" of laughter is not a single burst, a detached fragment, nor is it the essence[25] of a burst—it is the repetition of bursting—and the bursting of repetition. It is the multiplicity of meanings as multiplicity and not as meaning.—Jean-Luc Nancy, "Laughter, Presence"[26]

Nancy's meditation on laughter's insurrection extends his labor of ekphrasis; laughter acts as the hermeneutic for reading aesthetic theory in terms of erotics and desire, and conversely erotics becomes paradigmatic for a different articulation of aesthetics. Charles Baudelaire's "The Desire to Paint" (1869) marks the point of departure of this meditation. Reading along the peripheries of the text (a poem but also prose together), Nancy exclaims: "it is along this edge that desire itself bursts into laughter" and later that "laughter might be the transformation of desire" (Nancy 1987, 721–722; 723). Laughter works on and against the limits of representation and presence, forcing a tremulous and vibratory negotiation that

---

25. This nod to "essence" is perhaps a critique of Baudelaire's essay on "On the Essence of Laughter," one that Nancy claims in a footnote he will not deal with, yet it seeps in. Tricky as laughter is the rupture of the limit and so it too does its own work on Nancy's writing.

26. Two very similar versions of this essay exist: "Wild Laughter in the Throat of Death" published in *MLN* (Nancy 1987); and "Laughter, Presence" in *The Birth to Presence* (Nancy [1988] 1993) from which this quote is drawn.

exceeds the rules of aesthetics and resists any terminal figuration. In Baudelaire's text laughter forces an alteric mode of reading and of writing, one that defines what Nancy names a new "erotico-esthetic program" (721). Nancy announces at the beginning of his article that "we" will read Baudelaire's poem together first in French and then in English translation. We read it twice and then again extended through Nancy's own close reading. Like laughter itself, Baudelaire's text returns and repeats throughout Nancy's, so that the sound and image of this particular woman who resists being painted constantly interrupts the discourse surrounding her. Baudelaire writes of the painter who not only desires to paint, but must keep painting, as he and Nancy must also keep writing; laughter's labor (like the work of desire) laughs endlessly. Listen:

Darkness in her abounds, and all that she inspires is nocturnal and profound. Her eyes are two caverns where mystery dimly glistens, and like a lightening flash, her glance illuminates: it is an explosion in the dark.

I have compared her to a black sun, if one can imagine a black star pouring out light and happiness. But she makes one think rather of the moon, which has surely marked her with its portentous influence; not the white moon of idylls which resembles a frigid bride, but the sinister and intoxicating moon that hangs deep in a stormy night, hurtled by the driven clouds; not the discreet and peaceful moon that visits pure men while they sleep, but the moon torn from the sky, the conquered and indignant moon that the Thessalian Witches cruelly compel to dance on the frightened grass!

That little forehead is inhabited by a tenacious will and a desire for prey. Yet, in the lower part of this disturbing countenance, with sensitive nostrils quivering for the unknown and the impossible, bursts, with inexpressible loveliness, a wide mouth, red and white and alluring, that makes one dream of the miracle of a superb flower blooming on volcanic soil. (Baudelaire in Nancy [1988] 1993, 369–370)

Laughter casts her face as landscape, as eruptive volcanic surface that displaces day for night; she incites a tempest calling the moon to earth to dance. Against these shadows, her laughter, feminized, illuminates painting as presence (not representation), reiterating the endless desire to paint her "disappearance or of her disappearing" (Nancy [1988] 1993, 379). Similar to dance, which must often contend with the accusation of its own disappearance, laughter reveals the failure of representation to capture the appearance of the fleeing subject. Yet, laughter is not beholden to either presence or disappearance, but imagines another economy, an "offering of a presence in its own disappearance" (383). And isn't this a deeply choreographic proposal, to seek an impossible beauty, an unreachable limit, gorgeous and difficult as a black intoxicating sun bursting from barren burnt ground? This resistance to representation resides in the force of her laughing mouth and like Hélène Cixous's Medusa we must not only look at her, but listen very closely as well. As Nancy explicates: "This is why laughter itself remains mysterious. It knows with a knowledge that not only remains hidden but is this very knowledge precisely in its own hiding. It shows itself as its hidden-ness. Laughter reveals that it comes from the hidden place, which it keeps hidden. The glance illuminates its own darkness *as* darkness, and this is laughter" (Nancy 1987, 724).

Knowledge arising from the woman's red lips resists any easy replication to reveal something secret, explosive, beautiful, annihilating. Reading Baudelaire through Nancy we move from laughter into desire, a movement from stumbling to bursting, that seeks an extremity of experience at the limits of presence—the presence of laughter and the presence of death. Laughter laughs, Nancy repeats, conjuring its own sublime, dare we say rapturous, entrée into knowledge that resonates along the limits of sensation and of language. Part of the impulse driving Nancy's text is a movement toward an aesthetic economy not tethered to theories of visibility, verisimilitude, or beauty. Instead, he describes an obscure desiring economy, "illuminated" by a dark glow that might only be approached through an uneasy acknowledgment of our own messy desires. But is it not strange that these peregrinations on laughter emanating from a woman's mouth, from her uncontained desire, appear along the edges of the grotesque, too much, cruel and delicious, witch or whore? It is another perversion that Cixous responds to when she calls out to Medusa, shatters her stone, listens to her laugh, thus perpetuating a scandal of another sort.[27]

Laughter is of the body and of the voice, yet it is explicitly of language, a strangled or unwieldy utterance that interrupts semantic and syntactic structures through gestural force. Laughter performs as disfunctioning supplement, an

---

27. Parvulescu reminds me in her close reading of Cixous's "Laugh of the Medusa" that under the influence of laughter, language becomes "old sclerotic words," a phrase she borrows from Nathalie Sarraute's novel *Do You Hear Them?* ([1972] 2004, 116). The citations and affiliations proliferate as we continue to move between writing and living, laughing and laughing, around and around again.

utterance of voice and of body that intimately intertwines physical and linguistic in the moment of its undoing; a choreographic maneuver distorting the very grounds from which I might try to think language, to engage its physicality and bodily force. It is a scandalous gesture that undermines philosophies of language and theories of gesture. *Laughter is language becoming choreographic*: a vibratory syncopation. It trembles as gesture and utterance combine in an undoing of linguistic signification. Laughter writes differently; it is an *"insurgent"* writing and a choreographic text (Cixous [1975] 1976, 880). As Cixous instructs us: "You only have to look at the Medusa straight on to see her. And she's not deadly. She's beautiful and she's laughing" (885). Medusa laughs, not in the self-conscious way of someone made uncomfortable, not in a mockery of social censor, but as a critical gesture, a gesture that revels in her beauty and intelligence that cannot be constrained by the laws of choreography or of time. Her laughter incites writing and discourse, transgressing physical and intellectual, syntax and semantics. Laughter is central to Cixous's writing as it locates the site of writing as the site of the body, not only a body hunched at a desk staring into a computer,[28] but also a body gripped by emotion and urgency to move and to speak. Language becomes gesture that is simultaneously pleasurable and painful, ecstatic and full of grief, figuring desire in all its beauty and abjection as her mouth opens to reveal a dark throat. Such embodied writing must attempt a sonic corporeality even if it is not intelligible as it externalizes an interior demand. As Cixous instructs:

Woman must write her self: must write about women and bring women to writing, from which they have been driven away as violently as from their bodies—for the same reasons, by the same law, with the same fatal goal. Woman must put herself into the text—as into the world and into history—by her own movement. . . . When I write, it's everything that we don't know we can be that is written out of me, without

28. During a *Conversation without Walls* event at Danspace Project, Avital Ronnel reminded me of the positions that writing takes in and through philosophy—not only sitting, but also walking, vomiting, turning, dancing: "I've often been concerned by the kind of immobilized choreography of the pedagogical situation with the docile bodies that were more or less referred to the kind of broken transference that is already indicated by the positions that people take and all sort of contracts that are implicitly drawn among those who sit and write. . . . That's already choreographically decided, the one who takes that seat and enthrones oneself is traversed by language to be sure [they are] already materially designated as the driver of thought in a certain way, assuming they're not too drunk in their steering" (Ronell 2011).

exclusions, without stipulation, and everything we will be calls us to the unflagging, intoxicating, unappeasable search for love. (Cixous [1976] 1980, 245, 264)

Writing, Cixous reminds me again and again in her essay, must not only be written but lived. Write, she implores with a fierce urgency: "Writing is precisely *the very possibility of change*, the space that can serve as a springboard for subversive thought, the precursory movement of a transformation of social and cultural structures" (Cixous [1976] 1980, 249). And when we write, our text will be a counter-writing, insurrection and anticipatory knowledge that returns us to our bodies, our desires, our territories: "erotogeneity of the heterogeneous: airborne swimmer, in flight, she does not cling to herself; she is dispersible, prodigious, stunning, desirous" (260). Cixous is fierce; her text, a crescendo rising from ocean, to astral skies, challenges the ways that history has been written and announces another coming to knowledge. Not coming exactly, a word Bataille and Nancy and Jacques Derrida[29] deploy, but rather an "un-thinking" (*dé-pense*, from *penser*, to un-think but also to spend) (252). Her writing as provocation incites another economy and so Medusa's laugh leads us explicitly to the question of desire.

Insurrection: Laughter to Desire

with you

or alone

no

languages

only

grunts

moans

murmurs

chattering teeth

---

29. Jacques Derrida notes that Nancy's exposé on laughter is not only contracting but also "coming," and so for Bataille, Nancy, and Derrida the proximity of death to laughter is not only the death of thought, of body, but another little death as well (Derrida [2000] 2005, 118). It is a death that Cixous will not remain beholden to theoretically or otherwise; she wants to go further, not just "take the edge off," she writes ([1976] 1980, 247).

shuffling

only sounds

no languages

with meanings

no words

or signifying gestures

no

languages

. . .

no languages

just

you

me

sounds

of bodies without

bodies

sounds

with barely body

hearing

before sound

invisible

inaudible after

no

languages

no

only

what

is

only—DD Dorvillier, *Choreography, a Prologue for the Apocalypse of Understanding, Get Ready!*[30]

---

30. DD Dorvillier/human future dance corps presented *Choreography, a Prologue for the Apocalypse of Understanding, Get Ready!* at Dance Theater Workshop, New York, NY, in January 2009. *CPAU, Get Ready!* was directed by Dorvillier and created in collaboration with performers Heather Kravas, Amanda Piña, Joaquím Pujol, Elizabeth Ward; composer Zeena Parkins; lighting designer Thomas Dunn.

Apparitions projected in the dark theater: the words emerge slowly at first and then in alternating rhythms: *with you or alone no languages only grunts moans murmurs.* ... Each word takes its own time to appear: *me* pause *sounds* pause and then black screen *of bodies without* pause *bodies* pause then black screen. ... I read in silence until interrupted by a single tone played by Zeena Parkins off to the side of the stage. *unnameable* pause *sounds* then a chord resonates *only* pause *grunts.* ... The video-text (included above as epigraph) continues until the screen is consumed with a strange proliferation of mushrooms and goes black as bells, harps, and dissonant tones fill the space. Dorvillier's text renders a paradoxical dramaturgy along the peripheries of language—as murmuring shuffling words push language toward its debilitating point. The words intimate a desire to be outside of language, yet still must use language to convey this tension, performing an infelicitous partnering with meaning to reveal the fault lines between sensuous experience and the language we use to describe it, between the materiality of flesh and its linguistic counterpoint. It is as if the stutters conjured by Dorvillier's semantic partnerings attempt to elide the very terms they represent, instead slowly arousing the audience, stimulating our interest. These words act as foreplay for the piece; the timing of their advance is essential to cultivating a slower sensuous experience. This is not dance as virtuosic spectacle, but a seductive invitation, sexy awkward surprising. Dorvillier's negotiation of erotics and semantics, of language and gesture, of words and dance calls attention to the work of language as a choreographic force, and particularly to the labor of and toward desire as a process for rethinking what language and choreography might do together. Here choreography also confronts the historical imperatives of dance, such that Dorvillier's choreographic provocation is not only performed by the dancers on stage but also in the silent hesitations, stillness, sonic interruptions, questions, sculptural assemblages, saturated colors, patterns of light.

Choreography, a Prologue for the Apocalypse of Understanding, Get Ready! (2009) intimately plays the in-between of choreography and language, communication and desire, or as Cixous reiterates "work[s] (in) the in-between, inspecting the process of the same and of the other without which nothing can live" ([1976] 1980, 254). There is something of the relation between laughter and desire that evokes this same and other, and always the *in* in-between that Cixous intuits. Perhaps if we hold these modalities—choreography, language, communication— together we might begin to understand the disfiguring complexities, agonies, and pleasures of laughter and desire. So now as we dance with Dorvillier deeper into the realms of desire coming undone in language or language coming undone in dance in desire, these many transmissions imagine a choreographic as something else, a different temporality and spacing (figures 2.2–2.3).

The pas de deux continues as Dorvillier and Joaquím Pujol lie on the ground in sweatshirts revealing sections of their backs to the audience framed by black microphone cords.[31] Slowly sitting up, still facing away from the audience, Dorvillier howls faintly and then with more volume as her voice reverberates a strange emotional even animal cry. When she finally stands and turns to the audience and to Pujol, she asks: "Can you hear me? Can you see me?" This confusion of seeing and listening and feeling continues as she narrates her indecision and anxiety surrounding the making of the choreography while he translates her words into Spanish and responds with his own interpretative movements. Here the difficultly of creating a dance corresponds to the fragile seductions of courtship as Dorvillier and Pujol carefully move closer together and drift farther away, whispering into their microphones, startling us with admonitions as the microphone cords cross and uncross, coil and recoil. Their words enact a subtle dance, teasing questions along the surface as if trying to obscure the more complicated physical intimations happening in the gaps and silences between bodies and voices. This sensual relay informs the perceptual work of the piece as Dorvillier's choreography constantly reaches toward different modes of communication and of understanding not limited to linguistic structure and meaning. When I asked Dorvillier why language is so foregrounded in *CPAU, Get Ready!* she answered:

Language is the fault of a desire, whether conscious or not, for communication. I have an interest in the expansion of means of communication, and therefore in the expansion of language and of its definitions, as well as those means of communication that slip away from linguistically inscribed forms of cognition. . . . There's a kind of reactionary almost utopic, and I think quite funny, abdication of language, as an exclusive means of sharing knowledge and experience. Yet the video consists solely of words (language), inciting raw sound and movement,

---

31. This scene resonates with Dorvillier's earlier work *No Change, or, "freedom is a psycho-kinetic skill"* (2005) in which Dorvillier and dancer Elizabeth Ward appear in the beginning slumped on the ground of the space that is traversed with microphone cords and stands and also draws on the partial reveal of bodies in poses from *Nottthing is Importanttt* (2007).

2.2–2.3 DD Dorvillier, *Choreography, a Prologue for the Apocalypse of Understanding, Get Ready!*, 2009. Photographs by David Bergé.

shuffling, and an absence of language as a truer means of reaching consciousness, or understanding together. I'm trying to tap into regions of cognition that function like music but are not music. (Dorvillier 2009a, 6)

This seduction with and suspicion of language extends from the piece, requiring a critical tuning not only to her intentions for the work but also to our dialogic duet as we work toward an elusive understanding together. As the title reminds me: this is a prologue, an opening, illuminating the perceptual and sensual forces of words surrounding not only meaning, but also their sonority. Within this phenomenal terrain, Dorvillier's choreographic gestures interrupt what she refers to as dancing's ontology of "inexhaustible movement" to instead illuminate the fatigue resulting from constantly (endlessly) dancing (2009a). As she explains, gestures function

like a signifying placeholder, a punctuation mark, or an image enacted in time and space. Gesture situates itself in the past, even if through repetition it somehow attempts to free itself from time. . . . I think what I'm attempting to do is to use gesture to bring about an exhaustion of an accepted understanding of dance, and also of an accepted understanding of cognition, knowledge, and artistic value. Eventually if gesture reads like language in my work, it speaks in tongues. (Dorvillier 2009a, 6)

To speak of choreography as the interruption of movement by gesture or as a play between gesture and movement also points to its dependence on systems of signification and their ideological force. Gesture has an aesthetic quality and yet it is also explicitly social and political. Dorvillier revels in this medial becoming quality of gesture as a choreographic strategy, playing with the excessive polyphonic affect of choreographic gesture as a means of rethinking language particularly as it approaches desire. Part Three amplifies this erotic entanglement of language and gesture through its structural design—an intricate score drawn over a photograph of the choreographer's naked body on an unmade bed framed with two words: CHOREOGRAPHY and UNDERSTANDING. Her body underlies a grid of coordinates as letters from CHOREOGRAPHY intersect with letters from UNDERSTANDING marking the horizontal and vertical axes and creating a set of points that will determine the sound and movement scores. The specific points—all the squares touching the edge of the choreographer's body—are then transposed to the dancers' bodies—knee, elbow, chin, lips, humerus—identifying how each will move and in which direction, with which velocity, and in what kind of kinesthetic relationship.

As Dorvillier explains: "a suite of movements could be translated from the following information: 1: (4R– 4E) escape diagonally 4 counts with eurhythmy letter 'R,' a vibrating horizontal right humerus . . . 3: (5E–5T) touch floor during 5 counts, maintaining body vertical, with eurhythmy letter 'E' while vibrating left radius and ulna" (Dorvillier 2009a, 7). Using a reproduction of the erotic body of the choreographer framed by text as the source of sound and movement material, Dorvillier constructs a very specific structural constellation that activates a multiplicity of "cross-perceptions" transposing letters and sounds and gestures and anatomies (7). Because the grid is placed over a photograph, no square is empty as it is always filled with the background, the bed, the window, the wall. These spaces without body construct a spatial dramaturgy for the piece through the relational play of what she calls the "value"—particular gesture, movement, sound, position.

To perform Part Three the four dancers appear in single-color unitards and white sneakers: Dorvillier in cyan, Heather Kravas in yellow, Amanda Piña in magenta, and Elizabeth Ward in black. The colors of the unitards correspond to CMYK, the separation of colors used in printing—colors that Dorvillier describes as "incompatible and that is why they function to produce other colors" and blur between colors. The idea to use these colors also draws on her personal history of watching her parents' printing press at work melding colors to create naturalistic images, in what she now recollects as a "physical transformation in the process of making text [and images] that is linked in my mind with the production of language, sense, and knowledge" (Dorvillier 2009a, 7). The four dancers begin seated around a keyboard. Then each dancer opens her mouth in a large "O" as her tone is played; again there is confusion among the values of sound, voice, instrument, and anatomy. Rising to stand in a line the dancers simultaneously execute sequences of gestures and movements invented from the values of the grid. Each gesture—arms circle in front of each dancer's body, one arm stretches into a diagonal as head turns, arms swing to sides of body resting on hips, hands cross in front of chest then quickly circle and return to hips, hands paw in a circular motion—is accompanied by a sound, a different phoneme for each detail of the gesture. Watching I am reminded of the rigorous stylization of Merce Cunningham's movement (and the unitards play off this as well), yet Dorvillier is less concerned with a virtuosic body performing (or falling apart under the gravity of) chance and more engaged in a structural saturation as color, gesture, light, and sound mingle and separate. In one section, one of the dancers will interrupt the sequence and strike a pose; in this moment all the other dancers, lighting designer, and composer must focus only on this single color so that everyone is supporting Magenta, as an example. Alternating between stilled gestures and more frantic combinations of movement-gestures amplified by the shifting lights and sound score, the dancers at one moment appear as silhouettes and at another as frenetic figures barely in control of their simultaneous repetitions. Similar to the grid that inspired these combinations, there is a dense layering effect as the sound score of collaged rehearsal footage of the dancers speaking cuts over mechanical tones. Dorvillier runs across the stage with arms out, head shaking, as Ward stands convulsing on the front of the stage as Piña runs along the perimeter head shaking, arms crossing and uncrossing in front of her chest as Kravas traverses the center of the stage bending over and rising until she stands facing the back wall, arms out and circling as she undulates her hips and pelvis.

Difficult to watch and to narrate, Dorvillier's choreography invents a series of movement phrases, sonic sequences, lighting cues as a dense intramedial multisensorial event. Within this relational saturation each element struggles against its own limitations and gifts, disrupting use-value and function, so that we must always attempt an impossible translation across image and sound and movement and color and light simultaneously. Not simply synesthetic, Dorvillier's process approaches something closer to Clarice Lispector's revelation of music as means to clarify something of writing and reading: "You don't understand music: you hear it. So hear me with your whole body" (Lispector [1978] 2012, 4). In the instant of writing, Lispector forces a slippage of sense, a choreographic rupture of sorts that breaks from narrative and intention to embody something of consciousness or living. For Dorvillier, this consciousness also equates with a mode of embodied knowledge production. So when she explains that *CPAU, Get Ready!* is invested in "reaching consciousness, or understanding together . . . trying to tap into regions of cognition that function like music but are not music" (Dorvillier 2009a, 6), she points to an impossible series of transpositions that seek to undercut the primacy of linguistic and visual with the immersive intimacy of the sonic, exchanging semantics and syntax for tones, volumes, cadences, rhythms; other textures of experience all influenced by the sensuous body underlying the grid.[32]

---

32. Dorvillier's attention to the sonic extends further in *Danza Permanante* (2012), a quartet for four dancers who each enact one instrument from Beethoven's *Opus 132 in A minor*. The dancers become sound through movement and timing, yet without sound creating what she calls

This grid generates points of contact between the two axes—choreography and understanding—all along the surface of a very specific body reclining on crumpled white sheets. This representation of the choreographer extends the possible erotogenous zones to the entire surface of the body and at each point a distinct sensation becomes visible. The transposition of this score to the dancers' bodies further disperses these zones as they now stand vibrating, shaking, trembling, seizing on stage. Dorvillier's labor activates very specific points in the body similar to laughter—diaphragm, sphincters, risorius, trapezius—yet is never contained by them.[33] The contractions, convulsions, and undulations incited by laughter's intensity and by Dorvillier's choreography embody (for a moment) the flows of desire as a means toward a mode of knowledge we don't yet understand, one that is tied to but not determined by language, or in which we must rely on the explicit failure of language to approach.

Dorvillier's choreographic proposal invites us to reconsider Bataille's processes of nonknowledge particularly when he speaks of nonknowledge as an inability to recognize oneself or other (Bataille [1953] 2001, 133). In this context, I hear Dorvillier asking Pujol: "Can you hear me? Can you see me?" even as she stands next to him on stage. Nonknowledge requires an intimate proximity even as it disorients, provoking anxiety at the uncertain and illegible tremors, whispers, laughs of a choreographic erotics. Bataille's and Dorvillier's disparate practices do not erase all previous experience, but rather disperse my/her/our knowledge into something else. In this strange temporality of laughter and of nonknowledge, pasts and presents collide in convulsive breath, awkward silences, gasps, groans, spasms undoing how we think, write, choreograph desire not only in its pleasurable moments but also in its crueler states.

"visual music" (Dorvillier 2011). Again Lispector intercedes: "Beethoven is the stormy human elixir searching for divinity and only finding it in death. As for me, I've got nothing to do with music, I only arrive at the threshold of a new word. Without the courage to expose it" ([1978] 2012, 6). Neither Dorvillier nor Lispector, in her less self-effacing moments, lacks this courage; both arrive at other thresholds of dancing writing. *Danza Permanante* opened in New York City at The Kitchen on September 26, 2012. Created by Dorvillier; score transposed by Dorvillier and composer Zeena Parkins with dancers Fabian Barba, Nuno Bizarro, Walter Dundervill, and Naiara Mendioroz, and rehearsal assistant Heather Kravas. Lighting design by Thomas Dunn; acoustic environment by Zeena Parkins.

33. See diagram "Muscles activity during the laugh" included in Antonia Baehr's *Rire/Laugh/Lachen* (2008, 7).

Darkness, Desire: Repeat

Dance . . . makes the negative body—the shameful body—radiantly absent.—Alain
Badiou, "Dance as a Metaphor for Thought"

Cruelty is never far from pleasure or so Baudelaire's taunting witches remind us,
as does Gilles Deleuze when he writes of difference as the substance of repetition.
That which (witch) is not the same is cruel, distinct; it is in repetition that we face
this difference, again and again and again. Over and over and over, like laughter,
repetition echoes and contracts. For Deleuze this moment of contraction, or rather
this moment, this moment, this moment, reveals time as always out of joint (think
Hamlet's ghost) as past collapses into present signaling the future within an
instant.[34] If Deleuze were to speak of ontologies, which he usually avoids, being
would take the form of contraction or rather a series of accumulated contractions
even "modifications" as its very condition of difference (Deleuze [1968] 1994, 79).
Repetition reveals these differences constantly and thus works against repression
and representation; it is both "a theft and a gift" (1). Establishing his distance from
Sigmund Freud's theory of repetition that restricts repetition to a compulsive drive
to replay the experience of the identical, of pleasure without the possibility of
fulfillment,[35] Deleuze celebrates the transgressive powers of repetition, its ability to

---

34. Here Deleuze connects his thinking to that of Henri Bergson whose book *Matter and Memory*
([1908] 1991) argues for a concept of duration, of virtual experience, as a cone of suspended
memories filtering to the point where it touches the plane of experience. Bergson also offers much
to Deleuze, in this moment figuring an alternative to Freud's concept of repetition aligned with
repression and later as a model for cinema and thought as processes of accumulative becoming.

35. Freud develops his concept of repetition across much of his writing from his early essay
"Screen Memories" ([1899] 2003) to "The Unconscious" (1915 [2000]) to find its apotheosis in
Beyond the Pleasure Principle ([1920] 1961). In this text repetition is linked to the death drive, as
one of the boys he writes of exclaims to his startled mother: "go to the fwont," "go to the fwont";
repetition as the process of disappearance and return is not only a child's game but also a way to

"make something new" (6).[36] Dance acts as a movement of thought propelling his concept in multiple directions simultaneously, so that repetition "puts law into question" (3). When Deleuze chooses dancing over leaping, he sides (like Bataille) with Nietzsche to challenge the regimes of representation and the same through an attention to the forces of nature and history. Remember that choreography historically and etymologically arises during a meeting between a priest and a young lawyer who desired to dance; thus from its very inception choreography is beholden to laws of church and state.[37] Following Deleuze, repetition offers choreography a transgressive gift, stealing back its forces of paradox as freedom.[38]

Instead of how do you do say dig your own grave

Instead of flimsy excuses say devious nature

Instead of almost there say scantily clad

Instead of heart felt say fell flat

Instead of lost cause say high standards

Instead of buck up say ass-fucked

---

process the conscious and unconscious effects of death and war to which we are never immune but must always turn to again and again ([1920] 1961, 15).

36. An example of this newness might be the unnamed animal Deleuze writes of in the midst of a discussion of "Repetition for Itself": "An animal forms an eye for itself by causing scattered and diffuse luminous excitations to be reproduced on a privileged surface of its body" (Deleuze [1968] 1994, 96).

37. In *Exhausting Dance: Performance and the Politics of Movement* (2006), Lepecki establishes a genealogy of choreography that begins when dancing and writing meet at the shared table of a lawyer and a ballet master in 1589. A "peculiar invention of early modernity, as a technology that creates a body disciplined to move according to the commands of writing. The first version of the word 'choreography' was coined. . . . *Orchesographie* by a Jesuit priest Thoinot Arbeau (literally, the writing, *graphie*, of the dance, *orchesis*)" (Lepecki 2006, 6–7).

38. One of Pina Bausch's dancers, Ruth Amarante, speaks of a perhaps similar difference generated within repetition: "when we dancers repeat the movements at least we don't stay the same person as when we started . . . these possibilities grow and accumulate on each other" (Amarante in Fernandes 2001, 30). Bausch was many things as a choreographer, among them a virtuoso of repetition as difference.

Instead of cold comfort say which way did they go partner

Instead of wrongly accused say all that meat and no potatoes

Instead of grave robber say bit part

Instead of roll over say play dead

Instead of beauty queen say black sheep

Instead of fat chance say spare change

Instead of shit or get off the pot say oopsy daisy

Instead of pitch perfect say lost innocence

Instead of say it isn't so say that's all she wrote

Instead of blank check say credit check

Instead of over say over and over and over and over . . .

(Kravas 2011d)[39]

   Over and over and over . . . lights out. Spoken by the nine dancers standing at the edge of the stage wearing only one boot and holding their dresses in front of their now naked bodies, choreographic repetition achieves a fierce dissolution of narrative. This final section of Heather Kravas's *The Green Surround* stuns as much in its immediate proximity as its durational force contrasting the opening mise-en-scène of distance when the dancers stand silently staring from behind dark glasses, and wearing white kerchiefs and white dresses, as we enter. We wait as the sound texture thickens to a droning electronic atmosphere that reverberates in the small downstairs theater perfectly repainted with a white band across the center of the black walls. Finally the women remove their dark glasses and gather in the center of the stage, sound cuts to silence and they begin repeating: *boot lick boot lick boot lick boot lick boot lick lick boot lick boot lick boot lick boot lick boot.* . . . while counting on

---

39. *The Green Surround* premiered at Performance Space 122 in New York City, May 4–7, 2011. Choreography by Kravas; performance by Laurie Berg, Milka Djordjevich, Cecilia E., Carolyn Hall, Lyndsey Karr, Sarah Beth Percival, Liz Santoro, Antonietta Vicario, Elizabeth Ward; sound design by Vorhees aka Dana Wachs; lighting design by Madeline Best; costume design by Maria Garcia.

their fingers until a harp interrupts and they remove kerchiefs and dresses, pull on white knee socks, and walk in black leotards to the back wall as if in ballet barre class. Or rather it is ballet turned burlesque, as they execute exacting combinations of pliés, arabesques, and kicks, hips undulating, head rolling, ass toward the audience, then turn to face us again. In one moment the dancers all slide down the wall together, with their red painted mouths opened wide, and urinate in unison. Walking to the audience with their mouths still open they bend over as if to vomit and then rise, remove their socks, and pull on black tutus to begin another dancing sequence. As their movements accumulate and repeat and retrograde under dimming lights I am reminded of William Forsythe's *Duo* (1996)[40] performed by two dancers at the edge of the stage in black leotards, yet with transparent gauze revealing their breasts and the ever present conditions of erotic voyeurism. Yet Kravas's choreography takes a more aggressive approach to desire and subjection in its fierce challenge to the dancers who are always pushed to the edge of failure. Later they kneel in three rows with small bells in front and a metronome counting time as they repeat in various patterns *boo hoo hoo boo hoo hoo boo hoo hoo boo*. Each time a dancer misses a cue she rings her bell and they begin again. Of course, as Kravas admits they become very skilled at this game and she had to devise more complicated patterns during the performance run to mess them up (figures 2.4–2.6).

There are few moments when the dancers are not forced to perform in unison, one when Liz Santoro balances in an extended arabesque looking out the window and another when Antonietta Vicario pulls on black boots and stomps back and forth across the stage. As Vicario repeatedly jumps up then crashes onto the floor, the other dancers exit the stage while counting and we hear them faintly as they march up and down the exterior stairs. Vicario's movement is violent, angry, she is a punk rock vigilante alone in the space.[41] *The Green Surround* is a relentless choreography that strives for an almost fascist perfection that revels in a gorgeous abject labor of dancing, stealing traditional techniques and claiming them again in

---

40. I refer here to a performance of *Duo* I watched danced by Allison Brown and Jill Johnson of Ballet Frankfurt at Brooklyn Academy of Music in September 2003.

41. Her bent-over posture and swinging arms are reminiscent of the young men circling at the Minor Threat concert captured in Dan Graham's video *Minor Threat* (1983). And then I think too of the Melvins' *Bootlicker* (1999); there is in these punk moments another annihilating use of repetition as noise.

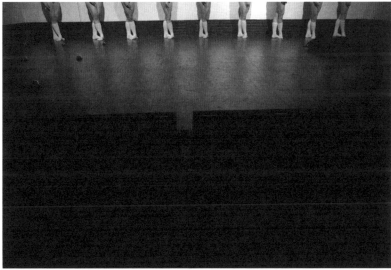

2.4–2.5 Heather Kravas, *The Green Surround*, 2011. Photographs by Ryan Jensen.

2.6 Heather Kravas, *The Green Surround*, 2011. Photograph by Ryan Jensen.

a difficult dark beauty. No longer will the ballerina remain mute, she will speak, she will dress and undress, on stage, and we will watch complicit.

In the solo that follows *The Green Surround*, Kravas makes the transgressive power of repetition even more explicit as she explains:

I'll work on a solo because I feel like I need to ask a pretty intimate question. Not even one that is necessarily something I can articulate. But, I need to go to a pretty internal place or I need to investigate something that is not as defined. I'll do that for maybe a year or two. Then there will come a point where all of the ideas and research, whether through a series of performances or something that's been kept more private, needs to be realized outside of myself. I need to see it. Generally, I consciously decide I want to step out and be more compositional about it. And, I like working in both ways and I hate working in both ways, too. (Kravas 2011b)

Dressed in a black Miu Miu cocktail dress and pink DG sneakers, Kravas stands with her hand on her hip, head tilting back as her eyes roll to almost white. Her face transforms from smile to grimace, quivering and distorted, as her amplified breath growls against the soundtrack of a catfight and howling and then silence. Painted in bright red lipstick, her mouth stretches open like a dark void emitting a silent prolonged scream. Spit slowly collects on her lips and falls onto her dress. She brushes it off and walks toward the altar of St. Mark's Church, approaching a large mirror on wheels that she pivots and rolls toward the audience. With each turn of the mirror a different section of the audience appears reflected on the surface. Placing the mirror at the edge of the audience, she stands facing it, removes her shoes and black lacy underwear, tapes up her dress above her waist with black gaffer's tape and stands in silent observation. Kneeling in front of the mirror her now bare ass and asshole facing the audience, she repetitively flexes her spine again and again and again accentuated by the loud syncopated braying of a donkey. Penetrating and penetrated—her virtuosic intensity and exquisite physicality render the velocity and violence of desire as her facial expressions morph with each repetition from what might appear as pleasure to pain to confusion to desire and on and on.

Kravas describes her solo *Kassidy Chism* that premiered at Danspace Project in October 2011 as the "underbelly" of her earlier group piece *The Green Surround* (2011a).[42] Shifting from an investigation of "perfection and precision" witnessed in the relentless repetitions of nine female dancers attempting and failing to execute various physical and linguistic tasks, Kravas's solo focuses on "the grotesque and un-repeatable. Like all of my work, it will strive to illuminate a sort of hideous beauty. Luscious, wet, monstrous" (Kravas 2011a). While *Kassidy Chism* still relies on extreme repetition and precision in its choreography, Kravas risks more as she explores "the presence and physicalization of appetite and desire" alone on a mostly darkened stage. The piece takes its name and the opening sequence from hip hop phenomenon Kassidy Chism, age ten, as Kravas reenacts

---

42. *Kassidy Chism* premiered at Danspace Project in St. Mark's Church in-the-Bowery, October 6–8, 2011. Choreographed and performed by Kravas; sound by Preshish Moments; lighting design by Madeline Best.

Chism's fearless dance.[43] Trading Chism's off-shoulder white T-shirt revealing a pink tank top, baggy black sweatpants, and white sneakers for a couture dress, Kravas expertly performs the shaking hips, wagging fingers, crotch grabbing, ass pumping gestures of the younger dancer set instead to a barking dog sound score designed by Preshish Moments (Michael Carter). What appears as naïve sexy play in Chism's piece descends into erotized punk rock in Kravas's rendition. As Kravas dances with her wide open red-painted lips, the smiling emulations of a young girl playing with sexual identity or simply enjoying dancing without necessarily understanding the content in it as witnessed in Chism's version is overshadowed by the sexual implications always present in aspiring adolescent dancing yet not usually explicitly revealed. Or when revealed, the audience is not asked to be a complicit witness in the same ways that Kravas requires.[44]

So part of the implicit cruelty (to borrow Baudelaire's description of the witch's dance and Deleuze's meditation on difference) of *Kassidy Chism* is that it taunts you with a tickling sensation of desire, drawing you in, seducing and exhilarating until it reaches the convulsive, darker, uncomfortable edges of desire; witness desire's complex economy of needs, fears, humiliations, vulnerabilities, risks, excesses, and shame. All of these emotional qualities are amplified by the soundtrack of animals fighting, barking, howling, in heat, a sound score that functions not only as metaphor but also as a more primal acknowledgment of desiring forces at work. In the barking dog section Kravas asked Preshish Moments to replace the lyrics and rhythm of Chism's soundtrack with barking dogs; and in the mirror section she asked that each of the repetitive back-bending movements correspond to the hees and haws of a braying donkey with speed changes (Kravas 2011c).

---

43. Kassidy Chism's dance can be found on YouTube: http://www.youtube.com/watch?v=loFHR9JoUMU (accessed December 10, 2013).

44. Speaking about the piece with Jodi Bender, Kravas describes not only watching it on YouTube, but also reading the comments—some celebratory and some vulgar, particularly about the ways that Chism dances with her mouth slightly open (a gesture that Kravas amplifies in her version) (Kravas 2011b). So while Kravas speaks about her own childhood dances as also drawing on this sexual content without knowing its meaning, per se, or as a rehearsal for an older identity, much of this exploration remained private in the bedroom and dance studio rather than circulated around the web. This marks an important difference in the timing of the dispersion of these economies of desire and its reception and audience (Kravas 2012).

Integrating these sonic cues into her movements, Kravas now stands in front of the mirror, shaking her head to the sound of trees falling, static; her left arm becomes a claw and she intones: *please*. Turns away from the mirror: *stop*. Turns back to the mirror: *please*. Turns: *stop*. Repeat. Lying down splayed out in front of the mirror, she brays: *maaaaaaaaa*. Her voice merges into the score, which crescendos as she walks to the front of the stage and performs an intense jumping thudding dance with her hands holding her breasts. The virtuosity required of this dance (of sound and of movement) casts a difficult dark beauty, one that stages the ambivalence of desire and the dangers of going too far as desire becomes disfigured through repetition and resistance. For Kravas, repetition allows a total exhaustion of gesture, movement, and sound that breaks what she calls the "fiction" of creating dance, instead drawing out more tenuous, precarious states as physicality and psychology meet (Kravas 2012). Witnessing these states is at times excruciating, but still I cannot look away.

Part of Kravas's labor, particularly when she is standing still with spit gathering on the edge of her lips, is to remain in one emotional or psychological state—smile, happy, grimace, frown, angry, sexy, grumpy, confused—that connects with her facial expression until it comes undone and moves into something else. As Kravas explains, once she can name and identify the state it has already passed and she shifts to the next (Kravas 2012). Her attempt to stay with a state extends her work with repetition and the inherent failure resulting in this obsessive durational performing of a gesture or expression. Describing her own work with "dancing states," choreographer Meg Stuart explains: "In states you work with oblique relations. The body is a field in which certain mental streams, emotions, energies and movements interact, betraying the fact that actions and states are separate. The internal friction and rubbing creates unexpected relations and by-products, revealing and concealing, expressing how people tend to control their mind and reactions most of the time" (Stuart 2010, 21). *Kassidy Chism* powerfully pressures control and social comportment—of the audience and of the dancer. Following Kravas as she jumps, trembles, drools, and brays, I am not only seduced and intoxicated but also anxious about where she might be taking me, worried that perhaps I am complicit in these patterns, that my own desires might seep, uncontained, into these aggressively uncertain and empowered terrains.

Economies of Desire

To write is to let oneself be swept along by a tongue of black ink that glides slowly without gestures or character, all the while imposing its will, giving away your self as if you were a murderer.—La Ribot, "Panoramix"

Desire like laughter can never only be narrated into semantic and syntactic forms, but floods in less expected ways across flesh and synapses: desire wakes me at night, it writes me, choreographs me, seductively disarming my critical and aesthetic apparatus (much like laughter but more intensely). The desiring labor of the choreographic incites other thoughts, other gestures, other words and deploys this generative potential in pursuit of an erotics of knowledge that is not only about sexual interest, but also explicitly about the desires and pleasures and pains of dancing, of writing, of thinking, of living, and all of these together. So perhaps it is not only coincidence that these choreographic projects by Hélène Cixous, Meg Stuart, La Ribot, DD Dorvillier, Heather Kravas, luciana achugar and I are all produced by women around a certain age, with a certain experience of work and life, who perhaps like Susan Sontag desire "an erotics of art" rather than yet another "hermeneutics" (Sontag [1964] 1966, 14).

In the opening moments of luciana achugar's *The Sublime is Us* (2008)[45] the five female dancers lean into and against each other. Writhing, twisting, their arms rise and fold as rippling effects of the spine (figures 2.7–2.9). The dancers become an organic force, an energetic resonance oozing an ecstatic viscosity distinct from the violent shattering ecstasy performed by laughter. Leaning into one another, arms intertwine as Hilary Clark rolls her head against Melanie Maar's undulating figure, a quality of movement that achugar describes as an "exposure of the fluids, turning the body inside out. [Moving] as if the arms were webbed and feeling in the body the history of the body's own evolution" (achugar 2009). Sliding toward desire, the dancers undulate against the studio's mirror, transforming conjoined group

---

45. *The Sublime is Us* premiered at Dance Theater Workshop in New York City, October 21–November 1, 2008. Concept and direction by luciana achugar; choreographed by achugar with performers including achugar, Hilary Clark, Jennifer Kjos, Melanie Maar, Beatrice Wong; music by Michael Mahalchick with Lucky Dragons; costume design by Icon; lighting design by Megan Byrne; set consultant, Mak.

2.7–2.9 luciana achugar, *The Sublime is Us*, 2008.
Photographs by Ryutaro Mishima.

movements as arms ripple from the spine to simultaneous solos against the cold surface of the mirror. They touch themselves, they touch each other, they overlap in delicate proximity. As Clark plays the piano, the others return to balletic technique, only to find that it too is empty and routine. Head wrapped in her dress, achugar leans into the piano, watching her dancers, watching herself becoming seduced by the sound, the crashing weight of her body falling onto the keys.

Here the choreographic is a feeling, as it participates in what Nancy calls a shared "ecstatic consciousness" that resonates between the dancers extending out to the audience who sit within the dance studio (Nancy [1982] 1991, 19). Importantly, this work takes place within the studio and not on the stage, calling attention to the work of making dance, as itself a desiring process, and this desire—physical, sensual, intellectual—is always an ongoing rehearsal, not an end product. It is also a disruption of audience passivity as we sit with the dancers facing the mirror. Watching the dance that surrounds us, we are also always watching ourselves watching the dancing, and each audience member maintains her own viewpoint, multiplying the perspectives across the space. Later we are invited to participate in the interior machinations of the dance, as achugar directs us to close our eyes, to focus on our own internal organs, to listen, to sense the weight and balance, our relationship to gravity compromised by sitting in these uncomfortable plastic chairs. With our eyes closed, achugar asks that we imagine our pelvis from the inside and then try to move our mind from brain to pelvis to butt, to momentarily suspend cerebral hegemony and to reorganize our thoughts through these other organs, to attend to other possible sites for initiating language and movement. Interpellated by my own interior sensations, I rock, undulating from sitz bones as the dancers crouch and crawl and slide along the floor.

achugar's work embodies a primitive or animal attention to the interiority of the body as impulse for gesture. While the work begins from a conceptual place— with *The Sublime is Us* the animating question is how to "perform desire"—the gestural content is "intuitive, visceral" (achugar 2009). The performers emanate desire, as their gestures originate from internal organs, inspire fluidity of limbs, loose and at times erotic expulsions of breath. Disrupting a dialogic interrogation of gesture by language and language by gesture, achugar attempts to "break language apart … destroying it." Not simply a naive aspiration toward a prediscursive process, she suspends language, moving toward its possible dissolution and resolution as a bodily practice, as language itself moves through the body, flashes up from different organs offering up the possibilities of utopic, social, and flexible communicability.

This desire works against representation; it wants instead to be experienced, to become presence. This labor requires a relentless repetition of gesture that seeks its own undoing. Clothed in navy blue dresses and sweatshirts, the dancers' utilitarian uniform signifies the labor of dance,[46] yet also reveals its dissolution as the gestures fall apart. As the dancers' hair loosens, buttons open revealing appliqué satin flowers on leotards underneath. As they remove parts of their clothing, tying them around their waists or on their heads, the expected labor of dance breaks down. Their pliés falter, the make-up smears, they appear almost bruised; their approach to desire is not easy, or direct. Rather through extreme repetition, a notion of work becomes undone through gestural disarray. This is the pressure of desire on dance—messy extreme.

Particularly in *The Sublime is Us*, this relational aspect reiterates through the use of the mirror that includes the audience as intimately part of this desiring collective. Here the choreographic takes on its critical and perhaps ethical force, engaging (momentarily) in an experiential process that simultaneously points outside itself. achugar's choreography invites us to participate in a rewriting of the somatic force of gesture. Her subversion of a notion of dance as a formal exhibition requires a subversion of structure, a dis-signification of gesture that moves away from language toward a more collective understanding that is simultaneously corporeal and sonic.

If *The Sublime is Us* stages a collective body between the dancers that extends into the audience through a scattering of viewing perspectives, then achugar's next piece shifts the terrain of desire to focus more individually and internally. Against the dispersive invitation or implication of *The Sublime is Us*, achugar designed *PURO DESEO*[47] with a singular perspectival framing in mind.

---

46. In *The Work of Dance: Labor, Movement and Identity in the 1930s*, dance scholar Mark Franko illuminates the political, cultural, and emotional relay between dance and labor. Taking "political emotion as its backdrop," Franko argues that "dance was not on the periphery, but at the center of politics; and . . . the bodies of chorus girls, modern dancers, and ballet dancers were protagonists in the class struggle" to reveal the mutually constitutive work of dance and work as governed by and governing ideologies (Franko 2002, 7).

47. *PURO DESEO* premiered at The Kitchen, New York, NY, April 29–May 2, 2010. Conceived and directed by achugar; created by achugar and Michael Mahalchick; lighting design by Madeline

Leaving the luminous studio and returning to the proscenium stage, achugar exchanges sunlight, windows, and mirrors for a completely darkened theater. Interrupted only by spotlights on the dancers or a dusk-like glow rendering a chiaroscuro ambiance that shifts to bright white light at the end, these cinematic effects focus my attention on achugar as she approaches and moves across the stage (figures 2.10–2.11).

PURO DESEO begins in darkness. achugar's whispers resonate across the saturated void of the theater: *Sana, sana, sana . . . colita de rana . . . si no sana ahora . . . sanará mañana.*[48] She sings quietly at first, accompanied by the sound of her shuffling feet and the rustling of her dress. Slowly moving from behind the audience onto the stage, her voice ascends in volume and intensity as this sweet lullaby repeats. Her shuffling movement creates a transverse path into the center of the stage that she continues to walk, forward and backward, while turning her head to stare out at the audience in the manner of Orpheus searching the darkness for Eurydice. Her turning feels like a direct confrontation as her gaze meets mine, an acknowledgment of the implicit voyeurism of the viewing relationship that she intends to quite literally turn, a dramaturgical decision further reinforcing the singular perspective of her gaze.[49] As her singing fades, she continues her trajectory across the stage and back, again and again until she falls to the floor. Now her pale skin glows underneath the gorgeously torn Victorian dress and the black gloves, her long black hair streaming over the layers of fabrics. A chain rattles from somewhere off to the side of the stage. Dim lights illuminate the other performer, Michael Mahalchick, who appears as a heap, a pile of black fabric, long hair, and beard splayed out, writhing slowly on the floor. Now lying down with her arms and legs spread, achugar repeatedly arches her back while opening and closing her arms and legs so they slap on the stage. The constant shifting of voyeurism toward different intensities invites us to watch, drawing us into one of the most subtly erotic moments as Mahalchick slowly curls and uncurls his hand: a pale gesture twisting in the shadows. If this is desire in its pure form, it remains hushed, repressed, tied

---

Best; costume design by Walter Dundervill.

48. achugar translated the lullaby for me as "heal heal little frog if not today then tomorrow" (achugar 2011).

49. The press image announced this intention in the form of a tightly cropped image of achugar's eye staring out from behind her long black hair.

2.10–2.11 luciana achugar, *PURO DESEO*, 2010. Photographs by Julieta Cervantes.

up in Victorian ribbons and gothic chains, breathing and murmuring like so many unsettled ghosts.

Removing her dress to reveal ripped lace tights and T-shirt, achugar undulates her hips and pelvis, movements that transform into viscous gestures and liquid limbs until she seems to lose balance and falls or throws herself to the floor. She rises and falls, rises and falls. We witness these movements only in fragments, captured by strobe lights as she falls through the air, her hair in disarray, and lies crumpled on the floor. As the sequence repeats, her vertiginous dance appears in photographic stills only. As breath merges with voice, the sonic quality of the piece taps into an interior anatomy, perhaps the nonlanguage place that she speaks of in relation to *The Sublime is Us*. And again it is not that this sounding is prediscursive, but rather that the intensities of breath and expulsion, of fatigue and labor force language into other forms. Part of the gothic impulse behind this work casts an ambivalent glow around desire, beauty, and abjection to suggest that these are never categorically distinct but are uncanny fragments and forms of a similar animation. Like laughter, a gothic aesthetics speaks through incongruence and layers and veils upon veils,[50] images that achugar makes literal in her and Mahalchick's costumes (designed by Walter Dundervill), but also extends in the sonic materiality of these fabrics and chains and bells set against the darkness. Shifting from the reflective Rorschach effects of *The Sublime is Us* that attempted to "perform desire," the choreographic force of *PURO DESEO* embraces presence in its vampiric draping, repetitions, falls, and dramaturgy of the gaze, casting a complicated image of desire danced.

Tracing multiple economies of desire requires an attention to corporeal and theoretical contingencies as flesh intertwines with syntax and gesture consumes utterance. Choreographic desire creates possibilities for sensuous encounter, yet these are never given, but always subject to failure and disfunction and misreading. Conflating corporeality with sexual and at times spiritual force demands a

---

50. Writing of gothic conventions in literature, Eve Kosofsky Sedgwick describes the exquisite layering of surfaces as part of the texture—literary, material, emotional, psychological—of the gothic. And she suggests that it is not only the layer of the "veil" that is erotic, but the fact of its covering that elicits desire, "both as metonym of the thing covered and as a metaphor for the system of prohibitions by which sexual desire is enhanced and specified" (Sedgwick [1980] 2007, 95).

vertiginous virtuosity to perform its sensuous communicability and its critique. This is an intensely affective labor that requires language as much as it resists it— reveling in an irruptive mode of communicability that trembles under the influences of physicality, of ideology, and of language to undo meaning and legibility. This is the labor of laughter of desire: an at times violent and spastic doing and undoing of relation, a sensuous entangling of physicality and discourse, a murmuring shuffling movement toward understanding, a surprising contraction of laughter, punk repetitions, and luscious drool, a gothic rattling of chains. These choreographic projects perform an ecstatic attention as they elicit desire and indict our complicity through language and through dance proposing yet another opening for an *Apocalypse of Understanding, Get Ready!*

3 Ecstatic Community

All right what are you going to show us today?
Whatever happens
Do you have any idea what you're going to do?
We'll just let ourselves go and see how it works out I'm really curious this is gonna be the first time and were kinda hot to find out what it's like
You didn't have the opportunity yet?
No somebody always interrupted us so we're here to finally do it together
And we're here to take a look at it
I hope you're gonna enjoy it
I really hope it's going to look beautiful that you are going to try all the possible variations and positions
I'm really hot for it.—Miguel Gutierrez, *myendlesslove*

Laughter rehearses the shaking tremors incited by desire and desire becomes entrée into the unworking of knowledge in its less recognizable ecstasies. Such a concatenation of laughter and desire produces a spasm—an intertwining as much corporeal as intellectual, a movement of thought and of body where gesture lacerates language and this wounding opens us to a mutual interrogation. To write of spasm is not to invoke a clinical language of seizure or madness (although the hysterical ghosts of Jean-Martin Charcot still haunt) nor is it tied to a depth model of psychology; instead a choreographic spasm images a more phenomenal rupture as the body attempts to escape from itself, from language, from demand. Gilles Deleuze evokes the word "spasm" as a sensate aesthetic effect that retains traces of an involuntary action, yet aspires toward a more phenomenological quality while resisting a universalizing impulse.[1] I imagine spasm as a sensational-perceptual

---

1. Writing about the sensational effects of the shadow in Francis Bacon's paintings, Deleuze describes the shadow itself as a moment of spasm "in which the body attempts to escape from itself *through* one of its organs in order to rejoin the field or material structure . . . the shadow has as much presence as the body; but the shadow acquires this presence only because it escapes from the body, the shadow is the body that has escaped from itself through some localized point in the contour" (Deleuze [1981] 2003, 16). In Bacon's paintings Deleuze sees the rendering of the

force that spreads out from the interior of the body and might be experienced as the kicks and pressures of a perpetual motion machine: at one moment I feel it like the becoming baby that rolls and shifts unexpectedly, calling attention to my own previously ignored interiority, tendons, muscles that remained invisible and numb before this other presence makes itself known. His subtle movements perform a series of spasms that arrive without warning, are out of my control, yet extend as force. Such a physical gestural phenomenon evokes Luce Irigaray's feminist phenomenology of touch (rather than vision), playing along language's perceptual edge without being contained by it:[2] "A touching more intimate than that of one hand taking hold of the other. A phenomenology of passage between interior and exterior. A phenomenon that remains in the interior, does not appear in the light of day, speaks itself only in gestures, remains always on the edge of speech, gathering the edges without sealing them" (Irigaray [1984] 1993, 161).

To touch as to dance: as I write I hear choreographer Miguel Gutierrez asking me why it is that to speak of dance and of body we always turn first to philosophy beginning from our bodies' very absence or as always already indoctrinated by

---

spasm as a limit not only of movement but also of a notion of subjectivity; the spasm performs the body at the edges of representation and of recognition, at the limits of sense as it moves into sensation thus marking a radical break from art-historical conceptions of figuration as he writes against periods, movements, biography, iconography, and social art history and focuses instead on aesthetics in terms of sensational movement. The spasm reveals the choreographic impulse, acting out what Deleuze calls "athleticism" (13)—a latent spasm effect. Witness the damage Bacon does to the image, the figure, and the subject in *Studies of the Human Body* (1970) when the figure lifts a leg and staggers or bends over bleeding into ground. The seemingly distinct figure becomes unrooted, falling into the inverted ground even as it attempts to walk across it. Bacon's triptych renders a serial instability that offers a glimpse of contracted movement at that very moment of its concealment. Bacon's working method notoriously moves between photograph and painting, as he claimed that he could only work from intimate photographs as live models were too disturbed by the violence he commits to their image. "What I want to do is to distort the thing far beyond the appearance, but in the distortion to bring it back to a recording of the appearance. . . . I would rather practice the injury in private by which I think I can record the fact of them more clearly" (Bacon in Sylvester 1975, 40–41).

2. Luce Irigaray's text explicitly critiques Maurice Merleau-Ponty's *The Visible and the Invisible*, *The Intertwining—The Chiasm* arguing against the abstract and masculine model of phenomenology articulated by Merleau-Ponty. Irigaray asserts the differences between languages, between sensations, between spasms such that the distinct intervals between visual and sensual are not collapsed one into the other, too easily eliding their differences and creative potentials.

language. And yet, Miguel, I open with your words spoken as a call and response, of sorts, an antiphonal conversation between you on stage and a video portrait that opens *myendlesslove* (Gutierrez 2006).[3] Love, even self-love, requires an other, a movement and utterance in relation, and perhaps here the choreographic touches upon a queer polyamorous ethics, an invitation to think these ecstatic qualities of spasm as so many darkening clouds and glittering showers: desire transgressing convention and a choreographic understanding rupturing the imperatives of dance (figure 3.1). So let us continue . . .

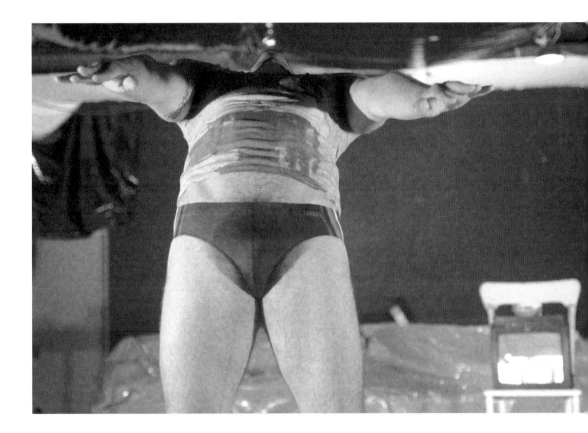

3.1 Miguel Gutierrez, *myendlesslove*, 2006. Photograph by Alex Escalante.

3. *myendlesslove* was commissioned by MIX: The Experimental Lesbian and Gay Film and Video Festival in 2006. Created by Miguel Gutierrez; performed by Gutierrez and The Fantasy Man; music by Gutierrez, Lionel Richie, Giorgio Morodor; text, set, video by Gutierrez.

I Went . . .

Following his opening conversation on love and sentimentality and waterfalls and distance and flowers, Gutierrez stands in high-heeled boots, argyle socks, underwear, a V-neck sweater worn over a square of pink plastic, while smoking and playing harmonica to Giorgio Moroder's theme song from *Flashdance* (1983). Behind him a television screens a close-up of his head and shoulders pulsing repeatedly on the floor as he occasionally turns to look at the viewer or rolls away. The video continues as he picks up a microphone and sings: *love you love you love you love you love you love you love you love you* [pedal click, repeat . . .]. Each series recorded and amplified creates an antiphonal saturation to sing with and against as he continues *I went online . . . I didn't meet anyone . . . I never do. . . . No one wants to know that shit. . . . No one wants to know. . . . No one. . . . No one. . . . No one . . .* The song continues as he rearranges the lights, undresses, and facing the audience in a sweeping lunge gyrates and shakes to Sonique's *It Feels So Good* (1998) using the pink square as a too-small stage.[4] He repeats this routine two more times carrying the stage with him to each new location and then carefully redresses. Lights out. Four television screens with headshots of men staring straight ahead in various expressions of indifference or pleasure illuminate the stage. Within the darkness Gutierrez intones: *I went to the city and realized I loved you I went to the buildings and realized I love you I went to the streets and realized I love you . . . I went to my toes and realized I love you I went to my bed and realized I love you I went to my dreams and realized I love you* (2006).[5]

As witnesses we are not allowed much distance, sitting on stage now enclosed in darkness; *myendlesslove* demands proximity as desire falls into sentimentality folds into pornography opens toward love. We refract these many approaches to longing and to love, perhaps like the Fantasy Man who holds up a mirror reflecting the dance even in the dark (until the very end when he supports Gutierrez as he falls

---

4. I am reminded here of Felix Gonzales-Torres's *Untitled (Go-Go Dancing Platform)* (1991) that features a man in a silver bikini and sneakers listening to music on his Walkman, dancing on a small raised platform lined with lights. As even when Gutierrez is not standing over the square, like the absent go-go dancer, the evocation of the performance and its potential, sexual and otherwise, remains.

5. Jean-Luc Nancy will argue that "I love you" is always "immediately destined to be its own lie" even as it remains a promise ([1982] 1991, 100).

to the floor crying *there . . . is . . . only . . . you . . . in . . . my . . . life . . .* each word suspended the length of a breath). In repetition love shatters, over and over and over again. As Jean-Luc Nancy notes discourses on love exist in exhausting plentitude yet all fail as they aspire toward an end: love is impossible, love is, love is. While the discourses can be endlessly enumerated, love resists. Instead Nancy and Gutierrez ask that we engage this "repetition differently" and "maintain that love is always present and never recognized in anything that we name 'love.' We will have to admit that the rendezvous, our rendezvous with love, takes place not once, but an indefinite number of times . . . Another love presence or another love movement: that is what the repetition should let emerge" (Nancy [1982] 1991, 93–94). For Nancy this is as much about loving as thinking and perhaps we can extend it to dancing, as a way of being "traversed by the other where its presence is most intimate and its life most open. The beating of the heart—rhythm of the partition of being, syncope of the sharing of singularity—cuts across presence, life, consciousness" (Deleuze [1968] 1994, 99). To dance, to think, to love, these all require encounters with alterity that open us to a limit perhaps even to joy.[6] It is a process along the limit that continues endlessly and like *myendlesslove* always moves toward "love, sex, and desire cumming and going, going, gone" (Gutierrez 2013).[7] So again, to invoke Gilles Deleuze, repetition becomes transgressive in these many "secret vibrations" that always "make remake and unmake my concepts along a moving horizon" (Deleuze [1968] 1994, 1, xxi). As a choreographic strategy, repetition invents a saturation of voices, of ghosts, of potential lovers, rendezvous, populating the stage visually, sonically, psychically, so that this solo is never quite that, especially as the Fantasy Man silently reflects it all.

Shattering, vibrating, going, going, gone these transitive qualities of laughter and of love echo across Gutierrez's work as so many ways of "cumming" to consciousness and to communication that not only embrace intoxicating velocities but also toxic sensations of rejection, shame, embarrassment that accompany the

---

6. Nancy will also write of "joying" as a transitive capacity for feeling joy: "she who joys is bedazzled" ([1982] 1991, 107).

7. Text taken from website http://www.miguelgutierrez.org/pieces/myendlesslove/, accessed August 20, 2013.

risks of coming to know self and other.[8] These qualities approach Bataille's conception of nonknowledge, an opening of self to a disorienting horizon that vertiginously shifts through rapidly altered states. To communicate such experience choreographically or otherwise leaves me breathless on an abyss, proposing a radical undoing of objective, subjective, scientific categories of experience, of thinking, and of writing. As Bataille writes:

Communication is diffuse: nothing is communicated from one term to another, but from oneself to an empty indefinite expanse, where everything is drowned. In these conditions, existence naturally thirsts for more troubling communication. Whether it be a question of hearts held breathless or of impudent lasciviousness, whether it be a question of divine love,[9] everywhere around us I have found desire extended toward a fellow being: eroticism around us is so violent, it intoxicates hearts with so much force—to conclude, its abyss is so deep within us—that there is no celestial opening which does not take its form and fever from it. . . . Nonknowledge communicates ecstasy—but only if the possibility (the movement) of ecstasy already belonged, to some degree, to one who disrobes himself of knowledge. (Bataille [1943] 1988, 120, 123)[10]

myendlesslove is troubling and even in some moments violent in its sonorous wails exposing the dancer coming undone. To reiterate: the dancer, not Gutierrez

---

8. To ask another way as Michel Foucault does: "How had the subject been compelled to decipher himself in regard to what is forbidden?" ([1982] 1997, 224).

9. In this moment, Bataille references the mystic writings of Angela of Fogina that he first encounters on a crowded subway in 1939. Crushed against the bodies of other passengers and shaken by the jarring of the train, Bataille exclaims "not knowing how to say how fiercely I burn—the veil is torn in two, I emerge from the fog in which my impotence flails" (Bataille in Hollywood 2002, 61). Of course given his intentional disruptions and deferrals of fiction and anecdote we cannot accept that this is a necessarily real story from his daily life, and yet, written during the beginning of World War II, this text records his fascination with Angela that inspired a radical shift in his approach to knowledge as it moved toward an atheological mysticism joining his descent into the mystic with his mediations on violence. In *Inner Experience* Bataille extends his initial seduction with Angela's writing to the foggy erotics of nonknowledge as a mode of communication—an ecstatic form.

10. This text from *Inner Experience* (1943) comes out of Bataille's early thinking about nonknowledge through ecstatic experience that is later extended to a consideration of laughter in "Nonknowledge, Laughter, and Tears" ([1953] 2001) as discussed in chapter 2.

himself, reaches toward this abyss. Part of the power of his work lies in its confessional honesty and virtuosic vulnerability, yet these elements are all designed within the arc of the piece; Bataille as well imagines his own fictional experience in the throes of passion, agony, love, as so many ways of warping and diffusing writing to approach this other, more ecstatic sensible form. What makes the work troubling is this constant slippage in between seduction and complicity and distance, so that as witnesses our own stories appear and fade among the fragments of narrative, music, image. We are lacerated, to borrow one of Bataille words, by the work as it ruptures our isolated position. Speaking specifically of lovers who "discover each other in mutual laceration," Bataille describes this incision as a spacing between lovers, rather than a cutting of one by the other ([1961] 1988, 152). This spacing and repetition animates Nancy's conception of community (lacerating, arriving, sharing, and also communicating) where artists and lovers act as singularities that incline toward one and another yet never collapse one into the other. Intimately haunted by Bataille's writing, Nancy allows ecstasis to fold into community. Here lies the tension of ecstatic experience: even as the terms of ecstasis and community merge in Nancy's writings, ecstasy requires a constant oscillation between singularities and community.[11]

Perhaps similar to the generative subversions of nonknowledge, Nancy describes community as happening only through "unworking": an "interruption, fragmentation, suspension" (Nancy [1986] 1991, 31). Again the limitations of language force us toward new syntax, new definitions of community as desire as "unleashing of passions" (32). As he reaches for these terms, Nancy draws on

---

11. Nancy is not uncritical of Bataille's intrigue with community and points to his momentary fascination with fascism as a model of community at its orgiastic limits. Bataille, as well, is repulsed by where this totalitarian excess ends, in death and piles of sacrificial bodies, and in his final writings turns away from a thinking of community altogether (Nancy [1986] 1991, 17). Nancy also notes that the horizon between totalitarianism and democracies that so horrified Bataille in the 1930s and 1940s remains the "general horizon of our time" as he writes in 1982, and I would suggest is still a concern in 2013 (Nancy [1986] 1991, 3).

Amy Hollywood points the shift in Bataille's thinking around sacrificial practice from the pre- to postwar years. In his early writings, sacrifice figures as a sacred and voluntary requirement culminating in the final suicide of the one who sacrifices, yet this conception radically shifts in the face of extreme violence and involuntary sacrifice happening during World War II. In his later work, he writes of sacrifice without death. Sacrifice works or perhaps unworks the subject: "through the fictionality of language and the wearing of masks . . . the subject is sacrificed while writing and communication remain" (Hollywood 2002, 58–59).

Bataille's passionate murmurs: ecstasy and community intertwine, conjuring a sacred space yet to be thought, yet to be lived. Through Bataille Nancy witnesses the violent toxicity of the individual subject separated from himself searching for another ontology. Being then cannot be grounded on a notion of the absolute individual or the absolute community. Being is always a being outside of it; it is always relational.

In our historical moment, we are faced with the failure of community—as the ruined legacy of the communist project and by the impossible alliance of individual subjects. Both of these doctrines—of communism and of the metaphysical (rational) subject[12]—omit the possibility of real community as Nancy sees it. In his attempt to reconcile a conception of community, Nancy is not suggesting that we return to some nostalgic bucolic or romantic cohabitation with others, but instead reminds us that community is at the limit of the human and the divine (Nancy [1986] 1991, 11). It is not what we have lost but "*what happens to us*" of our own invention and we remain "entangled in its meshes" (11; italics in original). Thus, community must be re-choreographed, experienced as sensual, relation flux, a joining not of discrete individuals but of singularities: "a body, a face, a voice, a death, a writing, [and a dancing?]" (6). These singularities or singular beings (he oscillates between these two terms) create community as a leaning toward or into each other, not a collapse, but a coming together, a spatial join.[13] This movement toward community also participates in a mode of communication that Nancy names "communicability": a sharing or a "bond that unbinds by binding, that reunites through the infinite exposure of an irreducible finitude. How can we be receptive of the *meaning* of our multiple, dispersed, mortally fragmented existences, which nonetheless only make sense by existing in common?" (xl; italics in original). For Nancy the work of community renders another way of being together; it is a choreographic practice that places ecstatic desire in relation to the other, staging a difficult and precarious encounter.

---

12. Subject and subjectivity are two distinct yet connected concepts for Nancy, whereas for Gilles Deleuze and Félix Guattari, the possibility of multiple assembled subjectivities exists even while a unified singular subject does not (Deleuze and Guattari [1980] 1987).

13. As Nancy meanders around this question of space, I hear Martin Heidegger whispering: the question of being aligns with a movement in and of space, "an ecstatically retentive awaiting of the possible hither and whither ... [this is not to] signify a position in space, but the open[ing to] directionality and de-distancing" (Heidegger [1953] 1996, 337).

Approaching Ecstasies

The dancer trembles, his body convulses as he bends over, thrashes, his head back, his mouth gaping open, his eyes rolling back into his head. Now standing in the center of the sanctuary, Jeremy Wade's movements slow to a subtle shaking, he focuses his gaze on me and begins to claw and grab at the space between us as if grasping for some invisible thread that might connect us, as if taking something away from my energetic field to process in his shamanistic dance. Speech becomes utterance becomes guttural plaint becomes disfiguring gesture, exhibiting his incredibly virtuosic distortion of face and anatomy. Against the now pounding soundtrack, he consumes my discomfort, my uncertainty, my fear. Yet, in these moments, the dance seems unsure of its initial invitation—am I engaging in a space of mutual address or witnessing at too close a range?

This scene from Wade's *fountain* (2011)[14] embodies the ecstatic force of the choreographic as a form of choreography deeply embracing limitations, illegibility, uncertainty, and psychological duress as modes of dancing and of addressing dance (figures 3.2–3.3). Wade's invitation requires a renewed negotiation of the ethics of witnessing and of aesthetics. Such ecstatic choreographic work shares with Gutierrez an attention to the messy, digressive, transgressive, and queer; imagining a practice of world-making within the studio, the stage, and beyond. Wandering toward the altar of St. Mark's Church in-the-Bowery, Wade intones: "we are pilgrims of small details" pointing to the rainbows of stained glass, repeating architectural domes, "frenzied geometries" of gray industrial carpet that seam the sanctuary (Wade 2011). Calling attention to the obvious yet usually unremarked upon environmental textures effects a "charging of the space" that the audience is asked to hold while we stand in a circle around him watching as he morphs from New Age charismatic to possessed shaman and back again.

When he asks that the audience join him on the stage (the sanctuary of St. Mark's Church in-the-Bowery or the back stage of Abrons Art Center playhouse in New York City or the floor of Hebbel Theater in Berlin),[15] Wade trespasses across

---

14. *Fountain* is choreographed and performed by Jeremy Wade; music by Tian Rotteveel; dramaturgy by Eike Wittrock.

15. These are the three places where I witnessed *fountain*. Initially at its premiere at the Hebbel Theater in Berlin in August 2011, a version that began with Wade telling a story about the difficulty

the invisible threshold of disinterested spectator expectations asking that we leave the safety of our autonomous positions and become part of a group experience; this entails wandering around the space, humming, lying on the floor, standing intimately in a huddle swaying back and forth, then circling around as he performs his dark satyr dance. If you choose to accept (and there is always the choice to remain on the periphery or in your seat), *fountain* requires a disarming vulnerability in order to be with, to incline toward other people, under the influence of Wade's directives. In these moments, he draws on the languages and rituals of spiritual and ecstatic and relational experience to create a temporary community. To think community through ecstatic practice demands a simultaneous attention to critical and physical process that flirts with joy, ugliness, pleasure, proximity, distance, touch, and separation, enacting an important counterpoint to the politics or ethics of what a community might be. In this mode of choreographic work the spasm is not only a theoretical convulsion, but also explicitly physical and emotional and energetic, figuring a choreographic that is gorgeously spiritual, secularly repulsive, transgressively baroque—ecstatic.

Another of Bataille's close interlocutors, Amy Hollywood, describes his work on the ecstatic as an "ethics of catastrophe"; a mode of writing that attempts "*to see the speechless body*" in such a violent and lacerating and fragmented form that it cannot simply be dismissed as a sign or become too easily assimilated to a general sensibility (and removal of our complicity) in this catastrophe (Hollywood 2002, 79, 83; italics in original). Here Hollywood's argument wavers as she tries to account for a mode of ethics that does not fall into a political project or action, but remains a mode of meditative witnessing of seeing suffering and refusing to recognize it as meaningful so that Bataille might "communicate it" (86). She describes Bataille's rendering of horror and ecstatic experience not simply as escapist fantasies, but as contemplative practices with spiritual and historical force. In the midst of ecstatic experience, consciousness oscillates along a threshold between perceptible and

---

of the past year—his father's death, his depression and fear, quitting smoking, the suicide of a friend and colleague in the NYC dance world—that continues into his solo in which he takes our fear and later blows it into plastic bags that line the stage and then concludes with a trio of dancers who join him in his ecstatic dance. The second version was performed in a joint evening with Heather Kravas at Danspace Project in October 6–8, 2011 (this version is described earlier), and the third as part of the American Realness Festival at Abrons Art Center in January 2012 (a version similar to the Danspace version but with a more intensified group experience).

3.2 Jeremy Wade, *I Offer Myself to Thee (Solo)*, 2009. Photograph by Anna Van Kooij.

3.3 Jeremy Wade, *fountain*, 2011. Photograph by Romain Etienne.

imperceptible conditions. Yet as Hollywood explains, Bataille's understanding of experience as neither a recoverable authentic narrative nor "immediacy and self-presence" proposes a more complicated and ambivalent understanding of the work of ecstasy and its revelation of the horror of his contemporary moment (40). And this question also speaks to Wade's investigation in *fountain*: how to communicate an ethics of the ecstatic through bodily sensations, movement, sound, language, spasms, trembling, shaking, growling, smiling, dancing, speaking to effect a "generative sphere of uncertainty" (Wade 2012)?

Wade's investigation of ecstasy in *fountain* draws on his more spectacular performance as pop-cultural shaman or spiritual guide in *I Offer Myself to Thee* that premiered at the *Politics of Ecstasy Festival* at the Hebbel Theater in Berlin in January 2009 (figure 3.4). *I Offer Myself to Thee* opens with Wade walking toward the audience with open arms, generously welcoming us with a hallucinogenic mix of New Age aspirations and cosmological projections—he becomes our "guide, trickster, and intergalactic fool" (Wade 2009). Flanked by hanging strands of light bulbs and musicians Brendan Dougherty and Keith O'Brien, Wade spins with his arms opening out as he speaks of "reciprocal exchange . . . communication between two groups . . . the science of feedback loops . . . the energy we feel or loss at its absence." Both wildly self-reflexive and sincerely emotional, *I Offer Myself to Thee* attempts a participatory aesthetics[16] that we might not only witness but also feel the

---

16. My use of participatory aesthetics draws on the impulse toward participation across a range of works as exemplified in Claire Bishop's anthology *Participation* (2006) including texts by Lygia Clark, Hélio Oiticica, Roland Barthes, Joseph Beuys, Guy Debord, Félix Guattari, Thomas Hirschhorn, and Jacques Rancière, as examples. This mode of participation extends Bishop's critique of Nicolas Bourriaud's conception of relational aesthetics initially elaborated in her essay "Antagonism and Relational Aesthetics" (2004). Against what Bishop sees as the lack of participation, but rather a spectacle of art world scene under the guise of capitalist critique through eating together, Bourriard argues for a new ethics of the "face" of art in *Relational Aesthetics*, a book and exhibition of his own design ([1998] 2002, 22–23). Shifting away from what he calls a "prosecutor aesthetics" that would tether art to only one aesthetic or another and then drawing on and distancing himself from Emmanuel Levinas's conception of face as a form of relational yet "interservility," Bourriaud turns to artist Rirkrit Tiravanija (his prime example) to identify "a form to invent possible encounters: receiving a form is to create the conditions for an exchange, the way you return a service in the game of tennis" (22–23). In this amazing writerly sleight of hand, we can move from the order not to kill to a game of tennis. And in this moment of Bourriaud's overwriting of an ethical aesthetic code lies the issue of relational aesthetics—it becomes too easy or slippery. The other animating question relates to media or rather how to avoid media as the defining characteristic. Is it sculpture or installation or relation? As evidenced

"golden energy" pulsates through our bodies under the influence of Wade's words, the trance effects of flashing strobe lights, and the accelerating sound score.

And yet, "participatory" is still not really the right term. What Wade incites is a more affective collaboration within the performance itself. It is a practice that resonates with what scholar Erika Fischer-Lichte identifies as a "performative turn" or "a *radical concept of presence*" ([2004] 2008, 18, 99; italics in original). Alluding to debates around the Cartesian mind/body split activated by readings of Maurice

3.4 Jeremy Wade, *fountain,* 2011. Photograph by Romain Etienne.

---

in the New York City gallery scene in Spring 2011, the distance is 2.5 miles between Joseph Kosuth's installation at Sean Kelly gallery and Rirkrit Tiravanija's exhibition at Gavin Brown.

Merleau-Ponty's phenomenology and hysterically argued against in the writings of art critic Michael Fried, Fischer-Lichte fixates on Marina Abramović's *Lips of Thomas* (1975) to argue that the performer's body is no longer either a phenomenal or semiotic thing, but is simultaneously phenomenal and semiotic, thus opening up a new definition of embodiment (82). Evidenced in works like Abramović's, performing bodies "function as the object, subject, material, and source of symbolic construction, as well as the product of cultural inscription" forcing a crisis in reception and ethics as "corporeality dominated semioticity" (89, 19). For Fischer-Lichte and for Wade, this process happens through a saturated materiality (of image, of text, of sound, of body) within the performance that moves along a "polymorphous" feedback loop (Fischer-Lichte [2004] 2008, 128). Particularly in Wade's work, his voice and its soundings release these multiplicities rendering the sonic as an equally material force within the work that requires a reconsideration of aesthetic critique from a more traditional alignment of work-production-reception to an aesthetics structured by social, political, and ethical atmospherics (Fischer-Lichte [2004] 2008, 128):

I can see it now . . . celestial event . . . is that consciousness? Am I? Am I? What am I thinking . . . no words . . . no words[17]. . . . I'm glad to see you because the world is really fucked up and these objects are part of it. . . . We flash. . . . We pulsate stronger than ever before. . . . We begin to separate like a star exploding. . . . One massive comet now separate entities floating in space. . . . Excuse me, my heart has always been too big. (Wade 2009)

Wade's narrative collapses celestial and anatomical, generating a disorienting vertigo as cosmic merges with intimate, my body sensing as his body sways and speaks, evoking a momentary energetic connection. This is the promise that Fischer-Lichte sees in Abramović as well, that the spectator "perceives the circulating energy as a transformative and vital energy" ([2004] 2008, 99). Wade quite literally acknowledges this reciprocal force as he casts a picture of a temporary joining, an inclining toward one another as Nancy proposes, that enacts the work of the ecstatic choreographic. For Wade this is a work not only of passion and generosity but also of love. In one moment in the performance, Wade merges

---

17. Wade's use of language to convey the impossibility of language also resonates with DD Dorvillier's use of text in *Choreography, a Prologue for the Apocalypse of Understanding, Get Ready!* discussed in chapter 2.

Bataille's sovereign lovers and artists, when trembling he whispers "I love you . . ." (2009). The lights go out and he disappears into darkness. Wade performs an emotional relation, yet his offer of himself on center stage as one who speaks and recedes plays, as he admits, with "paradox—is it possible to surrender or is it just a show?" (Wade 2010b). This is part of the research of the piece: to experiment with literally inserting text as a material and sculptural entity into the work and to use its effects as a vehicle for audience visualization, a process that he hopes effects a "shattering . . . through the chemistry of charismatics and a science of gesture" (Wade 2010a).

Part of the power of Wade's work lies in his deeply generous investment in sharing even at times against the audience's wishes. *I Offer Myself to Thee* and *fountain* invite submission to disorientation and fantasy as part of the choreographic work in an attempt to trespass into the ambivalent eros and uncertainty that ecstatic experience invokes. Listening to Wade's unfolding story and watching as he twists his arms spiraling his head and neck as if turning inside out, I am reminded of the opening lines of Shelley Jackson's evocation of the heart when she writes: "They give off a kind of light, but it is a backwards light that races inward away from the onlooker to hide itself from view, so this light, whose color we would so much like to know (maybe it's a color we haven't seen before, for which we must sprout new eyes), looks more like darkness than any ordinary darkness, and seems to suck the sight from our eyes, and make itself visible in the form of a blind spot" (Jackson 2002, 3).

We cannot understand the melancholic gravitational force of the heart and its desire through our existing organs and limbs, but must create new compositions or shifts in scale and attention so that the corporeal might coincide with the conceptual and expose the blindingly obvious through an encounter with darkness. And yet how do we get there?

Both Jackson and Wade perform the ecstatic choreographic as a working on the self in the presence of and toward something other. This relational movement is the heart of ecstasy. As art historian and curator Carolyn Christov-Bakargiev notes, the etymology of ecstasy derives from "the Greek *ex* (out) and *histanai* (to stand, to be in a place)," acknowledging the relational movement of ecstatic experience as it comes out of self and approaches another—another person, another experience, and also another temporality (Christov-Bakargiev 2005, 139).[18] Yet this approach to the something other of ecstatic experience is not a leave-taking of the self or of the present, but an ambivalent negotiation with presence. Novelist Milan Kundera describes this quality of ecstasy such that "to be 'outside oneself' does not mean outside the present moment, like a dreamer escaping into the past or the future. Just the opposite: ecstasy is the absolute identity with the present instant, total forgetting of past and future" (Kundera [1992] 1995, 85).[19] Stripped of its religious context but not its spiritual force, ecstatic experience imagines excessive, irrational (non-sensible), terrifying, and glorious ways of being, if only for a moment, that might act as ciphers for political and ethical engagement with self and formations of community, proposing an ecstatic choreographic as another mode of aesthetic practice.

Describing his curatorial conceit for the exhibition *Ecstasy In and About Altered States*, Paul Schimmel aligns the "utopian impulse" of community creation inspired by intoxication and ecstasy (in its drug form) in rave culture with contemporary artistic tendencies toward generation of utopian empathetic encounters (not necessarily under the influence of drugs). His opening essay "Live in Your Head" takes its title from Harold Szeemann's seminal exhibition *Live in your Head: When Attitudes Become Form* from 1969,[20] an exhibition that brought together artists including Robert Morris, Richard Serra, Eva Hesse, Mario Merz, and Robert Smithson, whose work rejected the transcendent aspirations of modernism and Abstract Expressionism in favor of an intrigue with immanence and experience reflected in the experiential and entropic qualities of the works themselves.[21] For

---

18. This essay is included in the exhibition catalog for *Ecstasy: In and About Altered States*. Curated by Paul Schimmel, the exhibition opened at the Museum of Contemporary Art, Los Angeles on October 9, 2005, and continued through February 20, 2006.

19. This quote by Milan Kundera is included in Lars Bang Larsen's essay "When the Light Falls," also from the *Ecstasy: In and About Altered States* catalog.

20. Rather than preselecting individual pieces, Szeemann invited artists to submit proposals for new works that might explore this connection between attitude and form. The catalog itself reflects his interest in encapsulating a particular moment and genealogy and breaks with conclusive curatorial statement and instead includes photographs of the artists alongside their proposals organized like a traditional paper phone book with letter tabs.

21. Christov-Bakargiev also discusses this shift from transcendence to immanence (Christov-Bakargiev 2005, 143).

Schimmel, the 1960s become a touchstone for thinking about the invitation of ecstatic experience proposed by the work of minimalist and conceptualist artists working in the 1960s and 1970s and here he explicitly references Andy Warhol's *Exploding Plastic Inevitable* (1966–1967) series of intermedia events as a historical precedent for this mode of working under the influence (of substance and of history). Captured in Ronald Nameth's eighteen-minute film shot over a week in 1966, *Exploding Plastic Inevitable* appears as a hallucinogenic mix of intensely saturated strobe and spot lights shifting among green, yellow, blue mixed with sound by Velvet Underground and Nico and simultaneous screenings of Warhol's durational films. At one moment, the film captures Edie Sedgwick dancing, her head swaying and her mouth slack and laughing. Her face turns green, then glittery yellow, then hazy cerulean blue as she undulates against a grainy backdrop of Warhol's *Whips,* slowly repeating black-and-white silhouettes of a leather strap snapping against a wall. *Exploding Plastic Inevitable* imagined an immersive aesthetics; sensuous pleasure pushed to extreme duration and breakdown under the violent and corruptive forces of rapture. As described by reviewer Michaela Williams:

To experience is to be brutalized, helpless. . . . The strobe lights blaze, spots dark, flickering pistol lights start in on [the audience] and their humanness is destroyed; they are fragments, cutouts waiving Reynolds Wrap reflectors to ward off their total disintegration. . . . Eventually, the reverberations in your ears stop. But what do you do with what you still hear in your brain? The Flowers of Evil are in full bloom with the Exploding Plastic Inevitable: let's hope it's killed before it spreads. (Williams in B. Joseph 2002, 91–92)[22]

Exploding Plastic Inevitable figured not only the gorgeous and glittery transcendence of choreographing ecstasies, but also the darker seductions and more nightmarish manifestations of a self-shattering. I want to hold onto this ambivalent force of choreographic ecstatics as a reminder that ecstatic experience is not only a pursuit of pleasure and freedom for self and with others (as Bataille has noted), but is always structured by a complicated dynamics of individual and social engagement. Put another way, it is in this ecstatic ambivalence that perhaps we

---

22. Branden Joseph notes that the final remarks in this description thrilled Warhol and were used for advertising of future events (B. Joseph 2002, 92).

might find an ethics of community that takes account of its impossibilities and necessary failures.

Facing Communicability

Naked, two dancers lie face down on the darkened stage. They tremble; a mild convulsion passes through their bodies, which transforms into a creeping mobility as they slowly peel their bodies from the floor, edging away from the light. No longer completely recognizable, their slow emergence from and disappearance into the darkness approaches larval abstraction as they ambulate using only their shoulders, chin, and hips. Thick muscular flesh slaps against the floor, amplifying their difficult horizontal mobility (figure 3.5–3.6). In these moments of *Glory* (2007)[23] choreographed by Wade and performed by Wade with Marysia Stoklosa, we encounter an extreme choreographic articulation of the spasm. *Glory* exhibits the generative excess of the spasm as the bodies attempt to expel themselves from their limits through what Wade describes as "a three-dimensional kinesthetic blur. Add levels of speed, levels of rhythm, add fluids, flesh, chemical, emotional, behavioral bodies, add detail, memory, position, history, character, add light, sound" (Wade 2007a). Now obscured in shadow, the bodies appear at one moment prostrated on the floor, at another as a messy pile of limbs becoming less visible and less distinct as if absorbed by the surrounding space. A low light illuminates part of a torso then flickers along the thighs or buttocks; yet as these figures make their way along the ground they remain only partially in view, haunted by the sound score—an industrial roar marked by moments of silence or the moaning tendons of the cello. In shadow, the sound acts as animal accomplice lamenting the painful, hysterical process of becoming, a process haunted by violent excess.

––––––––––––––––

23. The first version of *Glory* premiered in 2003 at the Kitchen in New York City as part of Dance Works in Progress and was performed by Wade with Lyndsey Karr. In February 2007, he performed a second version at Dance Theater Workshop with Jessica Hill; music by Loren Dempster and Michael Mahalchick; lighting by Jonathan Belcher; dramaturgy by Leigh Garret and Yvonne Meier. After moving from New York City to Berlin in 2007, Wade created a third version (described here) performed with Marysia Stoklosa; music by Loren Dempster and Michael Mahalchick; lighting by Fabian Bleisch; dramaturgy by Jenn Joy, which continues to be performed. As Wade writes, "We will continue to explore, tweak, question, and perform 'glory.' It is alive and malleable" (Wade 2007b).

3.5–3.6 Jeremy Wade, *Glory*, 2007. Photographs by Dieter Hartwig.

This duet of shadow and sound played across the body continues until the dancers pause at the edge of the stage. Stoklosa grabs Wade's mouth with her own, she appears to be chewing or consuming him as they roll over, onto, into each other. As they intertwine she whispers, building to a scream, "the road is long and I am tired and small." In this moment of the extended kiss, the mouth becomes, as Wade describes it, a "devouring machine" (Wade 2007a). Until this moment the states of spasm occur as individual gestures in parallel, as a duet or a mirror, yet in this phrase distance dissolves under the intensity of attraction disfiguring and refiguring their relationship. Sweat moves across and between bodies, limbs become more confused. This is communicability, as all consuming, submerged in an erotic and volatile physicality. It is a body almost possessed, desperate, messy, intimate, disorientated, and disfigured in a moment of relational-sensational plexus.

Witnessing the climax of the spastic duet convulsing into a singular spasm while recoiling from this intimacy reveals the spasm as beautifully grotesque gesture, relational yet resilient. The choreographic spasm poses an extreme anatomy of attachment and desire, even of violent disfiguration. Yet, in Wade's work the spasm resists a complete dissolving of subjectivity. Rather, the spasm functions as an interrogator of subjectivity and communicability. This becomes clear as the versions of *Glory* evolve. In the first version of *Glory* (2003), the dancers begin naked on stage, waiting for the audience to arrive. The process of becoming is already underway; the bodies have transformed into surreal objects and their sculptural flesh anticipates the event of movement. Yet in the second and third versions (Wade 2007b), it is the audience who waits, contemplating the empty space as Wade and Stoklosa walk onto the stage. Standing side by side, they pause. This dramaturgical shift directs attention to the quotidian presence of the bodies, to their easy orientation and calm physicality as if offering a foil for the drama to come. Clothed, the gestures seem less confused and vertiginous, forcing us to pay attention to the face, which alone remains open and naked to our gaze.

The dancers begin to smile, or almost, as a halting series of facial tics[24] morphs from smile to frown to yawn to gag. Her eyes roll back into her head. His tongue reaches grotesquely out of his mouth. Performing an atrophic virtuosity, the

---

24. As Deleuze and Guattari explain a tic is "precisely the continually refought battle between a faciality trait that tries to escape the sovereign organization of the face and the face itself, which clamps back down on the trait, takes hold of it again, blocks its line of flight, and reimposes its organization upon it" ([1980] 1987, 188).

dancers' faces appear to be choking on the very air that surrounds them. As their expressions accumulate and retrograde—eyebrows distort, tongues thrust, noses torque, mouths become gaping voids, issuing hysterical laughter—they transform from micro-spasms of the face to contorted staggering movements of the entire body across the floor. Wade's eyes roll back into his head, mouth open he drools as his knees collapse and his wrist twists into something more like a claw as he attempts to disfigure a legible image of the face.[25] Wade images a face attempting to deface itself, or perhaps reveals the face as always already defaced under the imperatives of virtuosic representation, and yet he resists. At the precarious edge of collapse, the dancers' bodies appear disarticulated and out of control, severing choreography's anticipated relationship to mobility and stasis, graceful expertise and beautiful uncertainty. Pausing, they remove their clothes, arranging them in abject piles at their feet and then carry them offstage.

Naked, the body becomes an extension of the face. Not only metonymically, but also quite physically as what begins as distorted expressions and tics across the face saturate their entire bodies transposed into stuttering, seizing, flailing movements that throw their bodies off balance. This intensely intimate, sensual, fragile, and at times violent dependency participates in the extreme gesture of the spasm as it "devours" a coherent conception of bodies and subjectivities, forcing an at times an illegible and distressing vision of the inability of language and movement to account for Wade's and our experience. Wade exposes a virtuosic failure or corporeal illegibility as his muscular flesh torques and seizes. This new opening section could be considered as an assemblage choreographed under the influence of what Wade calls the Deleuze-Guattari manual or "self-help with how to obliterate yourself" (Wade 2010a). It is a danger they recognize when they write: "Dismantling the face is no mean affair. Madness is a definite danger" (Deleuze and Guattari [1980] 1987, 188). Writing against the limitations of autonomous subjectivity and psychoanalytic depths, Gilles Deleuze and Félix Guattari imagine the face not as an anatomical entity or organism, but as a series of surfaces, "surface-holes, holey surface, system" that constantly works against singularity and signification (170). The face becomes a choreographic machine; and "body is not one of part-objects but of differential speeds" (172). In the Deleuzian-Guattarian

---

25. The opaque whites of his eyes call to mind an egg or the transpositions of eggs and eyes that the narrator of Bataille's *The Story of the Eye* describes of the ravished Marcelle in her fit of erotic and violent rapture (Bataille [1928] 2001).

cosmology,[26] subjectivity must constantly be undone through velocities and desires and assemblages to resist any symptomatic reading of subjectivity in light of its reparative economy. Wade's choreography does not illustratively perform their proposal, as this would contradict the very process itself, but perhaps works as additive accumulation.[27]

For Wade the face becomes a site of alteric and affective communicability. As he choreographs the momentary (seemingly) disembodiment of the face as a site of impossible speech interrogating possibilities of representation and language through expressions of despair, of shame, of pleasure, of pain, the bleed between these seductive and repulsive, recognizable and illegible expressions performs an excessive polyvocality not contained by the significatory logic of representation. Subverting a virtuosic notion of dance through an existential examination of extreme facial gesture, the dancers direct our attention away from the figure to the expressive potentialities of the face, a move not unlike Samuel Beckett's *Not I* (1972).[28] Also trapped in darkness, only a Mouth with glistening teeth is visible as she narrates her own coming into being, coming into language. She speaks of the impossibility of speech even when her own voice cries out, screaming, spasming against its limits, describing her own sound score as a "buzzing" not in the ears, but

---

26. Inserted near the end of this chapter on faciality, Deleuze and Guattari also include a program for art's potentiality: "For it is through writing that you become animal, it is through color that you become imperceptible, it is through music that you become hard and memoryless, simultaneously animal and imperceptible: in love. But art is never an end in itself; it is a tool for blazing life lines, in other words, all of those real becomings that are not produced only *in* art, and all of those active escapes that do not consist in fleeing *into* art, taking refuge in art, and all of those positive deterritorializations that never reterritorialize on art, but instead sweep it away with them toward the realms of the asignifying, asubjective, and faceless" ([1980] 1987, 187).

27. Victoria Anderson-Davies evocatively dissects the potentiality of faciality as choreographic hermeneutic in "Creative Endurance and the Face Machine: Roseanne Spradlin's *Survive Cycle*" (2009).

28. One recent version of *Not I* features actor Julianne Moore shot close-up so most of her face is obscured save her slightly crooked teeth and saliva accumulating on her tongue. Included in series *Beckett on Film: 19 Films by 19 Directors*, vol. 1 (2001).

in the skull (Beckett 2006, 411).[29] A kind of embedded, inscribed, inescapable soundtrack; here again face as voice, as language, as precarious communication.

Glory's faces use the choreographic function of the spasm to differentiate between language as a function of representation and communicability as a transitive poetic address. The face becomes a shifting surface moving from anatomy to speech to language that opens up an alteric reading of the ways that face figures discursively and ethically as a site of encounter or rendezvous. As Wade's dramaturgy reminds us, these compositions of body, psyche, and emotion are never far from violence, and while the histories differ, Wade risks violence in his trembling encounters with intoxicating intimacy and ecstasy. Struggling to interject an ethical responsibility into our phenomenological encounter with the other, Emmanuel Levinas writes of a face-to-face encounter as the limit of a particular kind of violence. The face appears as a "pure denuding of exposure without defense. . . . Extreme precariousness of the unique, precariousness of the stranger" (Levinas [1984] 1996, 167).[30] Importantly, Levinas reminds us that this face is not only a human face or anatomy but also an extension of the visage and voice transposed across the body, what Judith Butler calls a "catachresis" (Butler 2004, 132): "a particular way of craning their neck and their back, their raised shoulders with shoulder blades tense like springs, which seemed to cry, sob, and scream" (Grossman in Levinas [1984] 1996, 167).[31] Levinas takes a more oblique position relying on the adverb (as) as opposed to an ontological positioning (is) of this precariousness. Butler calls attention to his turn of phrase, suggesting that Levinas is not only speaking to our relation to the other but to the function and

---

29. The Mouth in *Not I* is not alone on stage. Her hysterical linguistic spasm is always attended by the choreographic presence of another. Completely cloaked in a black djellaba, the Auditor stands at an oblique angle to the audience on an "invisible podium" facing the Mouth (Beckett 2006, 405). Four times during her monologue the Mouth stops and the Auditor's arms rise and fall slowly from the sides of the body, "a gesture of helpless compassion" (405).

30. Writing against what he calls "the bourgeois peace of the man who is at home with himself behind closed doors, rejecting the outside that negates him," ([1984] 1996, 165) Levinas argues that we cannot think of peace only through nonviolence, but must attend to the fact that our approach to the other is always structured by the anxious tension and knowledge that we come from positions of violence seeking a way toward peace. We must articulate not only a political peace, but also an "ethical peace" (166).

31. Levinas's description of the face here quotes a passage from Vasily Grossman's *Life and Fate* ([1959] 1987).

responsibility of discourse itself. Discourse is, as both remind us, not only what is said, but the condition of experience as language, as saying. She explains: "For Levinas, the situation of discourse consists in the fact that language arrives as an address we do not will, and by which we are, in an original sense, captured, if not, in Levinas's terms, held hostage. So there is a certain violence already in being addressed, given a name, subject to a set of impositions compelled to respond to an exacting alterity" (Butler 2004, 139). If address contains the workings of violence as a condition of its ontological stature, then Levinas must speak and write from a more oblique place so that he is not in effect replaying the very problem he is attempting to address. This is also the ethical problem of representation as Butler reminds us: "representation must not only fail, but it must *show* its failure. There is something unrepresentable that we nevertheless seek to represent, and that paradox must be retained in the representation we give" (144; italics in original).

Giorgio Agamben's conception of the face as a zone of communicability that calls us to action takes up this catachretic potential of the face: "What the face exposes and reveals is not *something* that could be formulated as a signifying proposition of sorts, nor is it a secret doomed to remain forever incommunicable. . . . the face is, above all, the *passion* of revelation, the passion of language" (Agamben [1996] 2000, 92). Not only visage, a face moves toward a threshold of appearance within which we must negotiate and expose a radical politics of "communicability" (92). Agamben's choreographic imperative argues for a rethinking of political language as passionate gestural expression spreading out from the face that resonates with the disorientating decompositions and recompositions of the face in *Glory*. Here the spasm as choreographic address proposes an almost impossible body, one that rejects coherence and unity striving instead to articulate a more vertiginous flux of subjectivity. As Agamben calls us: "Be only your face. Go to the threshold. Do not remain the subjects of your properties or faculties, do not stay beneath them: rather, go with them, in them, beyond them" (100).

Ecstatic Surface

To exceed, to move beyond, to lacerate, within art and within discourse these possibilities propose "an activity of unframing, of rupturing sense, of baroque proliferation" (Guattari [1992] 1995, 131). For Guattari, the work of art is itself a moving encounter that reimagines aesthetics as a producer of alteric subjectivities.

His choice of "baroque" alludes to a kind of spiritual or ecstatic excess, a seductive and at times repulsive display of expression and sensuality rendered through the dark shades of chiaroscuro, waves of light, and shadow.[32] *Glory* performs the baroque in multiple ways as the dancers crawl into and out of darkness and even more specifically or perhaps art historically as the iconic image of *The Ecstasy of St. Teresa* tattooed on Wade's back shivers as he moves. Folds of flesh melt into the drawn folds of fabric draped across St. Teresa's body as she lies mouth open head turned from the attending angel.[33] Her fingers almost quiver, her toes are taut, her body trapped in the intermediary space of ecstasy, as Wade's body continues its stuttering ambulation across the floor. Drawing our attention to the "affective transport chiseled on [St. Teresa's] face," José Esteban Muñoz describes her ecstasy as a movement out of time or convergence of multiple temporalities within the ecstatic. Through Heidegger, Muñoz invites us to experience a "sense of timeliness's motion" that agitates against linear straight time—"a suffocating violence both visceral and emotional" and historical—placing us closer if only for a moment to something of pleasure and agony (2009, 186–187). When Wade dances this ecstatic temporality extends, quite literally inscribing an untimely convergence of flesh and figure.

Skin becomes another image surface participating in *Glory's* contingent unfolding. This is not to claim that these images become content for the work, but rather that the relational accumulation of images and movements engender multiple nuanced folds. In these moments, Wade's tattoo enacts a doubling of

---

32. Deleuze offers his own baroque explication of the baroque as "operative function" crossing disciplinary genres through an endless proliferation of folds as he moves across the writings of Leibniz to architecture, music, fashion, mathematics, and beyond (Deleuze [1988] 1993).

33. Here pain mingles with pleasure as St. Teresa describes her experience: "The pain was so great that I screamed aloud; but at the same time I felt such infinite sweetness that I wished the pain would last forever. It was not physical pain but psychic pain, although it affected the body to some degree" (St. Teresa in Janson [1962] 1991, 557). A representation of St. Teresa also serves as the cover image of Bataille's *Erotism: Death and Sensuality* ([1957] 1962). And to return to the work discussed in the chapter 1, I would gesture toward James Foster's mixed media sculpture *Self-portrait (Waaaay After Bernini's Ecstasy of St. Teresa)* (2009) that transposes Foster's face on Teresa's raised and reclined figure cast in black resin juxtaposed with a pile of translucent shards, also fragments of his face, and an impossibly illuminated lamp filled with concrete on the floor. So many modes of self-shattering etched across marble, flesh, resin, time. If we weave their disparate thoughts together, how might Bataille and Wade and Muñoz and Foster affect Bernini's angelic erotics?

ecstatic disfiguration. An image generated by intense sensation and commitment, the tattoo not only reveals duration as an inscription on the dancing body, but also more deeply animates body and skin through surface intensities. Speaking to its incisive force artist Ernesto Pujol writes:

A tattoo is a revelation. A tattoo is what lies beneath the skin and has decided to surface. A tattoo is the image that was always under the skin, taking a while to form, like personality, like deep complex thought, and is finally public. It is a risk, an admission, a challenge; and, sometimes, it is a concession to the world. It marks a moment, it signals a personality, it enshrines a life-change, a loss, a dream, a need, a want, a desire, an achievement. It sets a boundary, it dissolves boundaries, it intimidates and invites, it promises and withholds. It is generous and selective. (Pujol 2012, 31)

Pujol imagines the work of a tattoo not as a compulsion toward pain or a search for pleasure amid pain, but rather as a body's own choreographic promise lifted from the interior surfaces to the exterior through the careful attention of the artist's needle. A tattoo revels in the transitive sense of communicability, of coming into appearance as Agamben describes it. The image that is produced is deeply ambivalent: "a boundary, [and that which] dissolves boundaries," it admits and desires conflating temporalities of past experience and future anticipation as skin entraps ink. Inscribed in Wade's flesh, the tattoo of St. Teresa and the additions that complement her as *Glory* evolves from 2003 onward suggest another series of surfaces upon which Guattari's "baroque proliferation" might appear.

Guattari's words are never far from Wade's process as he carries his (and Deleuze's) writings to the studio, particularly *A Thousand Plateaus: Capitalism and Schizophrenia* (Deleuze and Guattari [1980] 1987), as so many scores for a "poetry of disorder" (Wade 2010a). This text serves as a manual for choreographic labor as it deploys writing as a constantly moving terrain of encounters, inciting collisions and disruptions across literary, psychoanalytic, and visual art and music as so many "lines of flight" and "becoming[s]" and intensities (Deleuze and Guattari [1980] 1987, 89, 239). As they write, always as an accumulation, always in plural, they describe ecstasy as a sonic refrain: "Chaos is not without its own directional components, which are its own ecstasies" (313). Similar to the work of improvisation, a technique both Wade and Gutierrez[34] rely on in their rehearsal processes, the chaos they describe contains a structure even at its limits generating the tensions of ecstatic experience that is always already physical, sonic, linguistic, oral, and odorous, as examples. For Wade, improvisation is not a random series of actions, but rather is a structure determined initially by the particular associations of words that are destabilized, subjected to precarious failures and ambivalent gestural oscillations as shame becomes ecstasy becomes anxiety in the process of experiential relational movement. He often works with Authentic Movement[35] and Scores[36] in his rehearsal process to locate gestures internally as the dancers move under the influence of specific words—empathy, anger, repulsion, shame, ecstasy, intoxication, anxiety, attraction. Subjecting the resulting gestures to the derepresentational play of improvisation, the extreme states of shaking, convulsing, trembling, falling are continually refined to interrogate language. Wade describes working with Meier as a "magnifying glass to my own perceptions ... [such that the] contour of my body becomes like a landscape with the potential for many different states [that] flows between hysterical, disoriented, transgressive. . . . A single pose of an old man turns grotesque and hard and melts into a feminine ecstatic religious pose and back to some slippery drunken state" (Wade 2010a). Transposing the practice of Authentic Movement to the linguistic directives of her Scores techniques, Meier introduces words into the improvisation so that the dancers must shift from one state—"genders, ages, levels of sobriety, sanity, class"—to another,

---

34. While both Wade and Gutierrez work with improvisational practice, including Authentic Movement and the "Scores" of Yvonne Meier, as some examples, they use these practices to different ends. As Gutierrez readily admits, improvisational labor is not easy; "I improvise to terrify myself into action" (Gutierrez 2011c).

35. In the practice of Authentic Movement, one mover begins lying on the floor with her eyes closed and follows the inner sensations of her body, transforming these sensations into images or impulses for movements, sounds, or words. Another individual witnesses the process of moving and later performs these same movements for the original mover. Scores can be created from these relational improvisations as an extended rehearsal strategy or transposed into the performance.

36. Developed by choreographer and performer Yvonne Meier, "Scores" is a technique of "essentially words, containing images, that we will learn to possess our bodies from head to toe. 'Scores' can be physical, emotional, psychological or spiritual" (Meier 2012). Meier's work with improvisation is also complemented by Authentic Movement and Release Technique (2012). Both Wade and Gutierrez have worked with and performed with Meier.

conjuring what Wade describes as a "nauseous amalgam of emotional-physical-physical" behaviors.

In addition to his work with Meier, Wade also collaborates with choreographer Meg Stuart whose description of states as a rehearsal process and technique resonates with his own practice:[37]

States may manifest in just one body part or just in your voice—I see them as frequencies and temperatures rather than things that can be easily articulated with words. The emotional underpinnings of particular states can be accessed through memory or through your breathing cycle. . . . In states you work with oblique relations. The body is a field in which certain mental streams, emotions, energies and movements interact, betraying the fact that actions and states are separate. The internal friction and rubbing creates unexpected relations and by-products revealing and concealing, expressing how people tend to control their mind and reactions most of the time. In the case of complete harmony, nothing is being revealed. As an observer, sometimes you don't recognize a state so easily, only aspects of it, like agitation in the eyes. The whole eludes you, as parts of the picture are scratched out. This partial opacity provokes the imagination of both the performer and the spectator. (Stuart 2010, 20–21)

Stuart speaks to the horizontal flows of sensation, image, emotion, and language that Wade triggers in his improvisational practice aspiring not toward meaning and sense, but uncertainty, disjuncture, and agitation as means toward imagining other spaces, other temperatures, other frequencies. The multiplicity and simultaneity required of this process enacts an assemblage of disparate forms and references and textures that touch, accumulate, repel one another.

This play with sensations and language enacted in the rehearsal studio and on the stage challenges techniques of representation and signification, creating new choreographic possibilities or what Agamben might refer to as communicabilities for excessive, spasming subjectivities to move. Here Agamben's theory of communicability (that also draws on his writing of the face) as a force of exposure—of ideas, of community, of "revelation"—is explicitly tied to reimagining the work of gesture as a profoundly political act. When he writes: "Exposition is the

---

37. Wade has worked with Stuart in multiple workshop contexts and as collaborator on the *Politics of Ecstasy* festival in Berlin at the Hebbel Theater in 2009.

location of politics," the visual and the gestural become intertwined, proposing a theory of politics as an always shifting encounter between image and movement located close to the realm of the animal that does not need to recognize herself or become trapped in appearance, but is instead open to improvisation and exposition (Agamben [1996] 2000, 93). His animal attention is an explicitly political project that resists communication as a polemical rational practice of truth or falsity and instead argues for a creative power of the choreographic as a generator of mutant identities and political potentialities. Wade's improvisational work explores such an animal attention, particularly in altered states, charismatic rituals, and the physical transformations of affective emotional and psychological meaning. Improvisation is a means to generate other physicalities, other senses of language, other difficulties, other situations, and this research is then structured into the piece. While *Glory* shifts over the course of its run, it is a set choreographic work. Yet, in Wade's continued investigations, improvisation becomes more foregrounded in the performance as well, calling out and speaking back to the too-easy dismissal or pejorative associations that accompany improvisation (as technique and pedagogy); instead, Wade deploys its oblique forces to disseminate multiple identities and images simultaneously.

This aggregate process also speaks to the use of images in Wade's choreographic research that draws on images not as literal references but as so many possibilities, visions, memories. Two struck me as particularly vivid: "images of the Jones Town massacre bodies sprawled out like dominos falling in an elegant pattern . . . a picture of a Pentecostal revival in which the congregation was in prostration face down with only their hands reaching upwards" (Wade 2008). Images of ritual death and religious communion, these pictures reveal the limitations of the ecstatic as a group experience or perhaps serve as a reminder of its passage into horror or redemption. The specificity and violence of these images question how images are appropriated and dispersed within the choreographic field. If part of the work of a choreographic ecstatics implies an ethics of address, we must seriously consider how to engage with these representations and their translation and dispersion. Bataille comes to mind as he describes in uncomfortably intimate detail a photograph of a tortured Chinese man (an image he returns to many times in his mediation on ecstatic experience). Bataille includes no other identifying characteristics of date or location or name, but details his wounded flesh, the cutting of his knee, and then confesses his love of this man who "communicated his pain to me or perhaps the excessive nature of his pain" (Bataille [1943] 1988, 120). His account disturbs as it seems to fall too easily into a seduction with the image without acknowledging the accompanying horror. And yet, his narrative forces Bataille and the reader to confront the image directly to see it and to keep seeing it; to examine what Hollywood describes as the "speechless body" in its extreme laceration (Hollywood 2002, 83). For Bataille an ethics of address would require that we see the wound without having recourse to do anything about it in the moment except meditate on this horror and suffering.[38] This wounded flesh gives us what Georges Didi-Huberman names the "rend," a violent opening of the body through wounding, the vanishing point of the image that we do not want to address. And yet Didi-Huberman, perhaps like Bataille, requires that we return to this site in order to rethink what ethical address it feels like, looks like, demands.

Approaching Community

Ralph Lemon: "I am not interested in belief anymore." He pauses. "I am interested in body conundrum . . . possession . . . spectators . . . translation across experience. . . . How to think about what a body can't do? If the form or container creates something knowable then what can't be held or contained?"

Jeremy Wade: "Choreography is the space of 'something else'[39] . . . ecstasy, disorientation, not knowing . . . sinking into numbness . . . nightmares . . . untenable. . . .

---

38. Bataille's meditation on the photograph of the tortured man also perhaps answers to Virginia Woolf's question asked at a similar historical moment (1936–1937) of whether "when we look at the same photographs we feel the same things" (Woolf in Sontag 2003, 4). And then she writes: "This morning's collection contains the photograph of what might be a man's body, or a woman's; it is so mutilated that it might, on the other hand, be the body of a pig. But those certainly are dead children, and that undoubtedly is the section of a house. A bomb has torn open the side; there is still a bird-cage hanging in what was presumably the sitting room" (4).

The details of Woolf's list are striking; the paratactic stall between the woman and the pig, the bomb, and the bird-cage juxtaposing something human become animal, something horrible and something mundane almost quaint. The specificity of the recognizable objects draws us in and yet in these pairings representation fails, or rather it points outside of itself so that we cannot help but witness the horror and be conscious of our own complicity or lack of recognition that may have preceded these events.

It gets me closer to god. I don't know what god is . . . a threshold to facilitate an experience . . . to destroy the solid gesture . . . there is glitter everywhere . . . ecstatic clouds."—Excerpt from conversation with Jenn Joy, Ralph Lemon, and Jeremy Wade, 2011

Close your eyes: Imagine glitter everywhere and ecstatic clouds.

Thought together the work of Gutierrez and Wade gorgeously complicates what artist Emily Roysdon calls *ecstatic resistance*, as much a theory as a set of tactics "to re-articulate the imaginary. . . . It wants to talk about pleasure in the domain of resistance—sexualizing modern structures in order to centralize instability and plasticity in life, living, and the self. It is about waiting, and the temporality of change" (Roysdon 2009). Drawing together the work of artists including Sharon Hayes, My Barbarian, Ulrike Ottinger, A. L. Steiner, Roysdon creates a constellation of strategies that undermine the distance between political protest and art-making, instead imagining alterity as so many forms for radical communicability. This focus on pleasure in resistance is part of the work of the choreographic, yet I want to hold onto the more difficult even toxic qualities of Wade and Gutierrez (and of achugar, Dorvillier, and Kravas discussed in chapter 2) as imperative to an ecstatic understanding of the choreographic. Here the choreographic always exceeds dancing and yet is still exquisitely, nakedly dance—emotional physical erotic intellectual sonic sculptural—with economies of difference constantly passing into and across each other as so many spasms exposing a vulnerability that is not always graceful, comfortable, or legible.

Turning to the audience during his solo *HEAVENS WHAT HAVE I DONE* (2010),[40] Gutierrez confesses: "I did not become an artist so I could make sense" (figure 3.7) . Walking across the space he scatters various objects on the stage: suitcase, cords, books, his father's medication list, yoga mat, his "sexual recovery

---

39. The "something else" refers to a question I asked Ralph Lemon and Jeremy Wade about how they imagine the work of choreography as opposed to "choreography" as the stand-in term for the "something else" of visual or other arts practices. I stole and slightly shifted this phrase (from something missing to something else) that Ernst Bloch takes from Bertolt Brecht on the utopian function of art more generally (Bloch [1964] 1996).

40. *HEAVENS WHAT HAVE I DONE* (2010) is created and performed by Gutierrez; lights by Lenore Doxsee; set by Gutierrez and Jason Simms; costume by Machine Dazzle; music by Vivaldi and others.

3.7 Miguel Gutierrez, *HEAVENS WHAT HAVE I DONE*, 2010. Photograph by Ian Douglas.

plan," coins, a friend's eulogy, Richard Shusterman's *Body Consciousness: A Philosophy of Mindfulness and Somaesthetics*,[41] Plato's *Symposium*, Elizabeth Grosz's *Volatile Bodies: Toward a Corporeal Feminism* (1994), a VHS tape on UFOs given to him by friend and collaborator Michelle Boulé. Changing into absurdly regal rainbow shorts, ruffles, and Marie Antoinette wig, he continues his monologue

---

41. Critiquing the "silent, limping" portrayals of embodiment in philosophy evidenced in writings of Merleau-Ponty, Simone de Beauvoir, Ludwig Wittgenstein, William James, and John Dewey, Shusterman looks to Foucault's later writings to find within philosophy a notion of body and self that is not as ontologically fixed but is socially constructed and therefore open to reinvention and play (2008, 49, 35). He then defines his concept of somaesthetics "as the critical meliorative study of one's own experience and use of one's body as a locus of sensory-aesthetic appreciation (aesthesis) and creative self-fashioning. It is therefore also devoted to the knowledge, discourses, and disciplines that structure such somatic care or can improve it . . . [working with and toward] philosophy's central aims of knowledge, self-knowledge, right action, happiness, and justice and designates three levels of somaesthetics: analytic, pragmatic/performative, practical (19, 23–26).

detailing his teaching experiences at P.A.R.T.S., his take on Sarkozy's racist policies, critiques of his work as "too messy" by one unnamed European curator, all interrupted by exquisite operatic crescendos of voice and movement (Gutierrez 2011d). At one moment he pauses with a sigh of disbelief to exclaim: "if only I had known that the cornerstone of philosophy was a bunch of men sitting around talking about their boyfriends." As Foucault might agree, *ascesis* or "care of the self" as a choreographic practice must happen at "the intersection of political ambition and philosophical love," all boyfriends, partners, lovers, teachers invited ([1982] 1997b, 229). And this process whether sung, danced, written, or lived is always deeply, repeatedly citational.

Beyond his performance work, Gutierrez engages this ecstatic consciousness as a constant unfinished and deeply participatory improvisational process through his teaching practice and particularly in *DEEP AEROBICS* (figures 3.8–3.9).[42] Described as a "communal political conceptual imaginational workout," *DEEP ELECTRIC EMO PROTEST AEROBICS* joins queer campy spirituality with political action as we don glittery drag to practice aerobics as resistance (Gutierrez 2009a). Rainbow lights transform the dark studio floor as we arrive and dress up in sneakers, glitter, torn tank tops, and chic headbands for this sweat-soaked retro 1980s aerobic dance party. Repetitions of arm extensions—a posture of "NO," an assertive negation of ruling ideologues, then jazz hands with swinging hips to accentuate our "YES" to something new, shoulders shrug an ambivalent "maybe" as Gutierrez's "Obama wand" (remember how hopeful we felt in 2008?) casts a feel-good glow over these chaotic encounters. This is not Jane Fonda or Tracy Anderson's workout aiming to isolate physical perfection or beauty, but a polymorphous-perverse joining of physical exuberance, absurd creative happening, and political action under the sign of queer utopic belonging.

---

42. In another of his workshops, INEFFABLE INTANGIBLE SENSATIONAL, Gutierrez invites translations of movement into action through sensorially motivated improvisation—hearing, seeing, touching, smelling, tasting, kineasthetic, balance, proprioceptive ("noticing the relative geography of your body in relation to the space"), space, time, energetics, composition, emotion, imagination, play (Gutierrez 2011b). Moving beyond the usual five, his conception of sensation encompasses a relational interaction with the other participants, the surrounding space (a decaying ballroom in the Alexandria Hotel in downtown LA), and our own imaginations and projections to cultivate movement as a "framework for complicated, nuanced, embodied meaning" (Gutierrez 2012a). These expanded senses act as filters for experience, interrupting habitual patterns and associations of movement and of language, and work toward an understanding of choreographic

3.8–3.9 Miguel Gutierrez, *DEEP AEROBICS*, 2011.
Photographs by Ian Douglas.

consciousness where dance and language, moving and speaking are not polemical discourses or metaphoric foils one for the other, but contingent categories that must be unworked and rearranged.

An intensely participatory event, *DEEP AEROBICS* enables alternate forms of communication and collaboration, exposing again Agamben's "communicabilities" through a mutant choreography of identities, political potentialities, and ecstatic becomings ([1996] 2000, 93). The workout exploits the political force of performance, creating for an hour or so a different world of imagination and abandon. Not outside the strictures and prejudices of social life, *DEEP AEROBICS* playfully breaks open a space of improvisation. As José Muñoz and Celeste Fraser Delgado write: "Improvisation links cultural memory in the here and now, where the meaning of dance is continually renewed to the (poly)rhythms of history in force in the present" (Muñoz and Fraser Delgado in Goldman 2010, 37). For Gutierrez, history is always explicitly a force to be choreographically reconciled in the present. As he reminds me: "Choreography is not only a language (at least, not a linear meaning making representational code), but rather a perceptual mode of value that gets placed in a space" and always in relation to contemporary dramas, personal and otherwise (Gutierrez 2011c).

Described as an "action" of contemplation, a durational process of attention and even a deep "meditation," his durational solo *freedom of information* calls attention to the difficult realities of reconciling history in the present, particularly in relation to freedom (Gutierrez 2009c) (figures 3.10–3.11). This project was originally performed for the last twenty-four hours of 2001 in his home studio in Brooklyn and then again for the last twenty-four hours of 2008 in a studio in the Barn, in the Greenpoint neighborhood of Brooklyn, along with thirty other artists across the United States.[43] Gutierrez's *freedom of information* began as a response to his "frustration" regarding the U.S. invasion of Afghanistan and as a way to "create solidarity with the people who were displaced by armed conflict, who do not have the basic right of rest . . . who instead have to remain ever-vigilant for violence . . . [I also wanted to] enforce both the disorientation that constant movement creates as well as the self-examination that happens when those basic senses are taken away" (Gutierrez 2009b). Countering the idea of movement as a "privilege," the piece forced a disturbing vision of freedom's precarious reality. The empathetic work of the piece called renewed attention to the limits of political, social, personal, and cultural freedom as we witnessed the artist—blindfolded and wearing ear plugs—

---

43. The piece was also performed as part of the *Politics of Ecstasy* festival at the Hebbel Theater in Berlin in January 2009 and so scenes from this piece will also be incorporated to give a sense of the gesture and movement quality, even though I focus on the New York performance.

choosing to engage in this difficult durational meditation. My own witnessing became more complicated as critical distance no longer seemed to hold and a more affective, personal (even diaristic) language and writing took over out of concern and interest.

When I entered the Barn at 10:00 a.m. on January 1, 2009, you had been moving for ten hours. The space is warm and quiet against the flurries of snow outside. An attendant lets me in and returns to her vigil by the video camera, alternately filling water bottles and removing bottles of urine. You walk backward toward the wall, passing a sleeping body on the floor. Your movement stutters, jumps, as if you are startled by something and then lurch and moan. Lying on the ground, your body slowly opens and closes as you drag your knees into your torso, sliding into and out of fetal position. The wood floor acts as a support, an escape from verticality. Rising you begin to walk around the room. Yet your walking feels haunted as if you have taken these steps already hundreds and hundreds of times. A red line smudged across the wall surrounded by scattered markings at hip level from your red sweat pants attests to the intense repetitions and returns of movements. A denser trace of red appears near the corner as if you have leaned against this particular part of the wall and then slid down, rose, and slid down, again and again. Even though movement remains imperative it is constantly plagued by the impossibility of continuing; the body's exquisite fatigue forces a slower, more careful procedure interrupted by spasms of manic energy. Time dilates and fatigue registers as specific physical history, a catalog of gestures always under the influence of the space itself. Both contained and supported by the space you stagger, wander, fall into virtuosic sequence or stand quietly standing by the window. One of the sleeping figures along the periphery snores. He or she or they remain/s anonymous, wrapped in a black sweatshirt and jacket with two cracked silver boots. You walk directly to where I am sitting and proximity intensifies; I draw closer to wall while desiring to touch, to let you know that someone is watching, but remain fearful of interrupting.

The blindfold appears likes a bandage over your eyes. A violent erasure of sight, it speaks to the intimate relationship between violence and witnessing—one that asks that witnesses not sit silently or with eyes closed, but that we become involved, affected, that we see. This blindfold across your eyes, a strip of fabric wrapped over a sleeping mask, reminds me of the paintings of Marlene Dumas, particularly *The Blindfolded Man* (2007) hanging across town in the Museum of

3.10-3.11 Miguel Gutierrez, *freedom of information*, 2008. Photographs by Ian Douglas.

Modern Art as I sit in this studio.[44] *The Blindfolded Man* is the color of bruises: purple smeared with blue laced with hints of black and brown; an eerie shading of cyan edges across his blurred smashed black nose and around the brilliant white gash of his blindfold. It is this white cut, opening to the gesso underneath, that defines the face and brings it into focus. Without the blindfold the face would be absorbed into the background, appearing only as an abstract effect of medium or dense pooling of marks; he would disappear. The face only comes to be seen through the closing off of its possibility of sight marking the difficult ambivalence resonating across Dumas's paintings. Sight, our sight and his, the painting suggests, is predicated on blindness. I come to see only through the other's blinding and write, or paint or dance, our history as a response to this condition. As Levinas reminds me: history itself is a "blinding toward the other" (Levinas in Derrida [1967] 1978, 94). Through Dumas's visceral disfiguration of sight and face—both revealed and concealed—Dumas forces us to witness again, and again, the anonymous disorientation of vision as it intertwines with subjectivity and history.

Not only a negation of vision, the blindfold destabilizes the body's relationship to balance and ground that if transposed from witness to painting, or even more explicitly from witness to performer and back, creates an empathetic pressure on the viewer. It causes me to question my own relationship to seeing, challenging me to inquire into my own modes of blindness and how this blindness becomes the condition for freedom or its limitation.

In your description of the action you write: "*freedom of information* is a practice of consciousness, an exercise in paying attention and engaging in the unknown, an opportunity to propose an alternative contemplation of the word 'freedom', and an attempt to connect empathetically with a host of real and imagined bodies" (Gutierrez 2009b). Yet, freedom is a suspect concept. If it alludes in one moment to the legislative act of July 4, 1964, that "allows for the full or partial disclosure of previously unreleased information and documents controlled by the United States government" (Gutierrez 2009b), it also speaks to the justification and imperative of empire and invasion, it also speaks to the rights and privileges of certain subjects in certain places in certain moments. Freedom is always already a

---

44. Marlene Dumas's exhibition, *Measuring Your Own Grave*, curated by Cornelia Butler, opened at the Museum of Contemporary Art, Los Angeles, June 22–September 22, 2008; traveled to the Museum of Modern Art, New York City, December 14, 2008–February 16, 2009; and to the Menil Collection, Houston, Texas, March 26–June 21, 2009. I refer here to the New York iteration.

provisional even paradoxical word that requires a more nuanced attention and negotiation of its terms and alliances as Foucault warns us in "What Is Enlightenment?":

If we are not to settle for the affirmation or the empty dream of freedom, it seems to me that this historico-critical attitude must also be an experimental one. I mean that this work done at the limits of ourselves must, on the one hand, open up a realm of historical inquiry and, on the other, put itself to the rest of reality, of contemporary reality, both to grasp the points where change is possible and desirable, and to determine the precise form this change should take. (Foucault [1984] 1997, 316)

Extending Foucault's conception of practices of freedom to the work of improvised dance, Danielle Goldman argues that improvised dance (like freedom) is not simply an open unrestrained process or concept, but is defined by constraint, a series of "shifting tight places, whether created by power relations, social norms, aesthetic traditions or physical technique" (Goldman 2010, 146). Witnessed in Gutierrez's durational improvisation, these practices of freedom appear explicitly constrained and restrained by blindness, by fatigue, by temperature, by hunger, by tedium, by isolation.

Is this what makes *freedom of information* difficult to watch? As I witness, a not-so-subtle nausea grows at my own complicity and blindness. Alongside this feeling, an affective charge circulates in the space, activating the utopic potentiality, not in the content of your stuttering, stumbling movements, but as a means to some other sense of labor, of inhabitation, of witness, of recognition, and of testimony. Importantly, this labor extends out beyond the walls of this studio to other studios and other dancers, literally performing difficult attentive meditations or simultaneous rehearsals for diverse and differentiated techniques of the self and practices of freedom.

Beating your fists together, you curl and crouch and moan. Slowly rocking on the floor, the movement crescendos to a churning propulsion of the body, an attempt to create momentum or heat or energy as the body opens and closes. You cry out, as if having a bad dream, and then your body is tossed by waves of intensity, as you yell. Standing in front of me, facing away, you shake and tremble, and retreat to the stained red corner with your arms behind you. Another witness enters and my vigil passes to your next silent partner. That night I watch you move online. Now you are dancing in the center of the room with open arms sweeping up and falling, no longer tentative. The studio is crowded with witnesses. The sound doesn't translate, so my soundtrack is the screaming from the bar outside my window. Yet in my mind you move—fierce and brave—no longer afraid of the walls; sitting down in lotus position you lie back.

Miguel, your work negotiates an intimate relationship between history and the present; it is critical without being hopeless. It gestures toward potentialities for a differentiated community, while resisting any singular or homogenous notion of communal belonging.[45] Here choreographic labor interrupts dominant paradigms with somatic intensity, feeling, pleasure, desire, sentimentality, stillness, smell, water, sweat, piss, moaning, writhing, exuberance. This is an ecstatic choreographic labor that refuses the failed legacies of community and of freedom in exchange for something other, an exquisitely visceral, personal, social, and communicative act. These projects are also explicitly queer in their stance and affective opening toward the other. To evoke Muñoz again: "Queerness's time is the time of ecstasy. Ecstasy is queerness's way" (Muñoz 2009, 187). To move into this ecstatic field is not to focus on our singular sensations; it is a movement toward and with one another. Speaking, dancing, writing, making, thinking, imagining—these are so many provocative strategies for a critical practice aligning multiple often illegible histories under a cascade of glitter and ecstatic clouds.

---

45. Miranda Joseph provocatively explicates the problems with community as an idealized or natural utopia in *Against the Romance of Community* (M. Joseph 2002).

4 **Outer Spaces** To Write, to Dance

This is not a lament, it's the cry of a bird of prey.

An iridescent and restless bird. The kiss upon the dead face.

I write as if to save somebody's life. Probably my own. Life is a kind of madness that death makes. Long live the dead because we live in them.

Suddenly things no longer need to make sense. I'm satisfied with being. Are you? Certainly you are. The meaninglessness of things makes me smile complacently. Everything surely must go on being what it is.—Clarice Lispector, *A Breath of Life*

And now we will dance—beyond the landscapes of the precarious, through echoing laughter and shattering tears into strange labyrinthine cosmologies always imagined and always real. Dancing across these thresholds into outer spaces and other worlds, we invent new choreographies as ciphers and scores, a becoming choreographic of shimmering violence and desire.[1] It is time to get lost, to walk, to laugh, to write, to dance as tears move slowly behind my eyes.

Did Carl Jung share such prismatic vision? His rivers (or shape-shifting snakes) serpentine through the many pages of *Liber Novus* (*Red Book*, 1914–1930) revealing an uncanny alchemy more fluid and curious than the frozen (even

---

1. There is a place where the fence breaks and jagged waves rise over dark rocks. Toxic wake collapses against skeletal rebar, pilings, traces of old industry and new, condoms, empty bottles, a projective surface for future encounters into which children now throw stones. From here I see shadows gathering across the East River refracting empty dreams where the new tower rises. I return to this shimmering liquid landscape to remember how to get lost; search this moving horizon to see if something of the choreographic still holds. In my often-consulted copy of Joan Didion's essay "Why I Write," the word "shimmer" is covered with my now illegible notes. For Didion images that "shimmer" appear as so many pixels for an inchoate narrative that she transforms into something else within the arc of the writing. Some of her examples ring nostalgic as well: the smell of butter in the train car between Berkeley and Sacramento, the bevatron in the Oakland hills, oil refineries surrounding Carquinez Straits, flickering conversational fragments she overhears in the casinos, bars, restaurants, streets of New York, Berkeley, Los Angeles, Las Vegas, East Coast meets West in the mind of a young writer (Didion 1976).

damming) universality of his later writings.[2] These early drawings and notes now appear as an opening narrative for the exhibition *il Palazzo Enciclopedico* (The Encyclopedic Palace) along another river in Venice.[3] The book rests in the center of a vast room encircled by reproductions of other pages: crystalline explosions, snakes, tree roots, monsters, many-legged dragons decapitated by errant knights, circles, mandalas, obsessively intricate faces, shifting patterns, aspirational hallucinations or so many perceptual dérives.

As hieroglyphic entrée the drawings evoke the myriad cosmologies resonating through the Arsenale and Central Pavilion of the Giardini: amorphous lumps roughly molded out of foam, sand, cement suspended from twisting planetary wires or glazed in ceramic growing out of moldy furniture; a slight odor preceding a foundation of bricks cast from the refuse of a local woman's prison; dioramas populated with childhood memories or proliferations of invented creatures; gorgeously drawn maps of spiritual worlds, some intricate mandalas or architectural odysseys in miniature, others pale spacious abstractions, sexual

---

2. "'You cannot step into the same river twice'—a heartening anthem, without a doubt" Maggie Nelson reminds me quoting Heraclitus in *Bluets* (2009, 80). Nelson cites a perfect antidote to Jung's later archetypal imperative. My students often ask why I don't teach Jung. I want to tell them that archetypes are like an empty marriage to a singular crushing idea that never delivers. I prefer Freud and his endless possibilities of reparative invention.

3. *il Palazzo Enciclopedico* (The Encyclopedic Palace) opened as part of the 55th International Art Exhibition of La Biennale di Venezia, June 1 to November 24, 2013. Curated by Massimiliano Gioni, the exhibition takes its title from a model of the Encyclopedic Palace—a museum to house all of the knowledge of the world—designed (and patented) by Marino Auriti in 1955. The exhibition mixes contemporary and historical art and talismanic, ritualistic, and anthropological objects to ask how knowledge might be produced and to what end. And is it mere coincidence or Gioni's at-times-prophetic curatorial vision for me to read an epigraph from Seamus Heaney in Gioni's exhibition catalog on the day of Heaney's death: "Who will say 'corpse' to his vivid cast? Who will say 'body' to his opaque repose?" (Heaney in Gioni 2013, 25). It is not merely coincidence, but a beautiful synchronicity. Against the pointed critique of the exhibition, particularly Benjamin Buchloh's chastising of its either naiveté or pretension, its embrace of a return to the myth of strange visions against art, I remain curious regarding Gioni's provocation that seems less about artist as mythic vessel and more about unmeasurable idiosyncrasy, about off kilter, marginal, failed cosmologies (see Buchloh 2013). Particularly staged within the grandeur of the biennale that at times feels like another more elegant version of an art fair, *il Palazzo Enciclopedico* seems even more potently to side with the messy and extreme in its many forms.

fantasies, or manic cerebral video storms.[4] Curator Massimiliano Gioni describes it as "a show about seeing with your eyes shut"—so many ways of coming to knowledge and the failure of all these omniscient aspirations crashing somewhere between joy and despair (this last thought he culls from theorist Christian Metz) (2013, 24).[5] Room after room of obsessive collections, figures distended, undone, reimagined, futile attempts to understand something of our desire and relationship to space, to history, to ourselves: bestial landscapes cry luminous starry tears while virulent tentacled creatures writhe in their undersea volcanic terrains; chimerical equations in chalk become a stage for two dancers curling together on the floor, she sings a moaning elegy in his ear that he translates into a quiet gestural dance and then they exchange roles, again and again; scattered architectural fragments from a Catholic Church in Vietnam; molding coffee, stained cardboard, glue, photographs of animals, collaged with trinkets and plastic lids shadow a collection of rare stones—variscite, agate, amethyst, crystal.[6] These many juxtapositions pose an intense proximity among quotidian materiality, ecstatics, cosmology, theosophy, and some perhaps take hesitant steps toward an aesthetic theology. Even austere forged steel whispers a mystical homage (if we are to take Richard Serra at his word) that grounds a room filled with vast oceanscapes rising to a dark horizon.[7] Or, more metaphysically, James Lee Byars's gilded marble column wrapping permanence in gorgeous flaking elegance returns me to the precarious urgency of all these

---

4. The works referred to are by these artists in this order: Phyllis Barlow, Jessica Jackson Hutchins; Rosella Biscotti; Andra Ursuta and Levi Fischer Ames; Augustin Lesage, Lin Xue, Guo Fengyi, Hilma af Klint, Hans Belmer, and Stan VanDerBeek.

5. I include the quote in its entirety as its elliptical unfolding enacts this process of attention that Gioni seeks in this constellation of works and ideas (not that these are ever exclusive): "a shared state of amorous passion . . . temporary breaking of a very normal solitude . . . the particular joy which lies in receiving from outside images which are usually internal, images which are familiar or not too dissimilar, and seeing them set down across a physical space, and thus discovering in them something almost attainable which was quite unexpected, and feeling for a moment that they are not perhaps inseparable from the mood which most often trails after them, that sense of the impossible, so common and accepted, which is for all that a mild form of despair" (Metz in Gioni 2013, 25).

6. The works alluded to here are by the following artists in this order: Jakob Julian Ziółkowski and Eugene Von Bruenchenhein; Rudolph Steiner and Tino Sehgal; Dahn Vo; Uri Aran and Roger Caillois.

7. Serra titles this work *Pasolini*; the landscapes are by Thierry De Cordier.

sensuous provocations.[8] It is as if the spectral solidifies in sculpture, so that even the spare geometries speak as golems, whispering against history and restraint.[9] Perhaps like the pale shrouded figures who populate Andra Ursuta's miniature rooms of stained wallpaper, leaning crutches, scythe, shovel, meat grinder, tiny paintings or narrow bed all encased in glass, these creatures conjure a psychic or emotional residue of place and of object that so often burdens memory (figure 4.1). In a sense Ursuta's works are aggressive reminders of what we cannot (or do not want) to see, so much affective substance leaking into our personal and collective memory.

Gioni's aspiration that we see with our eyes closed is like the Encyclopedic Palace itself a paradoxical ruse or beautiful impossibility that asks that I submit to a different mode of attention more internal and fantastical, yet also active. His choreographic approach invites me to witness the works again differently as after-images, to access the invisible behind or even in front of thought. In this he follows Georges Didi-Huberman's demand that we "require *vision* to assassinate *perception*" to rail against the imperative formalities of representation and imagine form itself as a dialectic of "operative violence" (Didi-Huberman 2007, 17, 1). Didi-Huberman turns to the writings of Carl Einstein to trace a theory of picture as prophetic rupture that breaks with the messianic dialectic of Walter Benjamin to instill exigency of thought and act. Riffing (I imagine) on Antonin Artaud, Didi-Huberman asserts that we "have done with the judgement of taste" and arrived at

---

8. Byars's golden work, *The Figure of the Interrogative Philosophy* (1987–1995), correlates in my mind with the cryptic bronze rods of Walter de Maria's *Apollo's Ecstasy* (1990) that fill the final room though Byars strikes a more seductively Dionysian quality.

9. Across the canal the restaging of Harold Szeemann's exhibition *When Attitudes Become Form* (1969), an early portrait of the more mystical variants underlying the minimalist project (including Serra), was restaged at the Fondazione Prada in conjunction with the Biennial in 2013. Curated by Germano Celant and retitled *When Attitudes Become Form Bern 1969/Venice 2013*, the exhibition attempted a literal restaging of the 1969 version, including constructing similar rooms within the space. A moving tribute, particularly in catalog form, the works installed felt constricted to a formal dogma losing much of their 1969 attitude—but perhaps that is merely my own projected nostalgia. Yet the absent works, marked out in masking tape on the floors and walls and often paired with a photograph of the original exhibition, offered a more haunted quality that seemed to foreground the precarious materiality and tone of the pieces in the initial construction.

4.1 Andra Ursuta, *T, Vladimirescu Nr. 5, Pantry*, 2013. Wood, metal, glass, fabric, paint, 18.5 × 14.5 × 22.5 inches. Photograph courtesy of the artist and Ramiken Crucible.

"*a crystal of crisis*" (2007, 7; italics in original).[10] Such a crisis is not only aesthetic, but also explicitly epistemological and this is why Einstein (and Didi-Huberman) have finished with taste, form (in the formalist sense), iconography, immobility. Instead they call for movement—shattering oscillating instability as form becomes force. In Einstein, Didi-Huberman finds another muse, a soulful agitator against art history as passive chronicler of forms. "Seeing means setting *still-invisible reality* in motion. . . . We underline the value of that which is not yet visible, of that which is not yet know" (Einstein in Didi-Huberman 2007, 17; italics in original).[11] This movement will be violent: a dialectic of deconstruction that seeks a "potential future" in image (18). Unlike iconographic imagery Didi-Huberman explains this "image scrambles the messages, delivers symptoms, delivers us over to the still-elusive. Because it is dialectical and inventive; because it *opens time*" (18; italics in original). Gioni is also seduced by this temporal matrix that finds in art an overdetermined force of intuitive knowledge and/as action, a decomposing of reality into something more prophetic. Writing between the two world wars, Einstein and Benjamin demand of art something more than aesthetic disinterest: they want to reconcile, even avenge. As Einstein writes in a letter to his friend, Daniel-Henry Kahnweiler, in 1923: "I cannot give myself the luxury of thinking about such [exclusively theoretical] things, in the middle of all this continuously unfolding daily catastrophe" (Einstein in Didi-Huberman 2007, 19). And now, Gioni insists, *and now* what will we give ourselves the luxury of thinking about in the middle of all this continuously unfolding daily catastrophe?[12]

---

10. Antonin Artaud's *To Have Done with the Judgment of God* was a radio play of glossolalia, a screed against capitalism, America, and all things normative, written in 1947 after he was released from various asylums. Terrifying in its inchoate sonority, the piece was censored during its first release on French Radio.

11. In this essay Didi-Huberman draws much of his close reading from Einstein's treatises on cubism, specifically his writing from the journal *Documents* (that he worked on with Georges Bataille and Michel Leiris) and *George Braque* (1934), which finds in cubism a revelation of "anxiety—in the face of the crumbling of time and the subjective dissemination of space (Didi-Huberman 2007, 5–6).

12. Of course, historical events are always singular in their horror even as they are incessant. When I was in Venice, June 9–12, 2013, I watched an unfolding litany of tragedies on CNN every morning as I ran on the treadmill—the death of a young boy in Syria (this was only the beginning), flooding rivers in Germany and Austria, always bombings in Bagdad, and on and on and on.

Love and Deluge

Heaven and outer space outer space and heaven . . . back to matters of formlessness and form. Not as mere form but something messy with its own activating dynamics and generosity. It is important to me that it be generous and weightless, a levitating of theater, a dance, a film, a proposition transporting into something beyond its awkward immediacy making it earthbound.—Ralph Lemon, *How Can You Stay in the House All Day and Not Go Anywhere?*[13]

An old black man dressed in a fraying silver space suit climbs into his ship welded from scrap metal, a satellite dish, and with a pink carpet floor over wheeled castors. He lies down attempting to sleep, tossing and turning in irritated insomnia. Waking, he pulls on his helmet takes the wheel as the video cuts to blue sky sliced by white exhaust fume then black cosmic particles flicker blackout or turn into stars. Lift off. Sitting on stage across from the video screen, Ralph Lemon explains that this man, 102-year-old Walter Carter from Yazoo City, Mississippi, is his teacher and that Walter likes to hear about god so today Lemon will read aloud from Walter Benjamin's *Angelus Novus*. Like Lemon, I, too, remain entranced by Walter Benjamin and his prophetic angel even while suspicious of belief, of god (figures 4.2–4.5).

Lemon reads slowly as the video shifts from Carter in his space suit sitting in a plowed field to Okwui Okpokwasili in a rabbit costume to a close-up of Lemon wearing the same costume. The hare, he reads, is "a threat to Walter [Carter's] legitimacy, because truth cannot really be mentioned. The hare creates exquisite lies in order to share something mentionable to an unsuspecting world" (Lemon 2010). On screen Lemon (as hare) and Carter wrestle interrupted by black-and-white

---

13. Ralph Lemon's *How Can You Stay in the House All Day and Not Go Anywhere?* opened at Brooklyn Academy of Music (BAM), October 13–16, 2010, performed by Lemon with Djedje Djedje Gervais, Darrell Jones, Gesel Mason, Okwui Okpokwasili, David Thomson, and Omagbitse Omagbemi; videography for film talk by Mark Robinson, Luke Schantz, Louis Sparre, and Chelsea Lemon Fetzer; *Meditation* film/installation by Jim Findlay; dramaturgy by Katherine Profeta; sound consulting by Lucas Indelicato; lighting design by Roderick Murray. The piece begins with Lemon sitting on stage reading as video is screened across the stage from him. The video includes fragments from his last work, *Come Home Charley Patton* (2004), also performed at BAM. Both pieces have toured, yet I reference the versions I witnessed in their BAM incarnations.

4.2–4.5 Ralph Lemon, *How Can You Stay in the House All Day and Not Go Anywhere?*, 2010.
Photographs by Dan Merlo.

documentary footage of a white cop shoving his gun at a young black man, a black woman pushed into the gutter by a group of police, artist Bruce Nauman crawling on the floor of his studio, and then Lemon on the floor of another studio pushing a chair with his leg.[14] And then Lemon (in the video), dances while assaulted by a fire hose held by two of his dancers. He dances in the rising water, slides, falls, stands, staggers, dances, falls until the fierce deluge stops. Or does it? Ever? The dancers in the video spin, fall, rise, stumble, kick at the air, caught as if by some invisible force they crash and stand again, rage, beauty, fierce, flailing, for a long time. Against the frenetic dance, Lemon reads slowly: "something can happen beyond the seeing, a revelation. Love without rage is said to be powerless" (2010).

And then we move into the intoxicating ineffable of the choreographic as Lemon tells us about this new dance we are now witnessing, how the performers went into the studio and got drunk and stoned and danced and then learned it sober until it was perfect and then got drunk and stoned again and turned it inside out and again and again. In turn he speaks of his partner, Asako, her sickness, how they watched films together—Yasujiro Ozu, Bob Dylan concert films, Andrei Tarkovsky— and he would hold her hand and whisper details as she slept. After she dies he returns to Yazoo City and remakes Tarkovsky's *Solaris* (1972) casting Walter Carter and his wife Edna Carter as Kris Kelvin and his ghost wife Hari, in contrast to Tarkovsky's "sci-fi love rage" this will be a film of their "elegant ordinary love" (Lemon 2010). Lemon reads slowly as excerpts from Tarkovsky's *Solaris* intertwine with scenes of Walter lying on his plastic-covered bed fully dressed in cowboy boots with his rifle, the camera shifts and we see Edna sitting in a chair holding a rear view mirror watching him. They lie with heads touching on a plastic-covered couch. She moves to the floor. She disappears. "Poof," Lemon pauses, "What the fuck?" Again the video shifts to Lemon and Okpokwasili dancing, embracing, crashing into each other and against the floor, violently holding and held, consuming air and distance and tragedy, channeling the many avatars: Walter and Edna, Kris Kelvin and Hari, Lemon and Asako as the instrumental opening of The Cure's "This Is a Lie" laments love's failed promises: "A love before it was this love and now it's another love with no form and universal form, universal doubt. Existence. And love and love and love and love . . ." And from the within this devastating intimate agony

---

14. The excerpt of Nauman comes from his studio film *Wall Floor Positions* (1968). In his book *Come home Charley Patton* (2013), Lemon details his correspondence with Nauman around an earlier reinvention of Nauman's work in the context of his own.

the dancing erupts, now live, on stage as the dancers thrash—exquisitely choreographed weight spinning, disorientating, aerial elasticity against gravity, he screams into his sweatshirt, she slaps against the floor, dense virtuosity, later the dancing will stop and we will hear only Okpokwasili's cries, later still the stage will go black and white silhouettes of animals will gather, and finally Lemon and Okpokwasili will dance together again and Lemon wearing only one yellow sock (Lemon 2010).

Balancing on the edge of formlessness as if holding its breath, *How Can You Stay in the House All Day and Not Go Anywhere?* approaches an ethics of the choreographic as it negotiates violence in proximity to love and intimacy. Regarding his work with dramatist Antoine Vitez, Alain Badiou speaks of a similar scene: "I think that love is a thought and that the relationship between that thought and the body is quite unique, and always marked . . . by an irrepressible violence. We experience that violence in life. It is absolutely true that love can bend our bodies and prompt the sharpest torment" (Badiou [2009] 2012, 87). In his wandering conversation with interlocutor Nicolas Truong, Badiou begins with an image of love as complement to war, equating the "zero dead war" with the "zero risk love," arguing instead for love as event, as "disjunctive" space time against the ordinary (7, 28). Thought through Badiou's concept of event, love will not collapse into romantic fallacy but enact a "two scene" that looks out into the world (29). Lemon's layering of duets, of two scenes, of partnerships spectral and otherwise, exposes the generative power of these intensities without, I hope, falling into the paralysis of depression, narcissism, or fear. Lemon also asks that we think of these intimacies as deeply historical cultural scenes; let us not forget the duet between the cop and young man as one example of something unlike love and very close to violence.

Love and Ghosts

Open your eyes, open your eyes, follow the light, squeeze my hand
Open your eyes, open your eyes, follow the light, squeeze my hand
. . .
Are you with us? Are you here with us?
Are you with us? Are you here with us?
. . .

We can help you, we can help you

We can help you, we can help you

. . .

Open . . . squeeze my hand

Boots, are you here?—Miguel Gutierrez and the Powerful People,

And lose the name of action[15]

Passing into other worlds requires our submission to a different economy of
attention, even grace. We must be schooled by something outside our own habitual
thought patterns, grasp the sweating hands of strangers, feel the echoing vertigo.
"Are you nervous?" Ishmael Houston-Jones asks, "Don't be nervous. You are safe . . ."
and so continues *And lose the name of action* by Miguel Gutierrez and the Powerful
People (2012) (figures 4.6–4.8). We surround the stage on three sides underneath a
suspended parachute as Houston-Jones sits at the edge, directing our attention to
the empty center, instructing us to breathe, to connect energetically as the dancers
sitting with the audience sing an eerie antiphonal harmony morphing into a
complicated feedback loop. "Open your eyes, open your eyes, follow the light,
squeeze my hand. Open your eyes, open your eyes, follow the light, squeeze my
hand . . ." A shattering sound like crystal cymbals silences the repetitions and the
lights turn deep blue. It is the blue of somewhere else, a colored intensity of light as
space—"something of an ecstatic accident produced by void and fire" as Maggie
Nelson describes the saturation of blue produced by "the darkness of empty space
behind it" (Nelson 2009, 62). Her evocation of blue is one of many attempts to
follow the color's melancholic passion, to transcribe something of its pressure on
language and of its dispersive undoing of knowledge. Nelson intimates that she has
fallen under its spell, one that she follows and fights, a similar experience to being
with *And lose the name of action* as it unfolds in flashes of nineteenth-century
spiritualism tinged with the paranormal tempered with neurological hypotheses all

---

15. *And lose the name of action* premiered in New York, December 4–8, 2012, at Brooklyn Academy
of Music, Next Wave Festival. Created by Miguel Gutierrez in collaboration with the performers;
performed by Michelle Boulé, Hilary Clark, Luke George, Miguel Gutierrez, K. J. Holmes, and
Ishmael Houston-Jones; understudy James McGinn; lights by Lenore Doxsee; sound design by
Neal Medlyn; songs by Miguel Gutierrez; multi-channel film installation and writing by Boru
O'Brien O'Connell; costume design by David Tabbert; costume assistance by Matt Kessler;
production manager Natalie Robin; sound and video supervisor Jimin Brelsford; management
by Ben Pryor/tbspMGMT and Julie Alexander.

tested against daily experiences of mortality and of love. We are not allowed to linger too long in any of these particulars of reference or blueness as the light shifts into reds, oranges, yellows, even at times a nauseating pale green, then bright white, then blue and again. Color and sonority unite to undo any easy understanding of dance, filtering these many perceptual experiments through intimate narrative fragments and shape-shifting characters.

Under white light the dancers dance, debate, throw chairs as if there is something brilliantly rational about their project even amid the illuminated chaos. This saturation of white is mirrored in the video that runs through most of the piece of a pretentious thinker thinking and pacing an empty white space. This thinker evokes the titular character in Jorgen Leth's *The Perfect Human* who smokes, pauses, eats, sleeps, makes love, cuts his nails all with minimal affect as a disembodied voice narrates his movements, at times interjecting questions about happiness, the taste of boiled salmon and potatoes, touch, joy, reminding us to look, look, look at this perfect human. And like the ghost-wife Hari of *Solaris*, the beautiful raven-haired woman in silver boots or naked in bed with him is always silent, watching this perfect human live his perfect life in an endless white room. On stage, as color and sound erupt in the manic energy of the dancers, I sense a more perfect conception of humanity, one that is excessive, emotional, fallible, deeply affected by happiness, pleasure, loss, death, confusion, isolation, pain. Then against the sterilizing whiteness, the darkened stage feels deeply visceral, haunted. We see the dancers only in flashes, hear them gasp or cry as so many moving shadows or ghosts. As she rushes in the darkness Hilary Clark screams at Gutierrez something about "a space without function" and he yells in response yet I cannot understand.

We return to blue—the deeper purple of quiet contemplation as Luke George and K. J. Holmes conspire around a glowing white box, testing out movement phrases, gestures, relationships; lighter turquoise cyan as Michelle Boulé, diaphanous in black whirls an exquisite dervish crescendo until she falls prostrate, rises again interrupted by Clark and Gutierrez and their tentative courtship. They speak although we cannot hear and dance separately in parallel; her movements exude a generous empathy, his are fierce, restrained. She will catch him and release; leaning toward and into each other they stumble, stagger, desperately cling to each other. While these dances outline something of the ineffable, again, so many after-images of what we cannot quite see, they are also deeply erotic séances of sensuous awkward beauty. Here traces of spiritualist hypnotics resonate against the gravitas of improvisation as so many possibilities for intimacies sensed and performed.

Blue, as temperature and atmosphere, amplifies the dramaturgical and relational intensities of the work—quiet cool breathless. I sense it appears in moments of transition, as a way of distancing or distinguishing sensations one from another. Blue confuses categorically; or at least this is the way I remember Ralph Ellison's use of blue: blue-gray smoke, blue gingham dresses, blue fire to signal a more difficult ambivalence than black or white in *The Invisible Man* (1947). Blue

4.6–4.7 Miguel Gutierrez and the Powerful People, *And lose the name of action*, 2012. Photographs by Ian Douglas.

4.8 Miguel Gutierrez and the Powerful People, *And lose the name of action*, 2012. Photograph by Boru O'Brien O'Connell.

passes not only through the eyes but also the ears and conscience; it is sonority and visuality and blindness and desire and violence all intertwined, which returns me to David Hammons's spectral installation *Concerto in Black and Blue* (2002)[16] or to Derek Jarman's elegiac *Blue* (1993).[17]

I want to hold onto this digressive quality as it seems necessary to the work of the choreographic, specifically to an experiencing of dance as medium (of spirit, of art) whose timing is anachronistic, a "braiding of temporalities" as choreographer Tere O'Connor describes the many layers of syntax, information, history, that recede and gather within the work and our experience of witnessing it (2012). Or as Jacques Derrida explains in his theatrical conjuring of Karl Marx, such spectral presences evoke "a paradoxical incorporation, the becoming-body, a certain phenomenal and carnal form of spirit. It becomes, rather, some 'thing' that remains difficult to name: neither soul nor body, and both one and the other. For it is flesh and phenomenality that give to the spirit its spectral apparition, but which disappear right away in the apparition, in the very coming of the *revenant* or the return of the specter" (Derrida [1993] 1994, 6).

Indeed this is Derrida at his most clairvoyant evoking such an uncanny intellectual viscera; time and spirit are indeed "out of joint" (Derrida [1993] 1994, 1). The ghosts as so many citations gather as Derrida writes of Hamlet and his ghosts. Gutierrez too turns to Hamlet's notorious soliloquy on sleep and dreams for the title of this piece *And lose the name of action*. Under these many influences might paradox then act as condensation not only of flesh and spirit, but also of histories and futures within this densely saturated present? If this mode of action is possible, we could undo a certain idea of action aligned with progress, rationality, and linearity, instead opening to another perceptual quality of encounter.

---

16. Hammons often works with the myriad powers of blue. Here are but two examples: *Concerto in Black and Blue* at Ace Gallery in New York City, November 2002. I received a blue flashlight when I passed the threshold of the empty gallery. *Blues and the Abstract Truth* installed at Kunsthalle Bern in 1997 also revealed emptied galleries, or almost, all excerpt the final room, which displayed a mute drum set and a stuffed cat. Throughout Hammons covered the windows and skylights with blue foil, saturating the almost empty museum space with blue light and sounds of John Coltrane, Charlie Parker, and Muddy Waters.

17. Derek Jarman's *Blue* (1993) was included in the exhibition *Political Minimal* at Kunst-Werke Institute for Contemporary Art, Berlin, November 30, 2008, to January 25, 2009.

Gutierrez suggests as much in the beginning of the piece as Holmes, dressed in regal white and gold, confesses: "I'm an old man . . . I came about my knowledge without a teacher . . . this is uncommon yet here I am."[18] Gutierrez and Houston-Jones meet on stage also costumed in pale white, beige, and gold, ancient Greek meets Rodarte. They mirror each other, an exacting series of poses that will recur throughout the work in different contexts: arms extend, heads turn, almost embrace. Gutierrez falls into Houston-Jones. Initially he catches him and then he lets him slip away: "sorry," he says. In these opening exchanges, we learn something of the logic of this other world—that it has deep historical roots, that it is about knowledge but not in any traditional sense, that we must come to it senses open, arms extended, together, that at times we will become unrecognizable to each other, even to ourselves, that sometimes we will fall and no one will catch us.

Gutierrez incites a different understanding of knowledge, of language, of action, undoing or unworking these terms to generate something more contemplative, perceptual, political, another aspect of a choreographic ethics. Not only restricted to the stage, he also asks us to think about philosophy and neurology (and their many failures and blind spots), to consider consciousness through its illegibility. Hannah Arendt might describe such an ontology as a way of being in the world with others. When she writes of action it is always in relation to her conception of work—a production of objects that will distance us from our own futility—and labor—a collective metabolic condition. Action exceeds these prescriptive requirements of a life to offer something else intrinsically necessary and sustaining. Part of her project entails identifying how we live so we might reconsider "the human condition from the vantage point of our newest experiences and our most recent fears" (Arendt [1958] 1998, 5). Arendt is writing about the disasters resulting from nuclear technology, and we can fill in our own contemporary fears here. Yet her question still holds—what is it that makes a world? How are we attached to it? And how might the choreographic speak to these conditions?

18. I think of the school teacher of Jacques Rancière's *Emancipated Spectator*, yet while *And lose the name of action* indeed participates in an wildly generous distribution of sensuous sensibilities, I don't sense it emancipates in the ways that Rancière might propose, for instead we remain intimately complicit, seduced.

A Speculative Poetics

Meanwhile, the world. He went back out on it again. Rumpled land under the blue dome of sky. The ordinary sky at the equator in spring changed color day by day, it took a color chart to even approximate the tone colors; some days it was a deep violet blue—clematis blue, or hyacinth blue, or lapis lazuli, or a purplish indigo. Or Prussian blue, a pigment made of ferric ferrocyanide. . . . Iron blue. Slightly more purple than Himalayan skies as seen in photographs . . . Look very closely; sometimes it was a flow, sometimes the planck-planck-planck of individual stillnesses.—Kim Stanley Robinson, *Blue Mars*

For Arendt, for Benjamin, for Einstein the twentieth century dawned in catastrophe; in distinct ways each thinker contemplated these many minefields (literal, historic, and otherwise). If we listen now with an eye turned toward the future, the twenty-first century does not offer much relief—or so Kim Stanley Robinson would like us to believe of this "long emergency of the 21st century" (2013). Standing within Adrián Villar Rojas's *La inocencia de los animales (The innocence of animals,* 2013) an amphitheater and cavern of broken ellipses and architectural leftovers all constructed of flaking clay and concrete within PS1 MoMA,[19] Robinson details the immanently unfolding cataclysm perpetuated by the economic fallout of capitalism and devastation of the biosphere.[20] Similar to his science fiction novels, Robinson's lecture is filled with statistics—rising carbon dioxide levels in the atmosphere, ocean acidification, analysis of market algorithms—warning that soon we will no longer

19. Rojas's *La inocencia de los animales (The innocence of animals,* 2013) and Robinson's lecture are both part of the exhibition and event series *EXPO 1: New York,* May 12 –September 2, 2013, at PS1 MoMA and affiliate venues. The concept of the exhibition was developed by Klaus Biesenbach with Hans Ulrich Obrist and advisors Paola Antonelli, Peter Eleey, Pedro Gadanho, Laura Hoptman, Roxana Marcoci, and Jenny Schlenzka. In the press, the curators describe the exhibition as channeling a *"Dark Optimism* address[ing] ecological challenges set against the backdrop of economic turmoil and sociopolitical upheaval" (Biesenbach 2013). We will return to this question of optimism soon.

20. Speaking from the same platform, Samuel R. Delany points out our proliferating amnesia (cultural and historical) and references Emile Durkheim, Karl Marx, and Sigmund Freud as the thinkers to first describe the existence of "correlations" that until that moment had remained invisible. Durkheim notes the correspondence between unemployment and suicide, Marx the workings of capitalism, Freud the unconscious (Delany 2013).

have the luxury of walking any hypothetical middle road between utopia and catastrophe. It is "utopia or nothing." His warning confuses any definition of utopia as a nonplace of fantasy or representation or hope or futurity, further complicating Frederic Jameson's definition of utopia seen through Robinson's own *Mars Trilogy*[21] as "not representation of radical alternatives but imperative to imagine them" (Jameson 2005, 415). I sense Robinson reminding us that the defamiliarizing sensations speculative writing produces are not so speculative or at least not so distant, rather more coeval with our own experience, again a temporal braiding of spatial, psychic, emotional paradoxes that incite action as part of a critical imagination and "social technologies" (Robinson 2013). His conception of social technologies—not only technological, medical, and environmental engineering but also, and as important, social justice—proposes a complex of cognitive, material, corporeal, and legal processes that must be engaged simultaneously. This thinking not only underwrites his lecture but also does deep structural work across his epic *Mars Trilogy*, within which humans are given "treatments" to extend sentience for two hundred years, resulting near the end in complicated breakdowns of memory, amnesia, déjà vu, reawakening. As individuals participate in what were once only projected futures, age and mortality lose dominance to extended consciousness, particularly set against the velocity of planetary and social change wrought by terraforming. This simultaneous creation of inhabitable worlds on physical, cognitive, and planetary scales models a complicated suture between, as Jameson describes, "realism as the narrative of human praxis and ontology as the traces of Being itself" (Jameson 2005, 403). Terraforming embodies a Rolfing for the soul and for the planet.[22] Unlike some hallucinations of utopia that draw space and time differently, even as humans remain trapped in our limitations and appear as "utopian geologists" or tourists of the radically altered, Robinson imagines a

---

21. Robinson's *Mars Trilogy* includes *Red Mars* (1993), *Green Mars* (1994), and *Blue Mars* (1996), which trace a history and future of Mars from the arrival of its first one hundred inhabitants through a vast terraforming project and the struggle to maintain independence from Earth while inventing a new social-political life. All of these events will happen within a generation under the influence of new treatments for senescence: history and individual life approach parallel time scales.

22. Rolfing is mode of bodywork that focuses on realigning the deep fascia layers of the body, attending to both musculature and emotional memory to effect a different relation of self to physicality and consciousness.

luscious relationality shared by humans, animals, landscapes, sexuality, rendering a sensuous viriditas in all its many forms; humans fly as virtuosic birds over martian ocean or staggering volcanic cliffs.[23] At moments, Robinson's worlds take on an almost corporeal quality that resonates as much as it disorientates: "The landscape itself was now speaking a kind of glossolalia. The inchoate roar smashed at the air, and quivered their stomachs like some bass tearing of the world's fabric" (Robinson 1993, 546).[24] Yet all of this converging imagination takes time to unfold and requires a commitment that is exhausting, not unlike performance, in moments.

Such duration of experience is what Carolyn Christov-Bakargiev might describe as "timeliness" in her essay titled "The dance was very frenetic, lively, rattling, clanging, rolling, contorted, and lasted for a long time" (Christov-Bakargiev 2012, 34). If we linger long enough, even too long, on the shores of fantastical martian oceans, in a trance of blue light, or along the deserted roads of a tiny town somewhere in Mississippi or Italy or Germany, we might sense, feel, intuit, be blown or even blown away by knowledge in a subtler form. Perhaps we might even create "space for the inoperative and the imperceptible, for the not-quite-appearing" (2012, 34).[25] Christov-Bakargiev is also not immune to the seduction of the planetary as she opens her introductory catalog essay for dOCUMENTA (13) with a story of a work that exists in only in its absence: a proposal by the artists Guillermo Faivovich and Nicolás Goldberg to transport the thirty-seven ton meteorite, El Chaco, from Argentina to Germany. She asks: what if we could "see things from the position of the meteorite? . . . What is this *dis*placed position, generated by the perception of a simultaneous being in different spaces, where the collapse of time and distance

---

23. One of the space travelers in BADco's *A League of Time* (2009) reminds us we are all so many "utopian geologists" and these experiments are so many kinds of "blueprintism," parables or hallucinations to read while sleeping. This as the dancers balance on unsteady ladders, execute complicated labanesque phrases all within a stark stage.

24. And here I think of Steve McQueen's *Once Upon a Time* (2002) included in the *il Palazzo Enciclopedico* exhibition that pairs an endless series of slide images from NASA's archive with a glossolalia soundtrack, a strange mingling of linguistic dematerialization and scientific determinism each undoing the other.

25. Christov-Bakargiev's essay "The dance was very frenetic, lively, rattling, clanging, rolling, contorted, and lasted for a long time" opens the catalog for dOCUMENTA (13) (Christov-Bakargiev 2012, 30), an exhibition that occurs every five years in Kassel, Germany, or in her version, in a series of places and times constelling out from Kassel.

provokes a new sense of what it means to be always in one place, and not in another place?" (30). Her conception of a curatorial "choreography" embracing "*dis-placedness*," contortion, frenetic out-of-sync relations is deeply sympathetic with a choreographic ethics as she continues: "These are terrains where politics is inseparable from a sensual, energetic, and worldly alliance between current undertakings in various scientific and artistic fields and other knowledges, both ancient and contemporary" (31). Yes, yes. Not only are these contingent terrains, but the aporias in between them matter as well, becoming sites of awkward, passionate, even misunderstood, generous sharing; if we risk unrecognizability then something else appears. And then she quotes Vinciane Despret on love:

To "depassionate" knowledge does not give us a more objective world, it just gives us a world "without us"; and therefore without "them"—lines are traced so fast. And as long as this world appears as a world "we don't care for," it also becomes an impoverished world, a world of minds without bodies, of bodies without minds, bodies without hearts, expectations, interests, a world of enthusiastic automata observing strange and mute creatures; in other words, a poorly articulated (and poorly articulating) world. (Despret in Christov-Bakargiev 2012, 34)

Love, passion, desire, doubt—these many affective states circulate through Christov-Bakargiev's thesis, aspiring to undo a conception of art as legible and comfortable and instead asking anxiety-provoking questions and posing impossible parables; insisting that art articulate and communicate within the precarious spaces of life and that if we focus on "moments of trauma, at turning points, accidents, catastrophes, crises . . . matter comes to *matter*" (Christov-Bakargiev 2012, 31).[26] Then she reminds us: "War creates facts. Art also creates facts, of a different order. The question of oblique speech is related to this" (38). She continues to ponder the ethics of making art in places where one cannot speak, where silencing, censorship, and war are quite real daily events.

Far away from Kassel and Kabul, two of the sites Christov-Bakargiev intertwines in curatorial proximity, I wonder: might the oblique take on another function? This is what Paul Virilio and Claude Parent argued for before the events

---

26. In a more ironic although not insincere mode, Jan Verwoert asks how contemporary sculpture might perform its own articulate magic. He places sculpture somewhere between a ghost catcher (from the film *Ghostbusters* [1984]) a dream catcher by way of a highway restroom somewhere outside Prague, as so many "conductors of relational magic" (Verwoert 2011, 88).

of May 1968 in Paris, when it still seemed possible that architecture might free itself from the failed promises of modernism through transversal planes, mobility, transit, disorientation. Yet realized in concrete architectural form, the "oblique function" became another impasse rather than a crossing (Virilio [1966] 1997, iii). Theoretically, however, their work was deeply choreographic. As Virilio reflects: "The human at the basis of architectonics is never a dancer, but always Don Juan's statue of the commander! With the theory of the oblique function, we had placed ourselves at the deepest level of negation of this fixity, we were heretics refusing the recurrent dogma of orthogonality" (Virilio 1997, 8). Promiscuity of reference, disorientation of movement—these would not only alter the use potential of space (social, emotional, and physical) but incite other modes of perceptual encounter.

Stepping over Marianne Vitale's transversal railroad junction *Diamond Crossing* (2013), I wonder if Virilio's "oblique function" has indeed been laid to rest or if it still retains its provocation (figure 4.9). At one level, this lonely formulation leads nowhere, posing a cynical critique of the empty spectacle of art as economy; perhaps it invites a fictional peregrination along an unfinished trajectory that places us closer to the violent history undergirding westward expansion and the brutal labor required to realize these feats of colonizing and terraforming of another sort. As she explains: "my burned, bullet-hole-ridden sculptures borrow from history to create a fiction in the contemporary imaginary that allows us to be 'there' through being 'here'" (Vitale 2013).

Vitale's *Mercury* (2013) renders another impossible threshold, a burnt ruin signaling the violent dramaturgy of its fabrication, a pock-marked geology, dark and quite close (figure 4.10). *Mercury* is charred, spun too close to the sun or torched in the woods upstate. A curvaceous trellis cut from struts of reclaimed lumber or miniature bridge balanced uncomfortably on its pedestal. "This was not luxurious wood, but a single piece of catastrophe that walked by the fire and burned itself," Kim Rosenfield offers as ventriloquism for another puppet traversing oblique streets of speech, lies, and trauma (2004, 13). Vitale describes *Mercury* and the flattened geometries of her *Mars* (2013), the cantilevered bunker palace of *Earth* (2013) or the Rosicrucian-like gathering of triangular figures that becomes *Jupiter* (2013) as "manmade hieroglyphs, like giant divining rods of how the planets might be if only we could get close enough to touch them" (Vitale 2013). Smoldering runes and cynical fictions, the works ruminate on histories' violent passing but also on the

4.9 Marianne Vitale, *Diamond Crossing*, 2013. Manganese steel, dimensions variable. Installation view, Zach Feuer Gallery, New York, NY. Photograph courtesy of the artist and Zach Feuer Gallery.

4.10 Marianne Vitale, *Mercury*, 2013. Reclaimed lumber, 59.06 × 82.68 × 16.93 inches, 150 × 210 × 43 cm. Installation view, Le Confort Moderne, Poitiers, France. Photograph by Pierre Antoine; courtesy of the artist and Zach Feuer Gallery.

crippling desire to effect what cannot be reached without being affected oneself, landing us close to a representation of Robinson's catastrophe.

I am not ready to fall into this catastrophe just yet. Where else might these planetary vanishing points take us? I turn back again to see: a thick white octagon framing swirling terrain compressing cosmic and tertiary, a saturation of paint, plaster, magnets hanging slightly awry. Is this untitled work an aperture of pixilating distance or opaque mirror? James Foster's visceral dramaturgy renders distance simultaneously more precarious and more proximate. As mirror my reflection becomes tiny, a miniature tear on the surface of a marble, surrounded by an epic miasma of gray, white, purple colliding in threads of paint and plaster. As aperture I am surrounded by celestial spaciousness. Within the work, the photographic takes on a sculptural function, not as representation of a directive elsewhere, but as an operation that suspends me within the labyrinthine outer spaces of the work. His cantilevered frame frames my encounter and like Jacques Derrida's parergon it does not enclose to protect but to disturb and erupt careful beholding. As Derrida writes between two large ellipses, an abyssal graphics of sorts:

Economize on the abyss: not only save oneself from falling into the bottomless depth by weaving and folding back the cloth to infinity, textual art of the reprise, multiplication of patches within patches, but also establish the laws of reappropriation, formalize the rules which constrain the logic of the abyss and which shuttle between the economic *and* the aneconomic, the raising [*la relève*][27] *and* the fall, the abyssal operation which can only work toward the *relève and* that in which regularly reproduces collapse. (Derrida [1978] 1987, 37; italics in original)

How to navigate this abyss? Derrida would challenge me to stand up in relief *and* against rising and falling pendulum swings, to economize on my disorientation. And when he writes of the economic and its supplement weaving, folding, intertwining toward infinity, I imagine him channeling the many gifts, rituals, dark, secret proliferations of Georges Bataille's notion of expenditure, an experience that risks catastrophe, flirts with its seductions, turns these into additive layers. Of the abyss, Foster asks: "What does the proximal scale of emotional distance look like,

---

27. *Relève* comes from *relever*, which compared with the more anemic English "raising" also means to stand up again, to relieve.

how is it measured, where does it begin and end, how do we feel close to inanimate objects that are far away? Do we breathe life into that distance and relish our ability to overcome it? . . . Or wait until it firms up and falls on us, maybe . . ." (J. Foster 2013).[28] And if it indeed falls on us, what then? How does a Derridian economics save us? It doesn't, of course. Yet since I am not seeking redemption this vertiginous encounter embodies another kind of score, thinking as collapse, inscribing entropy with critical force, rendering sculpture as another choreographic operative shattering my depth of perception and altering my sense of gravity. It is sculpture experienced as science fiction. Lemon reminds me again: "science fiction is how we are now" (2010).

Love and Apocalypse

How jealous I am of those I have known afraid to sleep for dreaming. I fear those moments before sleep when words tear from the nervous matrix and, like sparks, light what responses they may. That fragmented vision, seductive with joy and terror, robs rest of itself. Gratefully sunk in nightmare, where at least the anxious brain freed from knowing its own decay can flesh those skeletal epiphanies with visual and aural coherence, if not rationale: better those landscapes where terror is experienced as terror and rage as rage than this, where either is merely a pain in the gut or a throb above the eye, where a nerve spasm in the shin crumbles a city of bone, where a twitch in the eyelid detonates both the sun and the heart.—Samuel R. Delany, *Dhalgren*

"Perfect . . . Just like the picture . . . Nice and quiet out here, huh? . . . So glad you called . . . It's not easy to find . . . I'm feeling a shift . . . Are we here yet?" Meg Stuart asks Benoit LaChambre and Hahn Rowe near the beginning of *Forgeries, Love and Other Matters* (2004) (figure 4.11).[29] Arms reaching out, Stuart spins slowly through

---

28. These questions speak to a complementary work *In through the Outdoors* (2012) that includes a found photograph of a meteorite, signed from father to son, if I remember correctly, juxtaposed with a constellation of miniature tinfoil planets and a tiny leaning cairn. Again, the photograph acts as talisman, operator, never merely a representation of a place we are not.

29. *Forgeries, Love and Other Matters* (2004) is produced by Damaged Goods and par b.l.eux. Choreography and dance by Meg Stuart and Benoît Lachambre; live music by Hahn Rowe;

the thick hung-over atmosphere as Rowe's gravelly, melancholic, synthetic blues crescendos. A chocolate-brown carpet creates an undulating hill across the space that ends in a golden metallic shield or wall; landscape images the shape of the dancers' despair. No longer a ghostly couple, although this work is deeply haunted as well, the dancers first meet on small stools at the edge of the stage. Stuart cries, distraught. Lachambre leans away. His hand comes to rest on hers. She flexes her fingers to grasp, touch, feel something underneath his skin, yet his gesture resists her dry brittle caress. He walks away. Passing through despair to desire to indifference and again and again, their dance tests the barriers of intimacy as they claw, crawl, wrestle, fight, collapse into and away from each other. They run up the looming hill only to slip, slide back down, deadweight bodies torqued by other less visible intensities. Many of these forces converge in the sonic, eviscerating obvious linear legible patterns as sonority becomes shadowy substance, perhaps as Samuel R. Delany describes the music of the ocarina: "Colors sluiced the air with fugal patters as a shape subsumed the breeze and fell, to form further on, a brighter emerald, a duller amethyst. Odors flushed the wind with vinegar, snow, ocean, ginger, poppies, rum. Autumn, ocean, ginger, ocean, autumn; ocean, ocean, the surge of ocean again, while light foamed in the dimming blue" (Delany 1968, 19). An imagined gypsy instrument, Delaney's ocarina works syncretic magic through the specters it casts.[30] Flickering forgeries, of a sort, substance-less viscera imaging thoughts inside of vision, Rowe's sound score, like the ocarina, conjures a fugitive even amnesiac narrative. "This is not how they described it," Stuart says breaking the trance (2004).

Lachambre crashes to the ground. Stuart attempts to revive him: blowing air into his fingers, exaggerated jumps to press on his chest, sit on his face, Rowe hands her a first aid kit and she covers Lachambre with an emergency blanket, crumples it and places it under her head, uses another tube to breathe air into his mouth. His legs stop trembling, he lies still. Tying themselves together with elastic bands, they climb and drag, fall and pull each other up the hill. Momentum and weight force a

---

dramaturgy by Myriam Van Imschoot; scenography by Doris Dziersk; costume design by Tina Kloempken; light by Marc Dewit; filmed and edited by Philipp Hochleichter. I saw it performed at Dance Theater Workshop (now New York Live Arts), April 20–22, 2006, New York City.

30. The ocarina, like the scorpions of Delany's *Dhalgren* (1974), holograms of light shaped as so many animals to disguise the wearers of the lens that casts them, is another mirage that feels physical.

different engagement of their elastic tension and attention. Stuart unties herself. Along the top of the hill, Lachambre runs back and forth undressing as he moves, releasing the elastic band belt, he flees from an unseen force naked, long hair now loose. Spotlights illuminate his exquisite musculature as he runs, objectified as Stuart (and the audience) watch, she through binoculars from the edge of the stage. In this glowing light, reflected by the metallic wall behind him, his run becomes less vertical and transforms into a gallop on hands and feet, as an animal, he howls. Stuart climbs the hill, holds him, carries, caresses him.

The choreography seizes, thrashes, yet is always precisely danced even though often improvised. As Stuart explains: "My performers rarely have fixed characters or behavior, so they can readily fall into the holes of alternate realities. They do this, as in life, as a way of escaping an uncomfortable present. In dance, I try to physicalize the noise, the distractions, the projections that one experiences when meeting another person" (Stuart 2010, 239). In *Forgeries, Love and Other Matters*, the landscape also offers literal holes in which to get lost, or find another escape. Opening a trap door underneath the carpet, Stuart pulls out a bag full of plastic bags and a costume change. She takes off her blond wig, heels, dress, pulls on a T-shirt and stuffs it with plastic bags using the last to cover her head. Meanwhile, Lachambre appears through a now uncovered window, dressed in white lab coat sitting in a white room under the hill listing the contents. Stuart enters and he removes each bag individually narrating each gesture: "a plastic bag, another plastic bag, a plastic bag with a small hole in it, a tubular plastic bag, a green plastic bag." Now naked, he continues to gently examine her with his hands: "movement beneath the surface … bruises … folds and creases … a soft surface" She climbs onto the table now pushed against the window, "red marks … an organized chaos … signs of discomfort … a body that needs coverage." He hands her a white lab coat. They continue together from within this underground laboratory.

4.11 Meg Stuart, *Forgeries, Love and Other Matters*, 2004. Photography courtesy of Chris Van der Burght.

There is no waiting in this place . . .

No reasons to even think in this place . . .

Nobody can get lost in this place . . .

There are no emotions in this place . . .

No laughter in this place . . .

No tears in this place . . .

There is no longing in this place . . .

There is no history in this place.

(Stuart 2004)

Spoken in low even tones, they list all of the things that cannot be found in this place: "hope, toxic feeling, sexual fantasies, migrations of friendship, falling in love, falling out of love, denial, darkness" (Stuart 2004). No, no, no, the word reiterates like the gestures within the dancing, fierce precision negation. Yet language is never to be trusted as it too participates in the many intimate forgeries, another costuming of psyche and emotion. Falling behind the hill, they reemerge in headless bear costumes cut from the same fabric as the hill. Now falling, still wrestling, camouflaged, their erotics takes on a poetic texture, rendering the choreographic as a polyamorous and anarchic encounter, so much relentless research as if we forget that these attachments often end in ways we might not desire. From within the duration of the work, they construct a more fragile history of love and perhaps this is part of the other matters that the title evokes. We repeat to remember against forgetting. In this moment history changes us. Or as Delany writes in his own eloquent memoir: "(History arrives only when we don't know what has happened. Only when we forget. Only when people disagree on what has happened. That is why a theory of history must always come into being at the same moment as history itself)" (Delany 1988, 543). At the end of the piece Stuart and Lachambre construct a tent from a sheet dyed with a desert sunset, lights dim and the sun seems to grow brighter. They climb inside as darkness falls to dream another history, another love, of other matters.

Are You Still Awake? Close Your Eyes. It Is Time to Dream

Crows did fly,
Through the sky.
I hear their cries,
Strange lullaby.
Close your eyes and try to sleep,
They wait for me in the middle of the night.
It's hard to believe it now,
But I know it's going to work out right.
Dreams will come,
And when they're done
It won't be long
Until the dawn.
So close your eyes and try to sleep.
Strange noises always make it difficult to sleep.
The dogs are barking in the street.
Crows did fly,
I hear their cries
From far and wide
Echo through the sky,
Strange lullaby,
Crows did fly,
Close your eyes and try to sleep.—George Bures Miller,
"Crows Did Fly (Kathmandu Lullaby)"

I write at the edge of awakening where images shimmer partial and inchoate. The haze upon waking quiets my frenetic dance, I sift through thoughts, reorganize them by temperature or sonority. This is also how I experience *The Murder of Crows*

(2008)[31] by Janet Cardiff and George Bures Miller inside the vast armory as sound alters scale foregrounding the background.[32] Walking through the amplified darkness, I approach the almost empty chairs gathered around an old gramophone resting on a small table within a circle of standing and hanging speakers and throughout the vast space. From the gramophone, Cardiff's voice hesitates and stutters:

I can't . . . it was . . . it was . . . it was a very bizarre dream . . . it switched, somehow, to the future again . . . and there were all these different machines. And each machine had a different thing that they put into it. Like on machine had cats fed into it. And the cats got all ground up, and then the blood was pouring out and another machine had babies fed into it. (Cardiff and Bures Miller 2008)

The first of a series of dreams relayed in relentless nihilist logic tells of children, entrapment, running, blood, slavery, decapitation, sometimes in a jungle, sometimes along the beach. At one moment, Cardiff describes pulling a bed sheet back to find a severed leg. Each recollection interrupts and is interrupted by an oceanic sound score, at rare moments illustrative as footsteps become heavy, doors crash, machines saw at metal or a dog barks, but more often more densely atmospheric as crows call across the speakers, waves crash and collide along the shore or rocks, an operatic interlude is sung about a severed leg, Alexander Alexandrov's *Svyaschennaya Voyna* (The Sacred War) marches across the space saturating distinct sections as it passes across the armory hall.[33]

All of the complicated algorithms required to allow sound to move, to feel as if it is whispered in your ear, or moving from a distance to stand beside you, are

31. I reference the iteration of Cardiff and Bures Miller's *The Murder of Crows* that opened at the Armory, in New York City, August 3–September 9, 2012.

32. In her essay "More Permanent than Snow," Lin Hixson writes that she "foregrounded the background and backgrounded the foreground" (Hixson in Heathfield 2004, 129).

33. Carolyn Christov-Bakargiev notes that this patriotic march was composed in 1941 the year Hitler invaded the Soviet Union by the composer who would go on to direct the Red Army Choir and create a national anthem for Joseph Stalin in 1944 (Christov-Bakargiev in Cardiff and Bures Miller 2009, 34, 44).

hidden so that lying on the ground I feel the vibrations and rising narratives as dreams. Not only in the dreams that Cardiff confesses, but also in the structuring of the work, *The Murder of Crows* relies on a logic of sleep. The artists call up this image through the dreamer depicted in Francisco Goya's *The Sleep of Reason Produces Monsters* (c. 1797) who lies face down, drooling puddles on his notes as bats, crows, and strange cats gather. In their script notes Cardiff and Bures Miller collage this image under their final narrative fragments: *He sings last line... STATIC VOICE—testing testing... The end* as if to return their work to the oneiric. Written while Cardiff and Bures Miller were waiting in Kathmandu in 2007, the installation shares the hazy surreal logic of this valley city intoxicated by smog fire fantasy. In their catalog, they reproduce images of Kathmandu meant to be seen through 3D glasses, yet without the glasses the stuttering images seem much closer to my memories.[34]

When I witness *The Murder of Crows*, stories, images, memories, ideas become sensate. I feel these many synaptic flashes as after-images seen behind vision. I am seduced, consumed, devastated inside a sonorous dark. *The Murder of Crows* is a dense affective event and one that resonates deeply with Lauren Berlant's conception of affect as a historical force felt physically. "Affect's saturation of form can communicate the conditions under which a historical moment appears as a visceral moment" (Berlant 2011, 16). Reading these affective atmospheres closely reveals that violence, trauma, and accidents are not exceptional experiences, but the very textures of ordinary life. Berlant describes the "ordinary as a zone of convergence of many histories, where people manage the incoherence of lives that proceed in the face of threats" (10). Precarious, trembling, to think along the

---

34. Some images: a man with a long sofa strapped to his back walking uphill, a freshly severed pig's head swinging from a boy's shoulders still dripping blood, fried oil, dough, and betelnut, concrete lingams dense with red yellow pigments, a crudely drawn portrait of Karl Marx in a house hidden in winding hills, constant taste of sulfur on my tongue, *Guns N' Roses*, legs prickling numb from hours of tabla practice, broken hospital windows and scattered needles, pale blond ghosts living in one green room, bike crashes, and rice. Cardiff and Miller were in Kathmandu waiting to take their adopted daughter home. I was told to marry the ancient court musician's grandson and take him home. *You can take one with you*, they told me. I fled.

choreographic requires falling into catastrophe to see where we land and to imagine other very real escapes. Cardiff's breathy speech, her nightmares of slavery and dismemberment set against the wash of waves along the shore and crows, always crows, conjures another ineffable choreographic exigency so many facts of art and of war again colliding. I cannot sleep, and yet I must. And when I wake, to crows mourning at dawn, crying over the waters, this too is another lullaby as requiem for action. Sweet dreams.

Conclusion A Return and a Refrain

Once upon a time
It was beautiful here
and the sun came down and set fire to the ground
until it was black, scorched and hard
There was nothing
nothing
nothing left here for us—Miguel Gutierrez, *When You Rise Up*

What is the landscape of your desire, of your longing? Who lives there? What language do they speak? In what dreams do they dance? Cloaked in darkness, Hilary Clark's voice resonates across the vast sanctuary of St. Mark's Church calling out to the many avatars and superheroes evoked in the opening to her dance. "Female warriors, where are we?" she cries (Clark 2012). Removing her Clark Kent glasses, she wanders around the space dragging the shimmering sequin towers into position. The fragile architecture of *Accessories of Protection*[1] acts as an accessory for future encounters and talisman of crystalline trajectories participating in her dance (figures 5.1–5.3). In the half-light Clark moves in slow extensions metabolizing the expanse of space as if contending with another force that is pushing against her. "I'm against your slowness. I despise your heaviness," she reads in the opening section. Balancing between two precarious structures, she lunges arms thrust forward and then she runs around and around the space, removing her flowing white dress and pulling on a tight fur jacket over her power belt, magenta tights, sheepskin merkin, and white leotard. Grabbing one of the smaller sequined boxes as she runs and placing it on her head like a glittering balaclava, she stands in the center of the altar illuminated by a blue square of light, fist raised as Rihanna's song "Diamonds" plays. Clark's repetitive gestures, arms rising in protest, call out to the

---

1. *Accessories of Protection* (2012) was performed at Danspace Project at St. Mark's Church in-the-Bowery, New York City, on December 14, 2012, and April 25–27, 2013, as part of *Solos and Solitudes* curated by Noémie Solomon and Jenn Joy. Choreographed and performed by Hilary Clark; lighting by Kathy Kaufmann.

punk prayers of Pussy Riot, as she explains: "part of their revolt is the repetitive action" (Clark 2013).[2] The blue light casts another shadowy layer, an immaterial fortress of sorts, steeling her against the melancholic violence underwriting "Diamonds," a ballad of hope sung after very public abuse. Rihanna sings of a very "cruel optimism," to return to Lauren Berlant's refrain, antithetical to the fierce feminism of Pussy Riot. Now standing between two other towers, Clark shakes, her entire body consumed in a tremulous possession simultaneously sexual and psychic as the sonorous melancholic plaint distorts. Slowness and heaviness descend as Clark screams without sound, punching in slow motion, her now toxic improvisation animated by flickering rap gestures or power poses on a sheepskin rug, so much rage turning inside out. Saturated by voices that are wailing, moaning, mechanical, alien, always echoing, I am lost in a dense visceral grief. Until the end when Clarks quietly sings: "I am a warrior and I'll go to war for her. I will defend her. I will try . . ." Her voice renders a fierce vulnerability and I hear Ralph Lemon whisper: "love without rage is powerless" (Lemon 2010). Again the ghosts gather within this sanctuary as the lights dim and towers shine as metallic totems from yet another outer space.

2. The Russian feminist collective Pussy Riot stormed the altar of Cathedral of Christ the Savior in Moscow on February 21, 2012, and performed forty seconds of their punk prayer asking for Putin's removal from power. Collective members—Maria Alyokhina, Nadezhda Tolokonnikova, and Yekaterina Samutsevich—were arrested and imprisoned on charges of felony hooliganism and religious hatred.

5.1–5.3 Hilary Clark, *Accessories of Protection*, 2012. Photographs by Tamara Johnson.

Accessories of Protection intertwines a subtle energetic body with desperate pop culture narratives and a virulent feminist force framing a precarious constellation of relationships always shadowed by violence and war. I sense as Clark sings her warrior song that these wars are not only cultural, historical yet also deeply personal and social; a fight against the material, emotional, lived conditions of entrapment, of loss, of fear. When she asks about the conditions of precariousness, of what makes a life grievable, Judith Butler demands a "restructuring of the senses" so that we might embrace a different relationship to war and the density of its frames. War is not only or not ever far away, even though it might seem that way, but is as she describes a deeply relational event to which we must respond (Butler 2010, xii). She continues: "Precariousness is not simply an existential condition of individuals, but rather a social condition from which certain clear political demands and principles emerge. . . . When the frames of war break up or break open, when the trace of lives is apprehended at the margin of what appears or as riddling its surface . . . there emerges the possibility of critical outrage, war stands the chance of missing its mark" (xxv, xxx).

Perhaps the choreographic might also incite a mode of "critical outrage" as it enumerates so many other ways of living, of consciousness along messier edges, never only utopic but also, as always, experienced, danced, cried, screamed. From within this place, I hear Miguel Gutierrez screaming from the balcony of St. Mark's Church following a performance of Juliette Mapp's *One* (2005), a piece that takes seriously the work of enumerating the dead, those we must grieve and not forgot. *One* begins as Anna Sperber places a chair in the center of the sanctuary counts 1, 2, 3, . . . The tempo of her counting replicates the gesture of her right hand sliding down her thigh. Other dancers, all women dressed in black, enter alone or in pairs, then in larger groups, positioning their chairs across the space at oblique angles to the audience. Leaning slightly forward, they continue counting, beginning at different points, but always speaking and moving with methodical intent. A group of dancers stop counting and blankly scan the audience, bending over they caress their faces in mock salute, as their arms cross they pull at their own hands, each grabbing their wrists as if in an attempt to restrain the gesture, and then their hands break away, slapping against their legs. The dancers now move in series, some in chairs, some on the floor, and others stand manipulating the still-seated women. Their progression alludes to a not so subtle militancy; a regime of women shifts from the chair to the floor. The thud of the fall confronts the abstraction of the numbers: one dancer falls, another falls, and another, one rises, another falls. *One* ends in darkness and silence.

And then, Gutierrez screams: *Yeaaahhh . . .* As the annihilating intensity of heavy metal guitar fills the sanctuary, the audience sings Black Sabbath's *War Pigs* (1970) with him in antiphonal response:

Generals gathered in their masses

Just like witches at black masses

Evil minds that plot destruction

Sorcerers of death's construction

In the fields the bodies burning

As the war machine keeps turning

Death and hatred to mankind

Poisoning their brainwashed minds, oh Lord, yeah!

Politicians hide themselves away

They only started the war

Why should they go out to fight?

They leave that all to the poor, yeah!

Time will tell on their power minds

Making war just for fun

Treating people just like pawns in chess

Wait 'till their judgment day comes, yeah!

Now in darkness, world stops turning

Ashes where their bodies burning

No more war pigs have the power

Hand of god has struck the hour

Day of judgment, god is calling

On their knees, the war pigs crawling

Begging mercy for their sins

Satan, laughing, spreads his wings, oh Lord, yeah!

(Black Sabbath 1970)

As the song ends Gutierrez and the musicians descend into the sanctuary for a whirling, shaking, tremulous, ecstatic dance against darkness.

The choreographic calls you: invites you, sometimes against your will, to look closely not only at the historical ghosts spiraling around present events and atrocities, but to think with and dance with these ghosts toward something else. As Avital Ronell reminds us, this was also Friedrich Nietzsche's provocation: he "wants philosophers to dance" (Ronell 2011). But not only that:

Nietzsche required of us that we think in terms of dance and dancing and choreography, but at the same time he was a philosopher. . . . Nietzsche was also a philosopher who wretched and threw up. That was his thing, not only a way of getting at Hegel because it's a reversal of dialectics (we assimilate ideas and digest thoughts). . . . [Nietzsche] puked it out. He detoxed. He was always in a methadone clinic of one sort or another as a thinker but that is another thing. . . . He was one who had once advocated dance and also needed to throw up. (Ronell 2011)

Ronell choreographs an extreme undoing of the rational sites and surrounds of knowledge, articulating the pressure of discourse on the body and calling out to its intoxicated, eviscerating responses. Passing again through the intensification of so many spasms and exploding under the influence, the choreographic disfigures desire and thinking at its limits, cascading out onto the floor. Lying on her back sliding along the lobby floor of Berlin's Hebbel Theater, Florentina Holzinger repeats: "I love, I love the taste of you, I love you, I love the taste of you . . ." as Vincent Riebeek vomits blue pigment all over her in their duet *Klein Applaus fur Scheisse* (2011). Perhaps here again we encounter a punk cipher, another messy and precarious provocation. Is this *choreography for the apocalypse*? If so, *get ready*.

References

achugar, luciana. 2009. Conversation with the author. New York, NY, January.

achugar, luciana. 2011. Conversation with the author. New York, NY, January.

Adler, Dan. 2011. "Us and It: Sculpture and the Critique of Display Cultures." Panel for College Art Association Conference. New York.

Agamben, Giorgio. [1996] 2000. *Means without End: Notes on Politics*, trans. Vincent Binetti and Cesare Casarino. Minneapolis: University of Minnesota Press.

Agamben, Giorgio. [2008] 2009. "What Is the Contemporary?" In *What Is an Apparatus? And Other Essays*, trans. David Kishik and Stefan Pedatella, 39–54. Stanford: Stanford University Press.

Albright, Ann Cooper. 1995. "Incalculable Choreographies: The Dance Practice of Marie Chouinard." In *Bodies of the Text: Dance as Theory, Literature as Dance*, ed. Ellen W. Goellner and Jacqueline Shea Murphy, 157–181. New Brunswick: Rutgers University Press.

Albright, Ann Cooper. 1997. *Choreographing Difference: The Body and Identity in Contemporary Dance*. Middletown: Wesleyan University Press.

Allsop, Rick, and André Lepecki. 2008. "Editorial: On Choreography." *Performance Research: A Journal of the Performing Arts* 13 (1): 1–6.

Anderson, Laurie. 1987. "Words in Reverse." In *Blasted Allegories: An Anthology of Writings by Contemporary Artists*, ed. Brian Wallis, 68–72. Cambridge, MA: MIT Press.

Anderson-Davies, Victoria. 2009. "Creative Endurance and the Face Machine: Roseanne Spradlin's *Survive Cycle*." In *Planes of Composition: Dance, Theory, and the Global*, ed. André Lepecki and Jenn Joy, 192–208. New York: Seagull Books.

Anderson-Davies, Victoria. 2012. "Reflecting Modernity: The Dance Studio as a Performative Space." PhD diss., Performance Studies, New York University.

Arbeau, Thoinot. 1589. *L'Orchésographie. Et traicté en forme de dialogue, par lequel toutes personnes peuvent facilement apprendre & practiquer l'honneste exercice des dances* [*Orchesography. A treatise in the form of a dialogue. Whereby all manner of persons may easily acquire and practise the honourable excercise of dancing*]. Langres: Jehan des Preyz. Facsimile available from Dance Instruction Manuals collection, United States Library of Congress, Washington, DC. graner.net/nicolas/arbeau/orcheso02.php (accessed January 27, 2014).

Arendt, Hannah. [1958] 1998. *The Human Condition*. Chicago: University of Chicago Press.

Austin, J. L. [1955] 1962. *How to Do Things with Words*. Cambridge, MA: Harvard University Press.

Bachelard, Gaston. [1943] 1988. *Air and Dreams: An Essay on the Imagination of Movement*, trans. Edith R. Farrell. Dallas: Dallas Institute.

Badiou, Alain. [1998] 2005. "Dance as a Metaphor for Thought." In *Handbook of Inaesthetics*, trans. Alberto Toscano, 57–71. Stanford: Stanford University Press.

Badiou, Alain, and Nicolas Truong. [2009] 2010. *In Praise of Love*, trans. Peter Bush. New York: The New Press.

Baehr, Antonia. 2008. *Rire/Laugh/Lachen*. Aubervilliers: Les Laboratoires d'Aubervilliers.

Barthes, Roland. [1964] 1977. "Rhetoric of the Image." In *Image, Music, Text*, trans. Stephen Heath, 32–51. New York: Hill and Wang.

Barthes, Roland. [1970] 1985. "The Third Meaning." In *The Responsibility of Forms: Critical Essays on Music, Art, and Representation*, trans. and ed. Richard Howard, 41–62. New York: Hill & Wang.

Barthes, Roland. [1977] 1985. "Right in the Eyes." In *The Responsibility of Forms: Critical Essays on Music, Art, and Representation*, trans. and ed. Richard Howard, 237–242. New York: Hill & Wang.

Barthes, Roland. [1980] 1981. *Camera Lucida: Reflections on Photography*, trans. Richard Howard. New York: Hill and Wang.

Bataille, Georges. [1928] 2001. *The Story of the Eye*, trans. Joachim Neugroschel. London: Penguin Books.

Bataille, Georges. [1943] 1988. *The Inner Experience*, trans. Leslie Anne Boldt. Albany: State University of New York Press.

Bataille, Georges. [1945] 1992. *On Nietszche*, trans. Bruce Boone. New York: Paragon House.

Bataille, Georges. [1951] 2001a. "The Consequences of Nonknowledge." In *The Unfinished System of Nonknowledge*, trans. and ed. Stuart Kendall and Michelle Kendall, 111–118. Minneapolis: University of Minnesota Press.

Bataille, Georges. [1951] 2001b. "Nonknowledge and Rebellion." In *The Unfinished System of Nonknowledge*, trans. and ed. Stuart Kendall and Michelle Kendall, 129–132. Minneapolis: University of Minnesota Press.

Bataille, Georges. [1951] 2001c. "The Teaching of Death." In *The Unfinished System of Nonknowledge*, trans. and ed. Stuart Kendall and Michelle Kendall, 119–128. Minneapolis: University of Minnesota Press.

Bataille, Georges. [1952] 2001. "Aphorisms for the 'System.'" In *The Unfinished System of Nonknowledge*, trans. and ed. Stuart Kendall and Michelle Kendall, 153–182. Minneapolis: University of Minnesota Press.

Bataille, Georges. [1953] 1986. "Un-Knowing: Laughter and Tears," trans. Annette Michelson. *October* 36 (Spring): 89–102.

Bataille, Georges. [1953] 2001. "Nonknowledge, Laughter, and Tears." In *The Unfinished System of Nonknowledge*, trans. and ed. Stuart Kendall and Michelle Kendall, 133–152. Minneapolis: University of Minnesota Press.

Bataille, Georges. [1957] 1962. *Erotism: Death and Sensuality*, trans. Mary Dalwood. San Francisco: City Lights Books.

Bataille, Georges. [1961] 1988. *Guilty*, trans. Bruce Boone. Venice: The Lapis Press.

Bataille, Georges. [1961] 1989. *The Tears of Eros*, trans. Peter Connor. San Francisco: City Light Books.

Bataille, Georges. 1985. *Visions of Excess: Selected Writings 1927–39*, trans. and ed. Allan Stoekl. Minneapolis: University of Minnesota Press.

Bataille, Georges. 2001. *The Unfinished System of Nonknowledge*, trans. and ed. Stuart Kendall and Michelle Kendall. Minneapolis: University of Minnesota Press.

Baudelaire, Charles. [1855] 2008. "On the Essence of Laughter." In *The Painter of Modern Life and Other Essays*, trans. and ed. Jonathan Mayne, 147–165. London: Phaidon Press Limited.

Bauer, Una. 2008. "Jérôme Bel: An Interview." *Performance Research* 13 (1): 42–48.

Bausch, Pina. 1987–1989. *Die Klage der Kaiserin*. Film.

Beckett, Samuel. 2006. *Samuel Beckett: The Grove Centenary Edition, Vol. 3 Dramatic Works*, ed. Paul Auster. New York: Grove Press.

Benjamin, Walter. [1921] 1996. "Critique of Violence." In *Selected Writings, Vol. I, 1913-1926*, ed. Marcus Bullock and Michael W. Jennings, 236–252. Cambridge, MA: Belknap Press.

Benjamin, Walter. [1931] 1979. "A Small History of Photography." In *One-Way Street and Other Writings*, trans. Edmund Jephcott and Kingsley Shorter, 240–257. London: Verso.

Benjamin, Walter. [1935] 1994. "To Max Horkheimer." In *The Correspondence of Walter Benjamin: 1910-1940*, ed. Gershom Scholem and Theodor W. Adorno, trans. Manfred R. Jacobson and Evelyn M. Jacobson, 508–510. Chicago: University of Chicago Press.

Benjamin, Walter. [1940] 1968. "Theses on the Philosophy of History." In *Illuminations*, ed. Hannah Arendt, trans. Harry Zohn, 253–264. New York: Schocken Books.

Benjamin, Walter. 1999. "N: On the Theory of Knowledge, Theory of Progress]." In *The Arcades Project*, ed. Rolf Tiedemann, trans. Howard Eiland and Kevin McLaughlin, 456–488. Cambridge, MA: Harvard University Press.

Bergson, Henri. [1900] 1999. *Laughter: An Essay on the Meaning of the Comic*, trans. Cloudesley Brereton and Fred Rothwell. Copenhagen: Green Integer Books.

Bergson, Henri. [1908] 1991. *Matter and Memory*, trans. N. M. Paul and W. S. Palmer. New York: Zone Books.

Berlant, Lauren. 2011. *Cruel Optimism*. Durham, NC: Duke University Press.

Bhabha, Homi. 1994. *The Location of Culture*. New York: Routledge.

Bhabha, Homi. 1996. "Aura and Agora: On Negotiating Rapture and Speaking Between." In *Negotiating Rapture: The Power of Art to Transform Lives*, ed. Richard Francis, 8–16. Chicago: Museum of Contemporary Art.

Biesenbach, Klaus. 2013. *EXPO 1: New York*. Press release. MoMA PS1, May 12–September 2.

Bishop, Claire. 2004. "Antagonism and Relational Aesthetics." *October* 110 (Autumn): 51–79.

Bishop, Claire, ed. 2006. *Participation*. London: Whitechapel.

Black, Joel. 1991. *Aesthetics of Murder: A Study in Romantic Literature and Contemporary Culture*. Baltimore: Johns Hopkins University Press.

Black Sabbath. 1970. "War Pigs." *Paranoid*. Vertigo Records.

Bloch, Ernst. [1964] 1996. "Something's Missing: A Discussion between Ernst Bloch and Theodor W. Adorno on the Contradictions of Utopian Longing." In *The Utopian Function of Art and Literature, Selected Essays*, trans. Jack Zipes and Frank Mecklenburg, 1–17. Cambridge, MA: MIT Press.

Bloch, Ernst. [1974] 1988. *The Utopian Function of Art and Literature: Selected Essays*, trans. Jack Zipes and Frank Mecklenburg. Cambridge, MA: MIT Press.

Bourriaud, Nicolas. [1998] 2002. *Relational Aesthetics*, trans. Simon Pleasance and Fronza Woods. Dijon: Les Press du réel.

Brandstetter, Gabriele. 1998. "Defigurative Choreography: From Marcel Duchamp to William Forsythe." *TDR* 42 (4): 37–55.

Brandstetter, Gabriele. 2000. "Choreography as a Cenotaph: The Memory of Movement." In *Remembering the Body*, ed. Gabriele Brandstetter and Hortensia Völkers, 102–134. Ostfildern-Ruit: Hatje Cantz.

Brooks, David. 2011. Artist's lecture. Sculpture Department, Rhode Island School of Design, September 27.

Browning, Barbara. 1995. *Samba Resistance in Motion: Arts, Politics of the Everyday*. Bloomington: Indiana University Press.

Bures Miller, George. 2011. "Crows Did Fly (Kathmandu Lullaby)." In *The Murder of Crows*, George Bures Miller and Janet Cardiff. Ostfildern: Hatje Cantz.

Butler, Judith. 2004. *Precarious Life: The Powers of Mourning and Violence*. London: Verso.

Butler, Judith. 2009. *Frames of War: When Is Life Grievable?* London: Verso Books.

Camus, Albert. [1942] 1988. *The Stranger*, trans. MatthewWard. New York: Vintage Books.

Cardiff, Janet, and George Bures Miller. 2008. *The Murder of Crows*. Performance text. Park Avenue Armory, New York, NY, August 3–September 9, 2012.

Cardiff, Janet, and George Bures Miller. 2011. *The Murder of Crows*. Ostfildern: Hatje Cantz.

Carter, Paul. 1996. *The Lie of the Land*. London: Faber and Faber.

Casid, Jill. 2011. "Epilogue: Landscape in, around, and under the Performative." *Women & Performance: A Journal of Feminist Theory* 21 (1) (March): 97–116.

Cavell, Stanley. 2010. "The Transcendentalist Strain: Stanley Cavell Talks with Bookforum." *Bookforum* (April/May): http://www.bookforum.com/inprint/017_01/5356 (accessed December 15, 2013).

Certeau, Michel de. [1980] 1984. "Spatial Practices." In *The Practice of Everyday Life*, trans. Steven Rendall, 91–130. Berkeley: University of California Berkeley.

Christov-Bakargiev, Carolyn. 2005. "Transcendence and Immanence in Some Art of Today." In *Ecstasy: In and About Altered States*, ed. Lisa Gabrielle Mark and Paul Schimmel, 139–151. Los Angeles: The Museum of Contemporary Art.

Christov-Bakargiev, Carolyn. 2012. "The dance was very frenetic, lively rattling, clanging, rolling, contorted, and lasted for a long time." In *The Book of Books, dOCUMENTA(13), Catalog 1/3*. Artistic direction by Christov-Bakargiev, publications headed by Bettina Funcke. Ostfildern: Hatje Cantz.

Cixous, Hélène. [1975] 1976. "The Laugh of the Medusa," trans. Keith Cohen and Paula Cohen. *Signs* 1 (4): 875–893.

Cixous, Hélène. [1976] 1980. "The Laugh of the Medusa." In *New French Feminisms*, ed. Elaine Marks and Isabelle De Courtivron, 245–279. Amherst: University of Massachusetts Press.

Clark, Hilary. 2012. *Accessories of Protection*. Performance text. St. Mark's Church in-the-Bowery, New York, NY, December 14.

Clark, Hilary. 2013. Conversation with author. New York, NY, April 25.

Damisch, Hubert. [1972] 2002. *A Theory of Clouds: Toward a History of Painting*, trans. Janet Lloyd. Stanford: Stanford University Press.

Dean, Tacita. 1997. *Trying to Find the Spiral Jetty*. Audio work. Marian Goodman Gallery, New York, NY, August 16, 2001.

Demos, T. J. 2012. Art after Nature: The Post-Natural Condition. *Artforum* 50 (8) (April): 190–197.

Delany, Samuel R. 1968. *Nova*. New York: Vintage Books.

Delany, Samuel R. 1974. *Dhalgren*. New York: Vintage Books.

Delany, Samuel R. 1988. *The Motion of Light in Water: Sex and Science Fiction Writing in the East Village*. Minneapolis: University of Minnesota Press.

Deleuze, Gilles. [1968] 1994. *Difference and Repetition*, trans. Paul Patton. New York: Colombia University Press.

Deleuze, Gilles. [1969] 1990. *The Logic of Sense*, trans. Mark Lester. New York: Colombia University Press.

Deleuze, Gilles. [1981] 2003. *Francis Bacon: The Logic of Sensation*, trans. Daniel W. Smith. Minneapolis: University of Minnesota Press.

Deleuze, Gilles. [1988] 1993. *The Fold: Leibniz and the Baroque*, trans. Tom Conley. Minneapolis: University of Minnesota Press.

Deleuze, Gilles, and Félix Guattari. [1980] 1987. *A Thousand Plateaus: Capitalism and Schizophrenia*, trans. Brian Massumi. Minneapolis: University of Minnesota Press.

DeLillo, Don. 2010. *Point Omega*. New York: Simon and Schuster.

Derrida, Jacques. [1967] 1978. *Writing and Difference*, trans. Alan Bass. Chicago: University of Chicago Press.

Derrida, Jacques. [1972] 1982. "Signature Event Context." In *Margins of Philosophy*, trans. Alan Bass, 307–330. Chicago: University of Chicago Press.

Derrida, Jacques. [1978] 1987. "Parergon." In *The Truth in Painting*, trans. Geoff Bennington and Ian McLeod, 15–148. Chicago: University of Chicago Press.

Derrida, Jacques. [1988] 1991. "Che cos'è la poesia?" In *A Derrida Reader: Between the Blinds*, trans. and ed. Peggy Kamuf, 221–240. New York: Columbia University Press.

Derrida, Jacques. [1993] 1994. *Specters of Marx: The State of the Debt, the Work of Mourning, & the New International*, trans. Peggy Kamuf. New York: Routledge.

Derrida, Jacques. [2000] 2005. "Nothing to Do in Sight: 'There's no "the" sense of touch.'" In *On Touching–Jean-Luc Nancy*, trans. Christine Irizarry, 111–134. Stanford: Stanford University Press.

Derrida, Jacques, and Christine McDonald. [1982] 1995. "Choreographies." In *Bodies of the Text: Dance as Theory, Literature as Dance*, ed. Jacqueline Shea Murphy and Ellen W. Goellner, 141–156. New Brunswick: Rutgers University Press.

Didi-Huberman, Georges. [1982] 2003. *Invention of Hysteria: Charcot and the Photographic Iconography of the Salpêtrière*, trans. Alisa Hartz. Cambridge, MA: MIT Press.

Didi-Huberman, Georges. [1990] 2005. *Confronting Images: Questioning the Ends of a Certain History of Art*, trans. John Goodman. University Park: Penn State Press.

Didi-Huberman, Georges. 1996. "The Supposition of the Aura: The Now, the Then, and Modernity." In *Negotiating Rapture: The Power of Art to Transform Lives*, ed. Richard Francis, 48–63. Chicago: Museum of Contemporary Art.

Didi-Huberman, Georges. [2003] 2008. *Images in Spite of All*, trans. Shane B. Lillis. Chicago: University of Chicago Press.

Didi-Huberman, Georges. 2007. "'Picture = Rupture': Visual Experience, Form and Symptom according to Carl Einstein." *Papers of Surrealism* 7:1–25.

Didi-Huberman, Georges. [2006] 2013. "Fragments from *Le Danseur des solitudes*." In *Solos and Solitudes*, trans. Noémie Solomon, 5–8. New York: Danspace Project.

Didion, Joan. 1976. "Why I Write." *New York Review of Books*, December 5.

Dorvillier, DD. 2007. *Nottthing is Importanttt*. DVD liner notes.

Dorvillier, DD. 2009a. "IN-DEPTH: DD Dorvillier with Jenn Joy." *Movement Research Performance Journal* 35:6–7.

Dorvillier, DD. 2009b. *Choreography, a Prologue for the Apocalypse of Understanding, Get Ready!* Video text.

Dorvillier, DD. 2010. Conversation with the author. Brooklyn, NY, July 30.

Dorvillier, DD. 2011. *Mutual Seductions*. Conversations without Walls. Curated by Jenn Joy. Danspace Project, St. Mark's Church in-the-Bowery, New York, NY, November 5.

Dorvillier, DD. 2012. Post-performance discussion with Maria Hassabi, Robert Steijn, and Ralph Lemon. Danspace Project, St. Mark's Church in-the-Bowery, New York, NY, January 10.

Eagleton, Terry. 1990. *The Ideology of the Aesthetic*. Oxford: Blackwell Publishing.

Eco, Umberto. [1980] 1983. *The Name of the Rose*, trans. William Weaver. San Diego: Harcourt Brace Jovanovich.

Ellegood, Anne. 2007. *The Uncertainty of Objects and Ideas: Recent Sculpture*. Washington, DC: Hirschhorn Museum and Sculpture Garden; Smithsonian Institution.

Ellison, Ralph. 1947. *Invisible Man*. New York: Vintage Books.

Fabian, Johannes. 2002. *Time and the Other: How Anthropology Makes Its Objects*. New York: Columbia University Press.

Fabião, Eleonora. 2005. "precarious, precarious, precarious." PhD diss., Performance Studies, New York University.

Fabião, Eleonora. 2009. "On Precariousness and Performance: 7 Actions for Rio de Janeiro." Paper presented at Performance Studies International Conference #15, Misperformance: Misfiring, Misfitting, Misreading. Centre for Drama Art, University of Zagreb, Croatia, June 24–28.

Felman, Shoshana. [1980] 2003. *The Scandal of the Speaking Body: Don Juan with J. L. Austin or the Seduction in Two Languages*, trans. Catherine Porter. Stanford: Stanford University Press.

Fernandes, Ciane. 2001. *Pina Bausch and the Wuppertal Dance Theater: The Aesthetics of Repetition and Transformation*. New York: Peter Lang Publishing.

Fischer-Lichte, Erika. [2004] 2008. *The Transformative Power of Performance: A New Aesthetics*, trans. Saskya Iris Jain. Abingdon: Routledge.

Forsythe, William. 1995. *Eidos: Telos*. Program sheet, Städtische Bühnen Frankfurt, Frankfurt am Main.

Forsythe, William. 2003. *Improvisation Technologies: A Tool for the Analytical Dance Eye*. Karlsruhe: ZKM Karlsruhe.

Foster, Hal. 2009. "Precarious." *Artforum* 48 (4) (December): 207–209.

Foster, James. 2011a. Studio visit with the author. Providence, RI, May 9.

Foster, James. 2011b. Artist Statement. RISD 2011 Graduate Thesis Exhibition catalog, 94. Providence: Rhode Island School of Design.

Foster, James. 2012. Artist talk. Rhode Island School of Design, Providence, March 6.

Foster, James. 2013. Email correspondence with the author. February 1.

Foster, Susan Leigh. 1986. *Reading Dancing: Bodies and Subjects in Contemporary American Dance*. Berkeley: University of California Press.

Foster, Susan Leigh. 1995. "Choreographing History." In *Choreographing History*, ed. Susan Leigh Foster, 3–24. Bloomington: Indiana University Press.

Foster, Susan Leigh. 1996. *Choreography and Narrative: Ballet's Staging of Story and Desire*. Bloomington: Indiana University Press.

Foucault, Michel. [1969] 1972. *The Archaeology of Knowledge and the Discourse on Language*, trans. Alan Sheridan. New York: Pantheon Books.

Foucault, Michel. [1971] 1977. "Nietzsche, Genealogy, History." In *Language, Counter-Memory, Practice*, ed. Donald Bouchard, trans. Donald Bouchard and Sherry Simon, 139–164. Ithaca: Cornell University Press.

Foucault, Michel. [1982] 1997. "Technologies of the Self." In *Ethics: Subjectivity and Truth*, ed. Paul Rabinow, trans. Robert Hurley, 223–252. New York: New Press.

Foucault, Michel. [1983] 1997. "Self Writing." In *Ethics: Subjectivity and Truth*, ed. Paul Rabinow, trans. Robert Hurley, 207–222. New York: New Press.

Foucault, Michel. [1984] 1997. "What Is Enlightenment?" In *Ethics: Subjectivity and Truth*, ed. Paul Rabinow, trans. Robert Hurley, 303–320. New York: New Press.

Franko, Mark. 1986. *The Dancing Body in Renaissance Choreography*. Birmingham, AL: Summa Publications.

Franko, Mark. 2002. *The Work of Dance: Labor, Movement and Identity in the 1930s.* Middletown, CT: Wesleyan University Press.

Freud, Sigmund. [1899] 2003. "Screen Memories." In *The Uncanny*, ed. Adam Phillips, trans. David McLintock, 1–22. New York: Penguin.

Freud, Sigmund. [1915] 2000. "The Unconscious." In *The Continental Aesthetics Reader*, ed. Clive Cazeaux, trans. James Strachey, 506–518. London: Routledge.

Freud, Sigmund. [1905] 1960. *Jokes and Their Relation to the Unconscious*, trans. James Strachey. New York: W. W. Norton & Co.

Freud, Sigmund. [1920] 1961. *Beyond the Pleasure Principle*, trans. James Strachey. New York: W. W. Norton.

Fried, Michael. 1998. *Art and Objecthood: Essays and Reviews*. Chicago: University of Chicago Press.

Fried, Michael. 2008. *Why Photography Matters as Never Before*. New Haven: Yale University Press.

Gilbert-Rolfe, Jeremy. 1985. "*Gravity's Rainbow* and the *Spiral Jetty*." In *Immanence and Contradiction*, 86–150. London: Out of London Press.

Gioni, Massimiliano. 2007. "Ask the Dust." In *Unmonumental: The Object in the 21st Century*, 64–77. London: Phaidon Press Limited.

Gioni, Massimiliano. 2008. *After Nature*. New York: New Museum.

Gioni, Massimiliano. 2013. "Is Everything in My Mind?" In *Il Palazzo Enciclopedico*, ed. Gioni and Natalie Bell, 23–28. Venice: Fondazione La Biennale di Venezia.

Godfrey, Mark. 2010. "Politics/Poetics: The Work of Francis Alÿs." In *Francis Alÿs: A Story of Deception*, 8–33. New York: The Museum of Modern Art.

Goldman, Danielle. 2010. *I Want to Be Ready: Improvised Dance as a Practice of Freedom*. Ann Arbor: University of Michigan Press.

Greenberg, Clement. [1961] 1989. *Art and Culture*. Boston: Beacon Press.

Greenberg, Neil, and Miguel Gutierrez. 2006. "In Conversation." *Movement Research/Critical Correspondence*. http://www.movementresearch.org/ criticalcorrespondence (accessed December 12, 2013).

Grossman, Vasily. [1959] 1987. *Life and Fate*, trans. Robert Chandler. New York: New York Review Books.

Grosz, Elizabeth. 1994. *Volatile Bodies: Toward a Corporeal Feminism*. Bloomington: Indiana University Press.

Guattari, Félix. [1992] 1995. *Chaosmosis: An Ethico-aesthetic Paradigm*, trans. Paul Bains and Julian Pefanis. Bloomington: Indiana University Press.

Gutierrez, Miguel. 2006. *myendlesslove*. Performance text. MIX: The Experimental Lesbian and Gay Film and Video Festival, New York, NY, February 11.

Gutierrez, Miguel. 2009a. *WHEN YOU RISE UP: Performance Texts*. Brooklyn, NY: 53rd State Press.

Gutierrez, Miguel. 2009b. *Politics of Ecstasy/Altered States of Presence*. Program notes. Hebbel Theater, Berlin.

Gutierrez, Miguel. 2009c. "Story of an Action: Freedom of Information 2009 for Politics of Ecstasy Festival." Performance handout. *Politics of Ecstasy/Altered States of Presence*, Hebbel Theater, Berlin, January 24.

Gutierrez, Miguel. 2011a. Interview with the author. New York, March 17.

Gutierrez, Miguel. 2011b. INEFFABLE INTANGIBLE SENSATIONAL workshop. Los Angeles, July 17.

Gutierrez, Miguel. 2011c. *Choreography under the Influence*. Conversations without Walls. Curated by Jenn Joy. Danspace Project at St. Mark's Church in-the-Bowery, New York, NY, December 3.

Gutierrez, Miguel. 2011d. *HEAVENS WHAT HAVE I DONE*. Performance, Abrons Art Center, New York, NY, January 6–9.

Gutierrez, Miguel. 2012a. Description for INEFFABLE INTANGIBLE SENSATIONAL workshop. Movement Research Winter MELT Festival, New York, January.

Gutierrez, Miguel. 2012b. *And lose the name of action*. Performance text. Brooklyn Academy of Music, Brooklyn, NY, December 4–8.

Gutierrez, Miguel. 2013. *Myendlesslove*. Performance press text.

Hassabi, Maria. 2010b. Email correspondence with the author. July 31.

Hassabi, Maria. 2012. Post-performance discussion with Maria Hassabi, Robert Steijn, and Ralph Lemon. Danspace Project, St. Mark's Church in-the-Bowery, New York, NY, January 10.

Heathfield, Adrian. 2007. "Thema/Theme #7: Was ist Choreografie/What Is Choreography?" *Corpus*. www.corpusweb.net/answers-2228-2.html. (January 15, 2009).

Heidegger, Martin. [1953] 1996. *Being and Time*, trans. Joan Stambaugh. Albany: State University of New York Press.

Herzog, Werner, and Lars-Olav Beier. 2010. "Cinema Legend Heads Berlinale Jury." *Der Spiegel*. http://www.spiegel.de/international/zeitgeist/0,1518,677080,00.html (accessed April 14, 2011)

Hewitt, Andrew. 2005. *Social Choreography: Ideology as Performance in Dance and Everyday Movement*. Durham, NC: Duke University Press.

Hoberman, J. 2005. "Werner Herzog's New Direction." *New York Times*. nytimes. com/2005/05/08/movies/moviesspecial/08hobe.html (accessed April 14, 2011).

Hollywood, Amy. 2002. *Sensible Ecstasy: Mysticism, Sexual Difference, and the Demands of History*. Chicago: University of Chicago Press.

Holmes, Brian. 2011. "Post-fordisms and Culture." Lecture organized by Creative Time, Cooper Union, New York, June 30.

Humphrey, Doris. 1959. *The Art of Making Dances*. New York: Grove Press.

Irigaray, Luce. [1984] 1993. *An Ethics of Sexual Difference*, trans. Carolyn Burke and Gillian Gill. Ithaca: Cornell University Press.

Jackson, Shelley. 2002. *The Melancholy of Anatomy*. New York: Anchor Books.

Jameson, Frederic. 2005. *Archaelogies of the Future: The Desire Called Utopia and Other Science Fictions*. London: Verso.

Janson, Horst Woldemar. [1962] 1991. *The History of Art*. New York: Harry N. Abrams.

Joseph, Branden. 2002. "'My Mind Split Open': Andy Warhol's Exploding Plastic Inevitable." *Grey Room* 8 (Summer): 80–107.

Joseph, Miranda. 2002. *Against the Romance of Community*. Minneapolis: University of Minnesota Press.

Joy, Jenn. 2011. *Ecstatic Alliances*. Conversations without Walls. Including Ralph Lemon and Jeremy Wade. Danspace Project, St. Mark's Church in-the-Bowery, New York, NY, October 1.

Judd, Donald. 1965. "Specific Object." *Arts Yearbook* 8:74–82.

Kant, Immanuel. [1784] 1996. "An Answer to the Question: What Is Enlightenment?" In *Immanuel Kant. Practical Philosophy*, trans. and ed. Mary J. Gregor, 11–22. Cambridge: Cambridge University Press.

Kant, Immanuel. [1790]. 2000. *The Critique of Judgment*, trans. J. H. Bernard. New York: Prometheus Books.

Krauss, Rosalind E. 1977. *Passages in Modern Sculpture*. Cambridge, MA: MIT Press.

Krauss, Rosalind E. 1978. *John Mason Installations from the Hudson River Series*. Yonkers: Hudson River Museum.

Krauss, Rosalind E. [1978] 1986. "Sculpture in the Expanded Field." In *The Originality of the Avant-Garde and Other Modernist Myths*, 276–290. Cambridge, MA: MIT Press.

Kravas, Heather. 2011a. Email correspondence with the author. August 4.

Kravas, Heather. 2011b. "Heather Kravas in conversation with Jodi Bender." *Critical Correspondence* (October 2): http://www.movementresearch.org/criticalcorrespondence/blog/?p=3931 (accessed November 4, 2011).

Kravas, Heather. 2011c. Email correspondence with the author. October 27.

Kravas, Heather. 2011d. *The Green Surround*. Performance text. Performance Space 122, New York, NY, May 4–7.

Kravas, Heather. 2012. Conversation with the author. New York, NY, February 3.

Kundera, Milan. [1992] 1995. "Improvisation in Homage to Stravinsky." In *Testaments Betrayed: An Essay in Nine Parts*, trans. Linda Asher, 53–96. New York: Harper Collins.

Lambert-Beatty, Carrie. 2008. *Being Watched: Yvonne Rainer and the 1960s*. Cambridge, MA: MIT Press.

Lambert-Beatty, Carrie. 2010. "Against Performance Art." *Artforum* 48 (9) (May): 209–213.

Langer, Susanne. 1953. *Feeling and Form: A Theory of Art*. New York: Charles Scribner's Sons.

La Ribot. 2004. "Panoramix." In *LIVE: Art and Performance*, ed. Adrian Heathfield, 28–37. New York: Routledge.

Larsen, Lars Bang. 2005. "When the Light Falls." In *Ecstasy: In and About Altered States*, ed. Lisa Gabrielle Mark and Paul Schimmel, 177–185. Los Angeles: The Museum of Contemporary Art.

Lefebvre, Henri. [1974] 1991. *The Production of Space*, trans. Donald Nicholson-Smith. Oxford: Blackwell.

Le Guin, Ursula K. 1969. *The Left Hand of Darkness*. New York: Penguin.

Lemon, Ralph. 2010. *How Can You Stay in the House All Day and Not Go Anywhere?* Performance text. Brooklyn Academy of Music, Brooklyn, NY, October 13–16.

Lemon, Ralph. 2013. *Come home Charley Patton*. Middletown: Wesleyan University Press.

Lepecki, André. 2004. "Inscribing Dance." In *Of the Presence of the Body*, ed. André Lepecki, 124–139. Middletown: Wesleyan University Press.

Lepecki, André. 2006. *Exhausting Dance: Performance and the Politics of Movement*. London: Routledge.

Lepecki, André, and Jenn Joy, eds. 2009. *Planes of Composition: Dance, Theory and the Global*. New York: Seagull Books.

Le Roy, Xavier. 2010. Lecture and conversation with Claire Bishop. CUNY Graduate Center, New York, May 7.

Levinas, Emmanuel. [1964] 1996. "Meaning and Sense." In *Basic Philosophic Writings*, trans. and ed. Adriaan T. Peperzak, Simon Critchley, and Robert Bernascon, 33–64. Bloomington: Indiana University Press.

Levinas, Emmanuel. [1984] 1996. "Peace and Proximity." In *Basic Philosophic Writings*, trans. and ed. Adriaan T. Peperzak, Simon Critchley, and Robert Bernascon, 161–169. Bloomington: Indiana University Press.

Linyekula, Faustin. 2012. Conversation on *Some Sweet Day*. Museum of Modern Art, New York, NY, October 27.

Lispector, Clarice. [1978] 2012. *A Breath of Life*. New York: New Directions Books.

Louppe, Laurence, ed. [1991] 1994. *Traces of Dance; Drawings and Notations of Choreographers*, trans. Brian Holmes et al. Paris: Dis Voir.

Mailer, Norman. 1983. *Ancient Evenings*. New York: Warner Books, Inc.

Martin, John. [1933] 1972. *The Modern Dance*. New York: Dance Horizons, Inc.

Martin, Randy. 1998. *Critical Moves: Dance Studies in Theory and Politics*. Durham, NC: Duke University Press.

Marx, Karl. [1939] 1986. "Grundrisse." In *Collected Works of Karl Marx and Friedrich Engels*, vol. 28. Moscow: Progress Publishers.

McCarthy, Cormac. 2006. *The Road*. New York: Vintage.

Meade, Fionn. 2010. *Knight's Move*. Long Island City: Sculpture Center.

Meade, Fionn. 2011. *Time Again*. Long Island City: Sculpture Center.

Medina, Cuauhtémoc. 2009. "Materialist Spectrality." In *Teresa Margolles: What Else Could Happen?*, 15–29. Venice: Fondazione La Biennale di Venice.

Meier, Yvonne. 2012. Description for Improvisational "Scores" workshop. Movement Research Winter MELT Festival, New York, January.

Merleau-Ponty, Maurice. [1961] 1964. "Eye and Mind." In *The Primacy of Perception*, trans. Careton Dallery, 159–190. Evanston: Northwestern University Press.

Meyers, James. 2004. "No More Scale: The Experience of Size in Contemporary Sculpture." *Artforum* 42 (10) (Summer): 220–228.

Michelson, Annette. [1969] 2000. "Robert Morris: An Aesthetics of Transgression." In *Minimalism: Themes and Movements*, ed. James Meyer, 247–250. London: Phaidon Press Limited.

Miles, Christopher. 2005. "A Thing for Things." In *Thing: New Sculpture from Los Angeles*, 9–16. Los Angeles: Armand Hammer Museum of Art.

Morris, Robert. [1966] 1968. "Notes on Sculpture, Parts I–III." In *Minimal Art: A Critical Anthology*, ed. Gregory Battcock, 222–235. New York: E. P. Dutton and Co.

Muñoz, José Esteban. 2005. "Utopia's Seating Chart: Ray Johnson, Jill Johnston, and Queer Intermedia as System." In *After Criticism: New Responses to Art and Performance*, ed. Gavin Butt, 101–116. Oxford: Blackwell Publishing.

Muñoz, José Esteban. 2006. "Stages: Queers, Punks, and the Utopian Performative." In *The SAGE Handbook of Performance Studies*, ed. D. Soyni Madison and Judith Hamera, 9–20. Thousand Oaks: SAGE Publications.

Muñoz, José Esteban. 2009. *Cruising Utopia: The Then and There of Queer Futurity*. New York: New York University Press.

Nancy, Jean-Luc. [1986] 1991. *The Inoperative Community*, trans. Peter Connor. Minneapolis: University of Minnesota Press.

Nancy, Jean-Luc. 1987. "Wild Laughter in the Throat of Death." *MLN* 102 (4) (September): 719–736.

Nancy, Jean-Luc. [1988] 1993. "Laughter, Presence." In *Birth to Presence*, trans. Emily McVarish, 368–392. Stanford: Stanford University Press.

Nancy, Jean-Luc. [2003] 2005. *The Ground of the Image*, trans. Jeff Fort. New York: Fordham University Press.

Nancy, Jean-Luc. 2008. *Corpus*, trans. Richard A. Rand. New York: Fordham University Press.

Nelson, Maggie. 2009. *Bluets*. Seattle: Wave Books.

Nickas, Bob. [2003] 2008. *Theft Is Vision*. Zurich: JRP Ringier.

O'Connor, Tere. 2012. Conversation with the author. New York, NY, October 16.

Paglin, Trevor. 2008. "Experimental Geography: From Cultural Production to the Production of Space." In *Experimental Geography*, ed. Nato Thompson, 27–34. New York: Independent Curators International.

Parrino, Steven. 2003. *The NO TEXTS: (1979–2003)*. Jersey City, NJ: Abaton Book Company.

Parvulescu, Anca. 2010. *Laughter: Notes on a Passion*. Cambridge, MA: MIT Press.

Pente, Stefan 2008. "Laughter. Minus-Laughter." In *Rire/Laugh/Lachen*, ed. Antonia Baehr, trans. William Wheeler, 98–107. Aubervilliers: Les Laboratoires d'Aubervilliers.

Phelan, Peggy. 1995. "Thirteen Ways of Choreographing Writing." In *Choreographing History*, ed. Susan Leigh Foster, 200–210. Bloomington: Indiana University Press.

Phelan, Peggy. 1997. *Mourning Sex: Performing Public Memories*. New York: Routledge.

Ploebst, Helmut. 2001. *No Wind No Word: New Choreography in the Society of the Spectacle*. Alton: Dance Books Ltd.

Pujol, Ernesto. 2012. *Sited Bodies, Public Visions: Silence, Stillness, and Walking Practice as Performance Art*. New York: McNally Jackson Books.

Pynchon, Thomas. 1973. *Gravity's Rainbow*. New York: Penguin.

Rancière, Jacques. 2007. "The Emancipated Spectator." *Artforum* 45 (7) (March): 271–280.

Robinson, Kim Stanley. 1993. *Red Mars*. New York: Bantam Books.

Robinson, Kim Stanley. 1994. *Green Mars*. New York: Bantam Books.

Robinson, Kim Stanley. 1996. *Blue Mars*. New York: Bantam Books.

Robinson, Kim Stanley. 2013. Keynote lecture. MoMA PS1, Long Island City, NY, June 9.

Ronell, Avital. 2011. *Irruptive Pedagogies*. Conversations without Walls. Curated by Jenn Joy. Danspace Project, St. Mark's Church in-the-Bowery, New York, NY, December 3.

Ronell, Avital, and Anne Dufourmantelle. 2010. *Fighting Theory*. Urbana: University of Illinois Press.

Rosenfield, Kim. 2004. *Tràma*. San Francisco: Krupskaya.

Ross, Kristin. [1983] 2002. "Lefebvre on the Situationists: An Interview." In *Guy Debord and the Situationist International*, ed. Tom McDonough, 267–284. Cambridge, MA: MIT Press.

Roysdon, Emily. 2009. "Ecstatic Resistance." Exhibition statement. Kansas City: Grand Arts.

Rugoff, Ralph. 1997. *Scene of the Crime*. Cambridge, MA: MIT Press.

Sarraute, Nathalie. [1972] 2004. *Do You Hear Them?*, trans. Maria Jolas. Normal: Dalkey Archive Press.

Schechner, Richard. 1985. *Between Theater and Anthropology*. Philadelphia: University of Pennsylvania Press.

Schimmel, Paul. 2005. "Live in Your Head." In *Ecstasy: In and About Altered States*, ed. Lisa Gabrielle Mark and Paul Schimmel, 28–39. Los Angeles: The Museum of Contemporary Art.

Sebald, W. G. [1988] 2002. *After Nature*, trans. Michael Hamburger. New York: Penguin.

Sebald, W. G. [1999] 2003. *On the Natural History of Destruction*, trans. Anthea Bell. New York: Modern Library.

Sedgwick, Eve Kosofsky. [1980] 2007. "The Coherence of Gothic Conventions." In *The Gothic*, ed. Gilda Williams, 95–100. London: Whitechapel.

Shklovsky, Victor. [1929] 1990. "Art as Device." In *Theory of Prose*, trans. Benjamin Sher, 1–14. Normal: Dalkey Archive Press.

Shusterman, Richard. 2008. *Body Consciousness: A Philosophy of Mindfulness and Somaesthetics*. Cambridge, U.K.: Cambridge University Press.

Sloterdijk, Peter. [1989] 2009. "Mobilization of the Planet from the Spirit of Self-Intensification," trans. Heidi Ziegler. *TDR* 50 (4) (T192): 36–43.

Smithson, Robert. [1972] 1996. "Spiral Jetty." In *The Collected Writings*, ed. Jack Flam, 143–153. Berkeley: University of California Press.

Solnit, Rebecca. 2000. *Wanderlust: A History of Walking*. New York: Penguin.

Solomon, Noémie. 2012. "Unworking the Dance Subject: Contemporary French Choreographic Experiments on the European Stage." PhD diss., Performance Studies, New York University.

Sontag, Susan. [1964] 1966. "Against Interpretation." In *Against Interpretation and Other Essays*, 3–14. New York: Picador.

Sontag, Susan. 2003. *Regarding the Pain of Others*. New York: Farrar, Straus and Giroux.

Spångberg, Mårten. 2002. "Something like a Phenomenon." *Frakcija Performing Arts Magazine* 24/25 (Autumn): 35–37.

Spångberg, Mårten. 2009. "Why 'The Art of Making Dances' Now? Between '-What is . . .' and Choreography." In *THE ART OF MAKING DANCES*, ed. Chase Granoff and Jenn Joy, 29–38. Brooklyn, NY: Self-published.

Spivak, Gayatri Chakravorty.1991. "Time and Timing: Law and History." In *Chronotypes: The Construction of Time*, ed. John Bender and David Wellbery, 99–117. Stanford: Stanford University Press.

Spivak, Gayatri Chakravorty. 1999. *A Critique of Postcolonial Reason: Toward a History of the Vanishing Present*. Cambridge, MA: Harvard University Press.

Steijn, Robert. 2009. "how Martha becomes Trisha/this is not a fantasy, it is a program of experimentation." In *THE ART OF MAKING DANCES*, ed. Chase Granoff and Jenn Joy, 25–28. Brooklyn, NY: Self-published.

Stewart, Susan. 2005. "Tacita Dean." In *The Open Studio: Essays on Art and Aesthetics*, 75–84. Chicago: University of Chicago Press.

Stuart, Meg. 2004. *Forgeries, Love and Other Matters*. Performance text. Dance Theater Workshop, New York, NY, April 27.

Stuart, Meg. 2009. Introduction to the performance *One Hour Laughing*. Hebbel
   Theater, Berlin, January 24.

Stuart, Meg. 2010. "Dancing States." In *Are We There Yet?*, ed. Jeroen Peeters, 20–21.
   Dijon: Les presses du réel.

Sylvester, David. 1975. *The Brutality of Fact: Interviews with Francis Bacon*. New
   York: Thames and Hudson.

Taylor, Diana. 2003. *The Archive and the Repertoire: Performing Cultural Memory in
   the Americas*. Durham, NC: Duke University Press.

Taylor, Jane. 2005. "Introduction." In *The Anatomy of Laughter*, ed. Toby Garfitt,
   Edith McMorran, and Jane Taylor, 1–10. London: Legenda and Modern
   Humanities Research Association.

Taylor, Steven. 2011. *Language or Something Else*. Conversations without Walls.
   Curated by Jenn Joy. Danspace Project, St. Mark's Church in-the-Bowery, New
   York, NY, December 3.

Teilhard de Chardin, Pierre. [1955] 1975. *The Phenomenon of Man*, trans. Bernard
   Wall. New York: Harper.

Verwoert, Jan. 2011. "The Devils Inside the Thing Speak to the Devils Outside." In
   Sculpture Unlimited, ed. Eva Grubinger and Jörg Heiser. Berlin: Sternberg
   Press.

Virilio, Paul. [1975] 1994. *Bunker Archaeology*, trans. George Collins. Princeton:
   Princeton Architectural Press.

Virilio, Paul. [1996] 2000. *A Landscape of Events*, trans. Julie Rose. Cambridge, MA:
   MIT Press.

Virilio, Paul and Claude Parent. [1966] 1996. *Architecture Principe: 1966 and 1996*,
   trans. George Collins. Besançon: Les Éditions de L'Imprimeur.

Virno, Paolo. [2001] 2004. *A Grammar of the Multitude: For an Analysis of Contemporary Forms of Life*, trans. Isabella Bertoletti, James Cascaito, and Andrea Casson. Los Angeles: Semiotext(e).

Vitale, Marianne. 2013. Email correspondence with the author. August 25.

Wade, Jeremy. 2007a. Email correspondence with the author. June 22.

Wade, Jeremy. 2007b. *Feed* and *Glory*. Program notes. Performance Space 122, New York, NY, January 19.

Wade, Jeremy. 2008. Email correspondence with the author. March 25.

Wade, Jeremy. 2009. *I Offer Myself to Thee*. Performance text. Hebbel Theater, Berlin, January 24.

Wade, Jeremy. 2010a. Skype conversation with the author. New York, NY, and Berlin, June 11.

Wade, Jeremy. 2010b. Conversation with the author. New York, NY, July 8.

Wade, Jeremy. 2011. *fountain*. Performance text. Danspace Project, St. Mark's Church in-the-Bowery, New York, NY, October 6.

Wade, Jeremy. 2012. Website. http://www.jeremywade.de/ (accessed May 10, 2012).

Wade, Jeremy, and Eike Wittrock. 2009. *Politics of Ecstasy/Altered States of Presence*. Curator opening remarks. Hebbel Theater, Berlin, January 23–31.

Wagner, Anne. 2004. "Splitting and Doubling: Gordon Matta-Clark and the Body of Scupture." *Grey Room* 14 (Winter): 26–45.

Waldrop, Rosmarie. 1998. *Blindsight*. New York: New Directions Books.

Weiss, Allen. 1998. *Unnatural Horizons: Paradox and Contradiction in Landscape and Architecture*. New York: Princeton Architectural Press.

Weizman, Eyal, with Jeffrey Kastner, Tom McCarthy, and Nato Thompson. 2009. "The New Geography: A Roundtable." *Bookform* (April/May). http://www.bookforum.com/inprint/016_01/3511 (accessed April 4, 2012).

Youngblood, Gene. 1970. *Expanded Cinema*. New York: Dutton.

Žižek, Slavoj. 2008. *Violence*. New York: Picador.

Index